The London Program
University of Notre Dame
Notre Dame, IN 46556-5639

Walking London's Parks and Gardens

Walking London's Parks and Gardens

GEOFFREY YOUNG

TWENTY-FOUR ORIGINAL WALKS AROUND LONDON'S PARKS AND GARDENS

PASSPORT BOOKS
NTC/Contemporary Publishing Company

First published in 1998
by Passport Books, an imprint of
NTC/Contemporary Publishing Company
4255 West Touhy Avenue
Lincolnwood (Chicago), Illinois 60646-1975
U.S.A.

ISBN 0-8442-4872-X

Library of Congress Catalog Card Number: on file
Published in conjunction with New Holland (Publishers) Ltd

Editor: Helen Varley
Design: Alan Marshall, Wilderness Design
Cartography: ML Design

Reproduction by Dot Gradations
Printed and bound in Singapore by Kyodo Printing Co (Singapore) Pte Ltd

Photographic Acknowledgments
All photographs were taken by the author with the exception of the following:
Front cover: Andrew McRobb/Royal Botanic Gardens, Kew; Plate 2:
John Fitzmaurice/Syon Park Limited; Plate 4: courtesy of The Museum of Fulham Palace;
Plate 6: Kensington Roof Gardens; Plate 8: courtesy of The Royal Parks Agency;
Plate 24: Andrew McRobb/Royal Botanic Gardens, Kew.

Front cover: The Palm House, Kew Gardens, built in 1844–48 and designed by the
Victorian architect Decimus Burton working with the engineer Richard Turner.

Contents

Preface

London is loved for its parks and gardens, and in this book we have chosen the best of them. They're the ones with the most historic interest; they do have a fascinating story and countless byways of their very own. And they've been selected because of the sheer interest of the trees or plant displays. Added to which, maybe, are the views – some parks in this book provide vistas, planned landscapes, unmatched anywhere in the world. Added (again) to which are the concerts and shows and other events that these parks and gardens host.

The routes I describe link the most interesting features of each park or garden, but there are often others, and clearly, in the case of large parks, Holland Park or The Regent's Park, for example, several very different routes are possible. So if you feel like exploring further, this book will have succeeded. Although we do give precise instructions as to where to walk, we'd hate you to resist the temptation to walk on the grass. The detailed map that accompanies each walk and shows the major features along the route should ensure that if you do leave the path, you won't get lost.

We've given some guidance on the distance each walk will cover and the time it will take, ranging from the very short for the Kensington Roof Gardens to a longish trek of maybe two or three hours or more in Richmond Park – or Kew Gardens, where there is also much to see. The routes have been timed at a slow walk, allowing for a breather after an uphill stretch maybe, but also giving time to look at interesting features – but not for having tea in a café or sitting on a bench chatting!

Admission to the majority of parks and gardens in this book is free; if not, the ticket prices are given in information panels at the beginning of each chapter. The panels also give such information as the location of the park and its distance from Central London, convenient buses or other transport, the opening times of cafés, seasonal features, and events that take place in the park.

At the back of the book, in Further Information, the opening times of linked houses or museums are given, together with the numbers of telephone information lines, and also contact numbers for groups of 'Friends' of the park or gardens, and other societies related to the park. They welcome new members.

This information, the walk details and the maps were up-to-the-minute correct when the book was printed, but remember that parks and gardens are dynamic places and much goes on in terms of management and restoration and planting programmes. Some details may change as a result and you may need to improvise at times when following the route map.

Geoffrey Young

Introduction

London has some of the most marvellous parks and gardens in the world and they are yours to enjoy. They offer more grass to walk on than you can usually find in the countryside – and many have a great deal more wildlife. But London's parks are not just green places, they're also memorials to the people who created them, worked in them, used them and wrote about them: to kings and queens; landscape gardeners and plant-hunters; diary-writers and duellists; and (in one case) star-gazers. And they are all dotted with discoveries: a very personal secret garden, for instance (in Regent's Park – *see* pages 68–9 to find it); a supreme view that takes you back two centuries (on Hampstead Heath – *see* page 71 to discover exactly where); what must be the most pert statue in London (in Green Park – revealed on page 114). To discover the secrets and beauties of London's parks and gardens you have only to walk them, and see for yourself what's round the bend in the path. Happiness on the hoof, you could say!

The parks

London's parks are museums of their own history. Some of the oldest are the royal parks, which were originally deer parks, enclosed, in the main, by the hunt-mad Tudors, especially King Henry VIII (1507–47), within which the deer were coursed (chased by hounds) or released into what was then open countryside roundabout, to be hunted on horseback. Country mansions also had their deer parks. These, being heavily grazed, took on a 'parkland' look, still to be seen in Richmond Park.

Hunting in London's parks largely ended in Stuart times and several of the deer parks were then opened to the public. For example, James I (1603–25) first allowed his courtiers access to Hyde Park, and Charles II (1660–85) later opened it up freely. The word 'park' then became used for any large green area open for public enjoyment, including the custom-built Victorian parks such as Battersea Park and Crystal Palace Park. By then parks usually also contained garden features.

The gardens

The Romans had formal gardens, but after the fall of the Roman Empire it was well into medieval times before anything similar was seen again. Tudor mansions had plots for herbs to treat illness (the medicines of the time) and for nosegays to ward off the noxious stench of the house – there is a delightful example at Kew Gardens (*see* page 144). But by then flowers such as iris, pansy and cowslip were also being grown for pleasure. These were often charged with innuendo; the wall-flower represented love, for example. By that time the concept of the garden was becoming imbued with symbolism. Entry to the Tudor Privy Garden at Hampton

Hampton Court was itself a symbol of privilege, and walks of various kinds within the garden were full of meaningful details, ranging from symbolic heraldic beasts on poles to formal knot gardens.

The Knot

By the 16th century the knot was an important part of garden formalism, perhaps developing from a square bed with raised plank edges. It was a geometrical pattern within the square. At first, the pattern was created with close-clipped lines of hyssop, lavender, rosemary and other plants, separated by paths of coloured sand or crushed brick. The compartments may have been filled with 'gillyflowers' (clove-scented carnations, first mentioned in the 14th century) and other flowers, but were often not. A development took place with the introduction in Tudor times of the dwarf Dutch box *(Buxus sempervirens* 'Suffruticosa') which could be neatly close-trimmed. It became usual to plant flowers or herbs within the knot 'hedges', with maybe one kind to each compartment.

Knots have been recreated at many places – at Fulham Palace, Kew Gardens, Ham House and Hampton Court, though not many have authentic plantings. The one at Hampton Court is filled with Victorian-style bedding plants, for example.

The Parterre

From the knot evolved the more elaborate and larger parterre, with a highly complex arabesque geometry. Flowers or coloured earths could still separate the box 'hedges' and there might be sanded paths, but trimmed grass often played a part. In fact in one variation, the pattern was cut in the turf. Ornamental fountains, urns, statues, or tall trimmed yew and box trees could be dotted through the design. The parterre was perhaps at its most elaborate by around the end of the 17th century, partly as a result of Dutch influence. The Great Fountain Garden at Hampton Court *(see* pages 164–5) became a detailed tapestry, and some of its stylistic elements can be seen in the restored Privy Garden there.

The Physic Garden

By this time, another type of garden had evolved, probably from monastic gardens. This was the Physic Garden, a specialized apothecaries' garden (apothecary being an old name for those who dealt and dabbled with medicines). As well as producing medicinal plants for use, it was also a teaching garden, where student apothecaries could learn to recognize medicinal (and poisonous) plants growing in the ranked beds. In time, plants from around the world were grown in them, also for teaching purposes. Not all these plants were medicinal, and the gardens became known as Botanic Gardens, but the marvellous Chelsea Physic Garden keeps its ancient title.

Specialized buildings

By the time the great parterres were laid and planted, the gardens of great mansions might also contain specialized buildings. Orange trees were first introduced into England during the reign of Queen Elizabeth I and, in time, orangeries were built to protect them in cold weather. The orangery at Ham House, built in 1670, is one of the oldest in Britain. There might also have been a banqueting house – a place where family and guests might take snacks or desserts of wine and sweetmeats – like the one at Hampton Court *(see* page 164).

Also during the 17th century, a 'wilderness' was a popular addition to the gardens of great houses. The wilderness was a plantation of hedges and trees creating outside 'rooms', and it was treated as an extension to the house. Ham House has a fine example *(see* page 156).

The Avenue

The Tudor mansion, with its walled, inward looking gardens was rebuilt or replaced in the early 17th century by the outward-looking Jacobean building, with large windows which begged a view. And when, after the Commonwealth of 1649–1653, the monarchy was restored under Charles II in 1660, the new king brought with him from exile in France a fancy for long vistas and avenues of trees. Such avenues could be regarded as a symbol of authority, reaching out into the park, uniting it with the house in a new way. Tree alleys (sometimes in the splayed form of a 'goosefoot') were planted at Greenwich and at Hampton Court. There is a late (Victorian) example of the kind at Kew Gardens. Hedged alleys were also planted in the form of a goosefoot or patte d'oie, of which there are outstanding examples in the gardens of Chiswick House *(see* pages 30–2).

The Canal and the Lake

The grand avenue could edge a straight canal – one example can be seen in The Long Water at Hampton Court *(see* page 165). The canal originally built in St. James's Park *(see* pages 117–8 was subsequently made to look more natural in the 18th century. From that time, the 'natural' look was adopted, when lakes became a part of customary park design everywhere. The lakes of Hyde Park and Syon Park are two of many examples to be seen in London.

The Natural Look

The royal parks tended to set or follow the latest landscape fashions, often as a result of changes introduced by royal personages, such as Queen Mary, wife of William III, Queen Anne; Caroline, consort of George II, and Queen Victoria's consort, Albert. They employed influential landscape designers and gardeners.

During the 18th century a number of key figures transformed the appearance of London's parks and gardens by replacing the formal style that had prevailed during the 17th century with the 'natural' look which became synonymous with English landscapes and gardens.

Charles Bridgeman and William Kent. Some first steps were taken by Charles Bridgeman, who died in 1738 and who worked at Chiswick Park and Kensington Gardens. But the man of real note in this development was William Kent (1685–1748), whose great contribution to the development of landscape design was to see nature as a garden. Kent was an artist, and his 'natural' garden style was composed of set pieces reminiscent of a painted scene: there were trees and grass in his landscapes, but temples and other Classical eyecatchers were set among them. He designed the gardens at Chiswick House, which remain a marvellous example. Quaint additions to the grounds (now called the park) subsequently became the norm, from the grottoes of Marble Hill House *(see* pages 168–9) to the temples and the Pagoda at Kew, built in 1761 to the designs of the influential architect, William Chambers (1723–96).

Lancelot ('Capability') Brown (1716–83). By the 18th century, poets such as James Thomson, who died in 1748, were opening eyes to the beauties of nature, to scenery 'embosomed thick with trees', for example, a liking we take for granted today. One famous gardener or landscape designer close to this enthusiasm was Lancelot Brown. He gained his nickname 'Capability', from his habit of extolling an estate's capabilities for improvement in this way. He created unified 'landscape gardens'. He worked at Kew Gardens and Syon Park, and was also master gardener (though he changed little) at Hampton Court.

Brown's trademarks were natural-looking swells of ground and grass, trees in apparently natural clumps, and lakes with serpentine banks having all the appearance of being a creation of nature, but which gave shifting vistas as you walked past (rather like countryside seen from a car). He often went so far as to fell formal avenues of trees and tear up terrace parterres, bringing grass right up to a house. He would also eliminate the need for restrictive walls or railings by using a ha-ha – a ditch that formed a barrier to straying animals, like the one at Ham House *(see* page 155).

Humphry Repton (1752–1818) was Brown's natural successor, famous for his 'red books' with overlays showing views before and after his improvements. In fact, he invented the phrase 'landscape gardening'. He has left a classic landscape at Kenwood House *(see* page 70). He heralded the great changes of Victorian times, reintroducing the planting of flowers beside a house (though not as part of the main vista) as he did at Kenwood. By the time John Nash (1752–1835) was working at The Regent's Park and St James's Park, flowers were firmly back in fashion as part of the Grand Design.

William Nesfield was one of many notable Victorian plantsmen and garden designers. By the 19th century there was renewed interest in flower gardens and regret at the destruction of the formal layouts of the past. This resulted in a backlash of a kind, with the creation of formal gardens inspired by Italian Renaissance gardens, such as the young example at Chiswick House *(see* page 33).

To make an Italian garden, an area might be taken from a lawn close to the house, and parterre-like beds cut, to be filled with greenhouse-raised bedding plants, the corners maybe marked by dwarf trees (tall trees were kept out). If the fall of the land allowed, there could be terraces and Italianate stone balustrades, as there were at Crystal Palace Park *(see* page 92) and sometimes a few statues, but there was no attempt to recreate the magnificence of Italian Renaissance gardens. Instead there was reliance on massing the colours of bedding plants. In Regent's Park there is a notable recreation of Nesfield's style *(see* page 65). At this time, however, as a result of this influence it became customary to add statues and memorials to parks and gardens, some as drinking fountains.

During the late 19th century, the herbaceous border became an enthusiasm. There is a marvellous example at Hampton Court *(see* page 158), another in The Regent's Park *(see* page 69), and a luxuriant variety on Victoria Embankment *(see* page 97). Also, for a new type of gardener, the owner of a small middle-class villa, the cottage garden was reinvented. It is, in essence, based on individual plants or clumps of them, and not the massed bedding beloved of the Victorians.

Plants from abroad

Few plants or shrubs in a garden today are natives by origin, since for centuries plants have been imported from other regions. The discovery of the New World in the mid-16th century was perhaps a turning point. The tomato and sunflower are two examples of plants that first reached Europe at that time, and which are now familiar to all. Key figures of this age of discovery were the Tradescants, father and son, whose work spanned the years 1570–1662. They brought the virginia creeper to Britain, and very many other plants. The Museum of Garden History in the Church of St-Mary-at-Lambeth (see page 105) is devoted to them, and many of the plants they collected can be seen in the 17th-century Tradescant Garden which now occupies the churchyard where they are buried.

In the 17th century, the Reverend John Banister sent back from America to Fulham Palace, the country residence of the Bishops of London, the first magnolia to be seen in Britain, and liquidambar, the sweet gum. Descendants of trees and plants he introduced still grow in the garden at Fulham Palace *(see* page 36). Exotic botany became not just a hobby but a profession – in the 18th and 19th centuries, the botanist Sir Joseph Banks (1743–1820) and later William and Sir Joseph Hooker were sponsoring plant-collecting expeditions, in part to exploit to the full the new lands of the Empire for crop and medicinal plants. Plants they collected are on show at Chelsea Physic Garden and at Kew Gardens. Heated plant-houses, called stoves and conservatories were built by those rich enough, to nurture new flowers and shrubs, camellias (from China and Japan) being one passion. These conservatories, which can still be seen at Syon Park, Kew and Chiswick Park, were virtual temples to the new religion of plantsmanship.

Bedding plants and exotics

The climax to this development was the building of greenhouses for the raising of thousands of exotics at a time, destined for planting out in preplanned park and garden beds. At Hyde Park for example, plants were being shown in bulk bedding barely two years after first being seen in Britain; and the first great flower shows were held in the Temple Gardens *(see* page 98). This appearance of bedding plants led to the garden industry of today, for the breeding and raising of new hybrids and varieties is something we take for granted. And the 20th century has seen developments not only in the production of plants but also in the embracing of different garden designs and styles, of which the Kensington Roof Gardens *(see* page 46) and the Japanese garden in Holland Park *(see* page 44) are outstanding examples.

Plant Introductions

The table below gives the date of introduction of some of the trees and plants referred to in the following pages:

Approximate date	Trees	From
1500	Holm oak	Mediterranean
1500	(Red) mulberry	Iran
1550	Strawberry tree	Mediterranean/Ireland
1550.	Stone (Umbrella) pine	Mediterranean
1580	Plane tree	SE Europe
1640	Horse chestnut	Balkans
1640	Swamp cypress	North America
1660	Cedar of Lebanon	Lebanon
1750	Tree of heaven	China
1760	Maidenhair tree	Japan
1760	Lombardy poplar	Italy
1795	Monkey puzzle tree	Chile

	Other plants	
1550	African marigold	Mexico via Africa
1580	Hyacinth	Turkey via Italy
1580	Tulip	Turkey via Holland
1600	Yucca	Central America
1600	Nasturtium	South America
1710	Red hot poker	South Africa
1710	Pelargonium (geranium)	South Africa
1790	Hydrangea	China
1880	Cotoneaster	China
1890	Russian vine	Russia
1900	Buddleia	China

Key to Route Maps

Each of the walks in this book is accompanied by a detailed map on which the route of the walk is shown in green. Places of interest along the walks – such as historic houses, museums and churches – are identified by the symbols in the list below. The opening times of houses and museums linked to the park are listed in Further Information at the back of the book, starting on page 170.

The following is a key to symbols and abbreviations used on the maps:

Symbols

	route of walk
	footpath
	railway line
	railway station
	Underground station
	building
†	church
	public toilets
	viewpoint
	café
	flower bed
	specimen tree
	woodland
	parkland
	statue
	fountain
	monument
	bandstand
	stairs
P	car park

Abbreviations

APP	Approach	PH	Public
AVE	Avenue		House
CLO	Close		(Pub)
COTTS	Cottages	PK	Park
CT	Court	PL	Place
DLR	Docklands	RD	Road
	Light Railway	S	South
DRI	Drive	SQ	Square
E	East	ST	Saint
GDNS	Gardens	ST	Street
GRN	Green	STN	Station
GRO	Grove	TER	Terrace
HO	House	UPR	Upper
LA	Lane	VW	View
LWR	Lower	W	West
MS	Mews	WD	Wood
MT	Mount	WHF	Wharf
N	North	WLK	Walk
PAS	Passage	WY	Way
PDE	Parade		

Map of London Parks

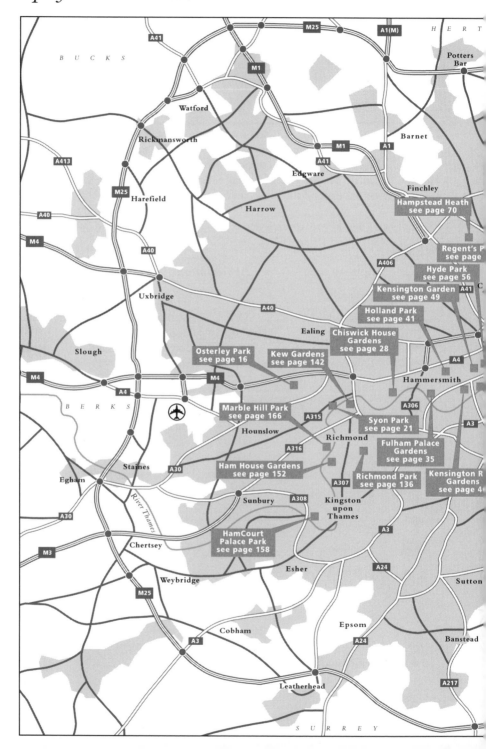

Cheshunt

Epping

M11

M25

A10

Chingford

ESSEX

A12

A406

A104

A12

Romford

A127

A503

Bloomsbury Squares
see page 76

A106

A406

Green Park
see page 109

A102(M)

A11

M25

Hackney

Barking

A13

St James's Park
see page 116

Rainham

...ster

A13

Aveley

A13

A206

Victoria Embankment
Gardens
see page 97

River Thames

Woolwich

Victoria Tower Gardens
see page 103

Greenwich Park
see page 83

Battersea Park
see page 122

Lewisham

A2

Chelsea Physic Garden
see page 129

Dartford

A2

A22

A20

Bromley

Swanley

Crystal Palace Park
see page 90

M20

Croydon

A225

A23

A21

A22

KENT

Biggin
Hil

A21

M23

M25

Sevenoaks

Caterham

Westerham

Osterley Park

Location	About 9 miles (14.5 kilometres) west of Charing Cross.
Transport	Osterley Underground Station (Piccadilly Line) is 15 minutes' (signposted) walk away. There is a car park (fee £2) at the end of South Avenue.
Admission	The park is open daily 09:00 hours until sunset or 19:30 hours. Admission is free.
Seasonal features	Spring blossom and autumn tree colour. Regency garden in summer.
Events	Dawn walks with the Royal Society for the Protection of Birds, spring Plant Fair, National Gardens Scheme Day, Community Fun Week in July with theatre, dancing and poetry. Concerts are held regularly near Middle Lake.
Refreshments	The Stables Tea Room and Tea Garden opens 11:30–17:00 hours when the House is open (*see* pages 170–3).

For some 300 years Osterley Park, an estate of 650 acres (263 hectares) was the largest park near London. At its core was a 'faire and stately building of bricke', completed by Sir Thomas Gresham, Chancellor of the Exchequer to Queen Elizabeth I, by about 1577. In 1761 Francis Child (or Childe), one of a family of wealthy bankers, commissioned the neoclassical architect Robert Adam to redesign it. Child died in 1763, but his brother Robert maintained the work. Adam kept the four Tudor turrets, but closed the front with the magnificent portico, and much of the interior was also transformed to his designs. The result was described by the writer Horace Walpole (1717–97) as 'a palace of palaces'. The house has remained virtually unchanged outside and in since Adam's day, the brightness of its interior decoration a surprise to modern eyes. The park had 'manie fair ponds', with the customary Tudor walled gardens beside the house. The Child family called in the architect Sir William Chambers (1800–83) to replace this formality with looser, more natural planning, and lakes were created from the small ponds.

In 1949 the 9th Earl of Jersey (a daughter of the Childs married into this family in 1802) gave the house and the park to the National Trust. The house was initially let to the Department of the Environment to cover management costs, but it reverted to Trust control in 1988, backed with management funds. The Trust has plans to restore more of the park's 18th century character. In the 1960s the estate was bisected by the M4 motorway. The southern half – covered on this walk – is 140 acres (57 hectares). This great reduction in area had no visual impact on the core of what is a unique survival, a great country estate within the embrace of London.

THE OSTERLEY PARK WALK
Start and finish South Avenue. *Time* Allow 1¼ hours.

South Avenue, the main drive leading to Osterley Park House, passes through fields of wheat and pasture, a rural touch which sets the scene for the character of its sur-park. The drive was created in 1870, when the new West London Railway built a station almost at the Park gates. It is lined with trees such as limes and horse chest-nuts, with drifts of daffodils beneath them in spring. There are some liquidambars or sweet gums along the path from the car park at the end of the drive. This tree was first brought to Britain in 1681 for Bishop Henry Compton *(see* pages 35–6). It is similar in appearance to maples, but with bobble fruit instead of the maple's winged fruit. The autumn leaves are equally colourful.

Garden Lake
The path rounds the end of Garden Lake and turns left along its north bank. Middle Lake, a larger stretch of water, lies to the right behind trees. These lakes are part of Chambers' improvements of around 1750, when the Park was 'naturalized' in the manner that was popular at the time. Before then, there was a formal, straight canal, partnered by avenues of trees.

There are likely to be black-necked Canada geese, mallard duck and coot on the lake, all reasonably tame. In summer, white waterlilies float on its surface. Out on the water is a curious Chinese Pavilion. It is a fairly recent addition, donated by the Hutchinson Whampoa company of Hong Kong in 1987, following a Chinese Festival held here. It also echoes Chambers' influence. He popularized the Chinese style with his Pagoda in Kew Gardens, and this pavilion is a copy of one that he designed for a lake at Kew. There is a record of a Chinese tea house at Osterley which has now disappeared.

The Cedar Lawn
Follow the path along the lakeside and when you near the house, take a detour round the Cedar Lawn to the right. Its magnificent cedars of Lebanon *(Cedrus libani)* were planted in the 1760s, which makes them close to 240 years old, and experts at the National Trust think they were probably planted to commemorate the birth of Sarah Sophia Fane, a granddaughter of Robert Child.

Cedars of Lebanon have become firmly linked with the country house image; they were not planted around town mansions because they cannot tolerate much smoke pollution. Although the diarist John Evelyn (1620–1706) makes no mention of them in his book *Sylva*, which was published in 1664, they were introduced at about that time, maybe via France – there is a delightful story of a Frenchman bringing the first seedlings to Paris using his hat as a flower pot. They come from Syria as well as from the Lebanon, and became popular not only for their tiered shape but also their Biblical links – they are mentioned in the Book of Psalms, for example – which made them superb commemorative trees. These Osterley Park cedars miraculously escaped damage in the two great night-time storms of October 1987 and January 1990 which cut swathes across the trees of southern Britain.

Replacements have now been planted, prudently. Other closely related trees on this lawn are the Atlantic cedar *(Cedrus atlantica)* from the Atlas Mountains in North Africa, with upward-angled branches and bluish needles, and the deodar *(Cedrus deodora)* from the Himalayas, with a pointed crown. At the southwestern corner is a venerable cork oak *(Quercus suber)* with massive horizontal branches, its trunk protected by railings. This Mediterranean tree, planted as a curiosity a couple of centuries ago, is a real find.

Past the Cedar Lawn to the left of the path are some swamp cypresses *(Taxodium distichum)* from the southeastern U.S.A., first recorded in Britain in 1640 and brought to Britain by John Tradescant junior *(see page 105–6)*. In wet or water-logged ground these trees grow curious root knobs sticking up above ground, to get air to the roots. When they were planted the water table was higher and the lake edges probably deeply marshy. The swamp cypress is a deciduous conifer with rather soft green needles which it sheds in entire leafy shoots each autumn. Just beyond them a mound marks the site of an 18th-century ice house, domed in brick, within which lake ice was packed in straw to last through the summer. It was filled in for safety reasons in 1939. Further along the path on the right are two ancient stag-headed oaks *(see page 137–8)* growing on a rise above wet ground.

The Great Meadow
Continue along the path, beyond the Ancient Oaks. To your right is the Great Meadow, enclosed with metal fencing. It is grazed by cattle – usually French Limousins, massive but benign animals with whitish coats – which lends a rural touch to the park. Ahead of you the path winds through a broad belt of trees called the West Woods, which hide the urban development beyond the park boundary. As you reach the edge of the wood, turn off the main path along a rough track leading to the right. A short distance ahead , the path emerges into a clearing, from where there is a good view of the west front of the house

Out on the open grazing land of the Great Meadow there are three large clusters of trees, surrounded by tangled undergrowth. They are known as Historic Tree Clumps and they were planted as part of Chambers' landscaping of the 18th century, with a mixture of trees, such as horse and sweet chestnut, oak and hornbeam, with hazel and hawthorn below. They have become invaded by sycamore and are now being cleared and replanted.

From the clearing continue your circuit of the Great Meadow, following the rough track. It is easy, in this rural landscape, to forget you are in London. The West Woods contain some interesting trees planted about 100 years ago by the seventh Earl of Jersey, such as Hungarian oaks *(Quercus frainetto),* distinguishable by their large leaves with many wavy lobes, and red oaks *(Quercus rubra)* from North America. These are spectacular when a cold snap in autumn turns the leaves to fiery colours. At the turn of the 19th century the oaks were supplemented by exotic trees, but in recent years the woods have been damaged by storms – two groups of cedars of Lebanon were lost in 1990 – and by invasion by sycamore and other scrub. Work has been carried out to clear this and to replant, with the aim of creating a wood with a better 'body'.

OSTERLEY PARK

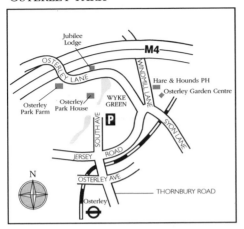

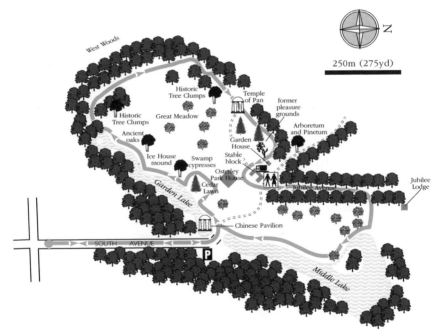

250m (275yd)

The Temple of Pan and the Pleasure Grounds

Once you reach the north side of the Great Meadow you see the gravel path ahead of you. Rejoin it and turn right. You soon see to your right the Temple of Pan, a kind of summer house where the family might picnic. It was designed by Chambers and is Doric in style – the oldest form of classical Greek architecture, with simple capitals at the tops of the pillars. Pan was the god of flocks and gardens, and the ruler of Arcadia (a province of Greece since ancient times). The temple is usually open in summer and its interior walls are decorated with Wedgwood-style swags in green and white. Behind it, evergreens have been planted, like those that would have originally been its setting.

Return to the side path and follow it as it curves to the right, round an area known as the Pleasure Grounds where there are some attractive cedars. Beyond the Pleasure Grounds stretch an arboretum, where trees of special scientific interest grow, and a pinetum, a collection of exotic evergreens such as the Colorado white fir *(Abies concolor)* – the Pinetum is sometimes referred to as an American Garden. There are also rhododendrons planted at the turn of the 20th century.

An orangery designed by Robert Adam (1728–92) stood on the Pleasure Grounds until 1950, when it burnt down, and as you approach Osterley Park House you see Adam's Garden House to the left, an attractive, semicircular building with round-arched windows and paired pilasters (projecting rectangular pillars). In front of it a Regency flower garden has recently been recreated. Originally, it would have been planted with exotic novelties; today it has beds of shrub roses, pinks, rosemary and sweet peas trained up wooden pyramids.

As you near the house you see that a few magnolias and old camellia varieties have been planted against its west front. Against the old wall of the stables to your left grow specimens of the spectacular evergreen *Magnolia grandiflora*, which bears huge, heavily scented waxy white flowers the size of dinner plates from June to September. This magnolia was a species collected by the first American-born botanist, John Bartram (1699–1777). He also courageously collected pines, maples and oaks from Red Indian territory to ship back to Britain, and he sent the first rhododendron to Britain, *Rhododendron maximum*.

Leaving the serpentine path, bear left around the stable block. This is a Tudor building, part of Sir Thomas Gresham's mansion of the 1570s, although it has since been altered. The central clock by Richard Street dates to 1714 and the Tuscan porch below it was built in the 1750s.

Middle Lake

Walk on toward the east front of the house and head along the avenue of trees you see to your left (running northward). This is Jubilee Avenue, planted to commemorate Queen Victoria's Diamond Jubilee in 1897. It leaves the grounds at Jubilee Lodge on a bridle path leading to Wyke Green, but turn right before you reach the park's eastern boundary and cross the open grass to Middle Lake.

Since it is relatively undisturbed (although it is not quiet, since the M4, which runs around part of the park's boundary, is fairly close by), a great deal of interesting wildlife can be seen at the lake's western end. Great crested grebe and herons compete with the fishermen, who claim that the waters of the lake contain pike. The ridge and furrow of medieval ploughland that was enclosed by the park are visible in the turf around the lake.

Turn right along the bank and stroll back toward the bridge at the lake's southern end. Across it is the path leading to South Avenue, where the walk ends.

Syon Park

Location	About 8 miles (13 kilometres) west of Charing Cross.
Transport	Syon Lane and Kew Bridge stations (overground trains from Waterloo and Clapham Junction); 267 bus from Kew Bridge to Brent Lea.
Admission	Gardens open daily 11:00–18:00 hours, £2.50 adults (£2 children).
Seasonal features	Spring blossom; displays of azaleas and rhododendrons in spring. Trees in autumn colours. Rose garden in summer.
Events	Tree dressing and flower displays, craft shows and fairs. Carriage-driving. The annual London to Brighton vintage car race begins at Syon. Christmas carols by candle-light.
Refreshments	Patio Café open daily 10:00–17:30 hours.

The grounds of Syon House, London's only ducal residence, provide one of the most attractive London walks. Its 55 acres (22.2 hectares) of gardens and parkland are noted for their fine native and exotic trees. They number more than 3,000, of which about 40 per cent are more than 100 years old, and close to 200 are 200 years old. The grounds were opened to the public in 1837, and a century ago the prestigious *Gardener's Chronicle* could write of Syon: 'Its History up to the present day is almost the most brilliant on record as regards practical horticulture, to say nothing of the interest attaching to the large and choice collection of rare trees...'.

In the 1400s, a convent stood on the site of Syon House, but after 1539, when Henry VIII dissolved the religious houses, the convent buildings fell into disuse. Their last use was as a prison for the hapless Catherine Howard, the king's fifth wife, before her execution in 1542. The Duke of Somerset, Lord Protector, subsequently built the core of the house that stands today on the cloisters of the convent, but he was beheaded in 1552, charged with wishing to fortify it, which counted as treason at the time. In 1594 Elizabeth I leased the estate to the powerful Percy family, earls and later dukes of the northern province of Northumberland, who were eventually given freehold ownership.

The interior of the house, then, is basically Tudor and there would have been formal terraces and gardens near the house in Tudor days, sheltered by brick walls. One of these seems to have been an early botanical garden, for a Dr. William Turner, author of a famous herbal and often described as 'the father of English botany', lived on the opposite bank of the River Thames in the 1540s, in the area

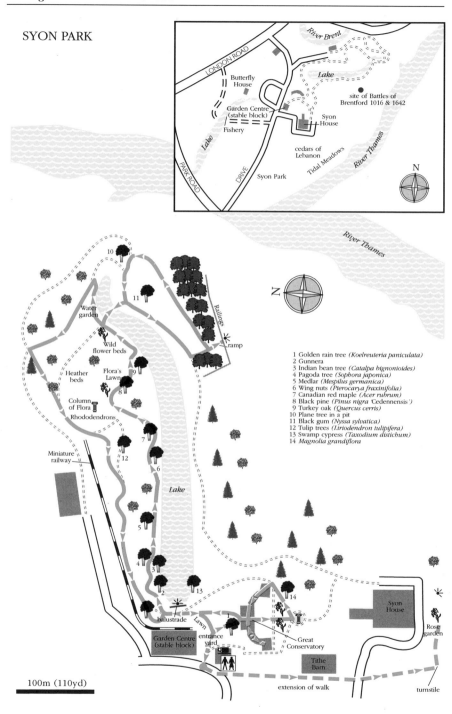

SYON PARK

River Brent

LONDON ROAD

Butterfly
House

Lake

site of Battles of
Brentford 1016 & 1642

Garden Centre
(stable block)

Syon
House

Fishery

Lake

cedars of
Lebanon

PARK ROAD

DRIVE

Syon Park

Tidal Meadows

River Thames

N

River Thames

N

10

11

Water
garden

Railings

ramp

Wild
flower beds

Flora's
Lawn

Heather
beds

9

Column
of Flora

8

Rhododendrons

7

Miniature
railway

12

6

Lake

5

4 3

2   13

14

Syon
House

balustrade

Rose
garden

Garden Centre
(stable block)

Lawn

entrance
yard

Great
Conservatory

Tithe
Barn

extension of walk

turnstile

100m (110yd)

1 Golden rain tree *(Koelreuteria paniculata)*
2 Gunnera
3 Indian bean tree *(Catalpa bignonioides)*
4 Pagoda tree *(Sophora japonica)*
5 Medlar *(Mespilus germanica)*
6 Wing nuts *(Pterocarya fraxinifolia)*
7 Canadian red maple *(Acer rubrum)*
8 Black pine *(Pinus nigra 'Cedennensis')*
9 Turkey oak *(Quercus cerris)*
10 Plane tree in a pit
11 Black gum *(Nyssa sylvatica)*
12 Tulip trees *(Liriodendron tulipifera)*
13 Swamp cypress *(Taxodium distichum)*
14 *Magnolia grandiflora*

which is now Kew Gardens, and rowed across the river to work at Syon. In the 1630s, the tenth earl commissioned the Renaissance architect Inigo Jones to improve the house, but it subsequently became a prison again, this time for the children of Charles I after the Civil War of 1642. During the 1760s the first Duke – then the richest man in the kingdom – had further improvements made by Robert Adam. His magnificent decoration remains, although in the 1820s the exterior of the house was fronted in Bath stone, which was then considered an improvement.

Around the time when Adam was redesigning the interior, the Tudor gardens were swept away by the first Duke. A painting by the Venetian painter Canaletto (1697–1768) of about that time shows that they had already gone. The landscape designer 'Capability' Brown, who was born in Northumberland in 1716 and who worked for the family in the north, was also employed. He introduced a new style, replacing formal gardens with grass and planting lawns right up to the house. He had serpentine lakes dug out and planted trees in clumps that were carefully positioned to look natural. A good many of the estate's fine trees have been planted since 'Capability' Brown's time. They have been sensitively selected and sited, to add to the appeal of his basic plan, and many are unusual or especially interesting.

Some of the most interesting trees along the walk are marked on the map and described below, but most of the exotic trees in these grounds generally have nametags. Some are quite hard to see, however, and they give the scientific name only, so it is a good idea to take with you on the walk one of the species recognition guides listed on page 173.

This walk takes place in the enclosed gardens to the north of the house, around the lake, but the Rose Garden to the south of the house. This is reached by leaving the garden by the yard and following the wall that surrounds the garden until you reach the turnstile leading into it. It is still quite a young garden, but with many old-fashioned roses and other, particularly beautiful varieties, such as 'Bush Chaucer' and 'Roserie de la Haie'. All are name-tagged. The view from the southern end of the rose garden is of open ground across the tidal meadows between Syon House and the River Thames. To the right is a scatter of storm-distressed cedars of Lebanon. In the great storms of 1987 and 1990 about 120 of Syon's trees were lost or severely damaged, and there has been replanting since.

As well as the rose garden, there is much else to see in Syon Park: The London Butterfly House, with living specimens of butterflies and other insects from around the world; an art centre; and an aquarium where exotic fish, such as piranhas, are displayed. The garden centre – the first to open in Britain, in 1965 – occupies the Riding School, designed by Charles Fowler, and the stables, designed by the neo-Gothic architect, James Wyatt (1747–1813).

THE SYON PARK WALK
Start and finish: The Entrance Yard. ***Time*** Allow 2 hours.

The entrance to the gardens lies through a yard, where there is a café and a shop. The glass dome of the Great Conservatory looms up behind it on the right, and once you are through the gate you can see its north door to the right. Close by it is an attractive golden rain tree *(Koelreuteria paniculata)* from Asia, with handsome clusters of yellow flowers in July and August, and papery, bladder-like fruits. After admiring it, however, continue along the path. Passing the miniature railway on the left, head left across the lawn and take the path that leads leftward to the lake. You are likely to meet your first peacocks as you start out, or hear one screech.

The Lake

The western end of the lake is marked by an iron balustrade that looks rather like a bridge. Pause beside the balustrade, from which there is a lovely view eastward along the lake. 'Capability' Brown was certainly employed at Syon, since there are records of payments made to him in the 1750s, but there are no plans or other paper evidence for what he did. However, this lake can be safely regarded as a 'Capability' Brown feature; a serpentine, natural-looking lake with carefully sculpted banks is his signature. The park had been extended to the north, and the old and new areas were separated by this manufactured stretch of water. 'It is well stored with all sorts of river fish and can be emptied and filled by means of a sluice ...' an observer noted at the time.

Follow the path right around the curve of the lake and continue along the north bank, passing a stand of gunnera looking like giant rhubarb, its feet in the water. This is a waterside plant from Brazil, but it is relatively hardy in the cool temperate climate of Britain (the giant foliage dies down in winter). Ahead of it, sprawling beside the lake, is an Indian bean-tree *(Catalpa bignonioides)*, a showy tree with broad, pale green leaves and masses of white flowers in upright clusters in summer, followed by hanging beans, which remain through the winter.

Syon's Trees

Continue following this meandering lakeside path. To the left is a grassy woodland area planted with magnificent trees. Growing just beside the path, beyond the Indian bean-tree, is a fine pagoda tree *(Sophora japonica)*, a mountain tree from Asia with panicles of white flowers; and a little way past it is a medlar *(Mespilus germanica)*, a small tree native to southern Europe, with rather twisting branches, pretty spring blossoms, and autumn fruits like large brown rose hips. It was a common feature of gardens from Tudor days.

As you walk on the path curves down to the lake shore and you notice that areas of the waterside are planted with an unusual border of herbaceous flowers and foliage plants. There are coots, mallards and Canada geese on the lake, and terrapins can often be seen basking at the waterside on warm days. Look out for a clump of wing nuts. These trees are, in fact, the suckers of a Caucasian wing nut *(Pterocarya fraxinifolia)*, which have grown tall; they have huge leaves composed of paired leaflets, and straight hanging chains of winged fruit.

At this point, the path forks. Bear right and walk on past a narrow-leaved ash *(Fraxinus oxycarpa)* that comes from the eastern Mediterranean. Continue past beds planted with azaleas, to reach another labelled tree on your left, the Canadian red maple *(Acer rubrum)*. The leaves of this splendid tree turn bright yellow or rich red or even deep purple in autumn.

The Column of Flora

Past this signpost red maple, you quickly reach Flora's Lawn, an open expanse of lawn set with herbaceous beds. At its northern end is the tall Column of Flora. It is a Doric column, the oldest and simplest Greek style, and is probably an 18th-century original, but the figure of Flora, the Roman goddess of flowers, on top of it is a fibreglass replica. Walk diagonally (westward) across the lawn and along a small pathway leading off it on the far side, and turn right. In the area ahead of you to the left, the beds of the old heather garden have recently been redug and planted with British wild flowers. Also to the left of this path is a small glade planted with some interesting oaks: the Hungarian oak *(Quercus frainetto)* with wavy-lobed leaves; and the American swamp white oak *(Q. bicolor)*; and on the right, overlooking the lawn, is a beautiful pine, *Pinus nigra* 'Cedennensis'. Further toward the lake stands a fine copper beech and, close to the lake shore, a magnificent Turkey oak *(Quercus cerris)*, which has rather feathery leaves for an oak. Now turn left along the lakeside passing to the left another bed of British wild flowers.

The South Bank

Follow the path round to the right and cross the footbridge over the lake. In summer look down into the water to see yellow native waterlilies floating on the surface. In summer, it is pleasant to stroll for a short distance along this south bank of the lake, where meadowsweet, with its tufted, cream-coloured flowers, grows high. Very soon, however, railings close off the grounds for private use, and the walk strikes off to the left across the open grassy meadow.

Walk about 100 yards (90 metres) up a slight rise toward the southern corner of the meadow. You are walking toward a dense line of willow scrub, but as you approach the corner, you can see that it is penetrated by a grassy ramp flanked, in summer, by cow parsley growing high. Walk right to the railing at the end of the ramp. From it you can look out across the open ground which lies between the house, visible to the right, and the river bank facing Kew Gardens.

The open ground ahead may be a relic of the work of 'Capability' Brown. A guidebook to London and its environs published in 1761 reported that 'a fine lawn extending from Isleworth to Brentford' had been created and that 'by these means also a beautiful prospect is opened into the King's gardens at Richmond (now Kew Gardens) as well as up and down the Thames ... even the Thames itself seems to belong to the gardens, and the different sorts of vessels which successively sail as it were through them, appear to be the property of their noble proprietor...' Somewhere on these tidal meadows are the sites of the battles of Brentford of 1016 and 1642, and some claim that this is the spot where Julius Caesar fought his way across the Thames in 54 BC. Wooden stakes found in the river mud could match his description of the defences of the Celtic tribes.

From the ramp, turn right and walk across the open grass to a giant plane tree which you can see ahead, surrounded by railings. This old tree stands in a stone-lined pit. One possible reason is that it was growing there before the soil was piled up from the lake excavations. Walk back along the path to the footbridge, passing, on the left, a fine black gum *(Nyssa sylvatica)*, a swamp tree from the northern U.S.A. whose leaves turn magnificent shades of red and orange in autumn. Recross the footbridge to the north bank of the lake.

The Water Garden

Take the path that leads right from the footbridge, and follow its twists and turns through a charming water garden planted with attractive evergreen and deciduous foliage. A small stream winding through it splashes over shallow water drops, and is crossed by a humpbacked stone bridge and stepping stones. On hot summer days this water garden is blissfully cool and very peaceful. Leave the water garden along the path to the right and follow it through the parkland on the south side of Flora's Lawn and around the back of the Column of Flora.

The Woodland Walk

Just past the Column of Flora you enter an area of woodland planted with rhododendrons. In spring it is aflame with brilliant colour. The path takes you through the northern part of the grassy area planted with specimen trees through which you walked earlier. Down by the lake there are beds of orange, pink, and yellow azaleas.

Leave the path from time to time and wander through the trees in order to see them more closely. Look out for a lofty copper beech, a tall-trunked hybrid Indian bean-tree, and dark-leaved Mediterranean oaks. Some of the trees in this park became popular because of their colourful autumn foliage: the North American liquidambar or sweet gum *(Liquidambar styraciflua)* and the maples are notable examples – and others because of their unusual or striking insect-pollinated flowers; native British trees, such as the oak, the ash, and the beech have only small, inconspicuous flowers, because they are wind-pollinated.

In the middle of this woodland area is an enormously tall tree with a primeval-looking trunk. This is a tulip tree *(Liriodendron tulipifera)*. Its foliage is far out of reach, but a younger one is growing nearby, and you can inspect its unusual leaf, whose shape is unlike that of any other tree, with a rather abruptly notched tip, looking as if it has been scissored across. The tulip tree was one of the first exotic trees to be brought from North American in the 1600s. It has yellowish flowers above folded-back sepals, which are rather cup-shaped, but do not look much like tulips. Past the tulip tree is an ancient sweet chestnut, very likely a tree planted by 'Capability' Brown. His plantings were mainly of native or long-established trees, and the sweet chestnut was brought to Britain in Roman times.

Rejoin the path at the western end of the woodland walk, which is bright with daffodils in spring, and walk back around the western head of the lake. Past the balustrade to the left, growing at the waterside, is a swamp or bald cypress *(Taxodium distichum)* from the southern U.S.A *(see page 18)*. The pond cypress *(Taxodium ascendens)*, a close relative, also grows on this lakeside.

The Great Conservatory

Now head southward toward the Great Conservatory, the climax of the walk. In the past, Syon had a magnificent Conservatory and a vast glasshouse area dedicated to horticulture over toward the River Brent. Exotic flowers were grown in them, pineapples, bananas and figs were ripened, and the first mangosteens – a fruit from the East Indies – to be grown in Britain. Those glasshouses have all gone, but the Great Conservatory remains. Erected in 1820–30 by Charles Fowler, the architect of Covent Garden Market in central London, is a mansion of its kind in Bath stone, cast iron and immense areas of glass.

Conservatories have an important place in British garden history. They first appeared in the 17th century, when, furnished with a stove to keep frosts at bay, they were called 'winter houses'. Soon after, when orange trees became a prized status symbol, they evolved into orangeries, and a new term, 'greenhouse', was coined for these buildings, which protected tender 'greens', as orange trees and other tender shrubs, such as pomegranates, myrtle, and bay, were called. Later, a new word, 'conservatory', became used to describe places to show plants off, and 'greenhouse' became the name for the glasshouses where they were propagated.

The first conservatories were stone or brick buildings, with a solid roof, for the importance of light as well as heat in plant biology was not yet fully understood. But by the early 19th century new technology brought a revolution in plant propagation: curved iron glazing bars (which enabled walls and roofs to be glazed with small panes of glass) were invented by J. C. Loudon in 1816; and although until 1845 all windows carried a prohibitive tax, it became cheaper to manufacture glass. The scene was set for the creation at Syon of this vision of curved tracery with a vista of the sky.

Walk through the north door and stand beneath the central dome. The scale of the Great Conservatory is astounding. It measures more than 100 yards (90 metres) from the end of one of its curved wings to the other, and the dome above you is 60 feet (18 metres) high. Walk along the west wing, to the right, to see a commemorative vine threading through its ceiling. It was grown from a cutting donated by the Australian government, to commemorate 36 cuttings sent from Syon to Australia in 1832, to start the white wine industry there. At the west end is a palm and fern display, which is kept humid by a pretty waterfall. Now walk along to the east wing, which is stocked with bedding plants and climbers, some of which are beautifully perfumed. At the end is a delightful cactus room.

Exit the Conservatory by the south door, and you stand onto a raised terrace, whose step is planted with old-fashioned roses. Embraced by the Conservatory's two wings is a formal garden with plots of lawn set with yew clipped into cone shapes. Descend the steps and walk along the path through the centre of the garden, where there is a pool with a fountain topped by a statue of Mercury.

Re-enter the Conservatory through the door at the end of the east wing, which leads into the cactus room, and along the eastern arm, stocked with perfumed bedding plants and climbers. When you reach the dome, exit by the north door, turn left, and follow the path to the entrance yard, where the walk ends.

Chiswick House Gardens

Location	About 6 miles (9.5 kilometres) west of Charing Cross.
Transport	Chiswick Station (overground trains from Waterloo via Clapham Junction) is 5 minutes' walk from the west side of the Park. Chiswick Park and Turnham Green Underground stations (District Line) are about 20 minutes' walk away. Buses are 190, 425, E3. There is a free car park off the Great West Road.
Admission	Open 08:30 am–dusk. Admission is free.
Seasonal features	Camellia collection in flower in the conservatory in early spring, but these gardens have interest all year round.
Events	Theatre and opera in the amphitheatre.
Refreshments	Burlington Café open daily 10:00–17:00 hours.

Chiswick House Gardens were created in the 18th century to set off the then innovative Palladian style of an enchanting new villa, which was designed and built by Richard Boyle, the third Earl of Burlington (1694–1753), on his Chiswick estate, during the years 1727–29. It was built beside an older Jacobean house and linked to it – if not, it had no kitchen (one wit described it as 'too little to live in, and too large to hang to one's watch'). The older house was demolished in 1788 and wings added to the new one. These wings were in turn demolished in the 1950s, leaving the free-standing building and its extension, which remain today.

Lord Burlington became the chief steersman for English taste in his day. He had made a Grand Tour of Europe during which he had seen the ruins of ancient Rome, and in England he implanted a passion for antiquity. The Palladian style, named after the Italian architect Andrea Palladio (1508-80), incorporated Roman motifs and was much to the taste of Lord Burlington and his peers, who saw themselves as the new Romans. They also admired the work of Inigo Jones (1573–1652), the first architect in England to build in the classical style.

Chiswick House was intended as a kind of gallery, a setting for works of art, for civilized talk and music, and near enough to the London of the time for the fashionable. It went down well. As the poet Alexander Pope said in 1732 'I assure you, Chiswick has been to me the finest thing this glorious sun has shined on ...'

The grounds of Chiswick house are full of classical follies. A key name was William Kent (*see* page 9), an artist and colleague of Lord Burlington, who also painted some ceilings inside the house. He planned gardens with an artist's eye, with set scenes like three-dimensional pictures which visitors could walk to, and which were designed to evoke memories and provoke ideas. He was greatly influenced by the artist Claude Lorrain (1600–82) who painted scenes of an invented Roman countryside with temples bathed by mellow light and saturated with nostalgia. But Kent made another impression on these grounds with the natural-looking lake and its rustic cascade, both first examples of their kind.

Kent's work in the grounds was probably finished by 1738. When Lord Burlington died in 1753, the estate was inherited by the fifth Duke of Devonshire and remained with the family until it was acquired by the local authority in 1929. With the Devonshires there came further changes – in the 1780s, serpentine paths were created in the wilderness, for example, and the classical bridge was built in 1774. More changes were made during the 19th century but some of these changes and additions were reversed in the 1950s to recreate much of the atmosphere of the original gardens as designed by Burlington and Kent.

THE CHISWICK HOUSE GARDENS WALK
Start and finish The main gate. *Time* Allow 1¼ hours.

The walk begins, as it should, at the main gate to Chiswick House. But if you drive to the house and use the car park off the Great West Road, don't miss the chance to glimpse something of what was once the working area of the old gardens. Surrounding the car park on the north side is a a mellow brick wall pierced by an iron gate. A glimpse through it recalls childhood visions of an enchanted wilderness. In fact, you are looking at an overgrown part of a walled vegetable garden.

To reach the main gate you should leave the car park through its main entrance to the south, and turn right along the Great West Road. Very shortly you see to your right the impressive, wrought-iron gate leading into Duke's Avenue. Go through it and walk down the long, tree-shaded avenue. The old brick wall to your right surrounds the northeast side of the walled gardens. At the bottom is Corney Road Lodge, designed by Decimus Burton. Bear right along the path, and you come to a wide lawn planted with fine old trees. They screen off the front of the house, which comes into view to the right as you emerge close to the main gate.

Chiswick House
From main gate, walk along the path overshadowed by great cedars of Lebanon toward the south front of the house. This has many classical allusions: the columns are copied from the Temple of Jupiter in Rome, for example, and the dome from the Roman Pantheon. Even the chimneys are shaped like obelisks, Egyptian monuments which had been admired by the Romans. Walk into the gravelled forecourt, noticing the termini, or terms against the hedging. These are stone columns carved with a human face at the top. They date from the 1720s, and are another echo of the ancient Romans, who used them to mark the boundaries of their estates. In their day the face would have been that of the god Terminus, who presided over boundaries and landmarks.

Alongside the steps up to the door are statues by Michael Rysbrack (1694–1770), a Flemish sculptor working in England in Kent's time. Now somewhat weathered, they are of Palladio (to the left) and Inigo Jones (to the right). Palladio himself would not have placed them there; he would have thought them too lively for the restrained design of a Palladian house. Turn back and then left along the path that leads past the west side of the house until you reach the lake (or 'river' as it is called).

The River and The Cascade

The layout of much of the grounds is rather formal, but if you look through the gap in the hedge to your right you see that a great lawn, planted with trees, spreads out from the front of the house, which sweeps down to the lake in a more natural way. The winding bank of the lake also looks natural. It is not; it was dug out to the pattern you see today. It was very probably William Kent (who 'first leaped the fence and saw all nature was a garden') who produced this early example of the famous English 'natural' landscape style: water following the lie of the land and set in open grass scattered with trees. Walk onto the hump-backed bridge. To the left is the cascade, a rustic, rocky edifice built to contain machinery to send water tumbling into the lake. It was an ambitious feature, for in 1746 an engineer was paid £182 for trying to make it work, and it was later given an engine. In 1996 a modern cascade was installed, and can often now be seen working.

The Terrace

Now leave the path and climb up the grassy bank to your left. This is the Terrace, a high bank, built with the spoil dug up when the lake was excavated, with a walk running along the top. This walk, which has now been restored and was opened to visitors just as this book went to press, once gave guests (and visitors, for grounds such as this were often open to visitors from among the gentry) a view over the surrounding meadows to the River Thames – today it is obscured by buildings. The bank was planted, as it is today, with flowering shrubs. It extends as far as the gate from Burlington Lane, and there are some superb tall trees further along the path.

Classical Follies

To the right at the end of the terrace is one of the classical follies that create points of visual interest in these gardens: an obelisk. The sculpture at its base (a copy of the original, which has been removed for safekeeping) is from a 2nd century AD Roman tombstone and shows two women and a child. This obelisk is the hub of a goosefoot, a point from which straight-hedged alleys radiate, each one usually closed off at the end by a built feature. The alley that runs straight ahead leads the eye to the back of a temple on the other side of the lake. This goosefoot is one of two in these gardens. They were probably first laid out by the designer Charles Bridgeman (*see* page 9), but in the 1780s, when the fashion in landscape design had moved from formal to natural, they were changed into winding paths. They were recreated in the 1950s, although perhaps not exactly to the same lines.

The walk proceeds along the alley to the left, which leads to the classic bridge. This alley is quite wide – it was converted into a carriage drive (it was usual to drive around at least the larger estates), but it has recently been planted with lime trees. A little way up, to the right, is a magnificent evergreen Mediterranean oak (*Quercus ilex*). Through the trees to the left you can see a large cricket field. Stop to admire

CHISWICK HOUSE GARDENS

1 Cedars of Lebanon (*Cedrus libani*)
2 Maidenhair tree (*Gingko biloba*)
3 Swamp cypress (*Taxodium distichum*)

300m (330yd)

the classic bridge when you reach it. It was built in 1774 to replace an earlier small bridge, probably to a design by the architect James Wyatt. From the bridge there are views along the lake shores, variously planted with pampas grass, dogwood with its red autumn twigs, and native meadowsweet.

The Amphitheatre

Ahead of you on the other side of the bridge a wilderness stretches ahead. It does seem quite wild (you may hear the screech of a jay or a woodpecker) with, today, some magnificent trees. The walk turns right, however, along a straight path bordered by formal, clipped hedges. It is, in fact, an alley of a second goosefoot, whose three alleys can be seen on the map above.

Over the centuries, this area of the gardens has undergone many changes. Whereas a plan of 1753 shows all three lines of the goosefoot, a plan of 1818 shows two of the three gone, and a network of serpentine walking paths. In the restorations of the 1950s, the paths were retained and the hedges of the two missing straight alleys were replanted.

As you approach the hub end of the alley, you come across an evocative scene, almost certainly the work of William Kent (the hesitation only because he was not accustomed to leave plans or notes, but often worked on site by eye alone). It remains much as it was in the 18th century. A break in the hedge to the right reveals a sudden view down into a miniature turf amphitheatre with an obelisk at its centre set in a shallow pool, and behind that a temple – the front of the temple whose back you saw from the obelisk. It is an Ionic temple (the Ionic order, one of the styles of decorating pillars and other architectural features in classical times, had spiral scrolls on the capitals at the tops of the columns). In summer, orange bushes in white tubs are set along the curving terraces of the amphitheatre as they would have been two and a half centuries ago. The temple, 'embosomed soft with trees' (to quote the 18th-century nature poet, James Thomson), was a captured memory of the classic Roman countryside – the kind of scene that appeared in the paintings of artists such as Claude Lorrain.

Beside the railings alongside the path is a stone memorial with a Latin inscription commemorating the burial beneath of 'Lilly, the most faithful of hounds ...'. And if you have not yet noticed, the grounds at Chiswick have plenty of dog-poop-scoop bins.

Continue to the end of the alley and the hub of the goosefoot, from which four alleys radiate. Look left along the middle alley and you see what appears to be an imposing building; it is known as the Bagnio. However, if you walk to the end of the alley, you will see that it is merely a façade, with empty niches for statuary.

The Exedra
The hub of the goosefoot is conveniently set with stone benches on which you can sit and admire the elegant northwest façade of Chiswick House. When you have rested, walk onto the lawn. To your right is the exedra, a kind of curved porch of closely clipped yew hedge, which is first hinted at on a map of 1733. Turn to face the exedra. These semicircular alcoves were a feature of ancient Roman villa gardens. They make a superb setting for statues, and there is (from the right as you face the exedra) one of the Roman-style terms, a lion, another term carved with the name Socrates in Greek, two urns, three stone figures, and then to the left, more urns, terms, and another lion.

Socrates was probably named for a reason: he opposed tyranny, and in the 1730s Lord Burlington was suspicious of the authoritarian leanings of the Prime Minister, Sir Robert Walpole. The three central statues (maybe Cicero, Pompey and Caesar, but nobody knows for certain) were possibly looted from Emperor Hadrian's villa at Tivoli, outside Rome. They were at first housed in the Temple behind the amphitheatre, but were in this position by 1748.

The Doric Column
Return to the hub of the goosefoot and walk a short way along the alley to the extreme right to a Doric column you see ahead. It was placed in this spot (by 1728, judging from paintings of the time) as something to glimpse across the grounds, to walk to and admire. The Doric order was the oldest and simplest of the Greek

orders. To produce an ancient Roman effect, there was a copy of a statue of the Venus de Medici on top of the column, but she has now gone. The rose beds at the foot of the column were not part of the original design. They are recent, but rose beds are first recorded at Chiswick House in 1811.

The Deer House

From the Doric Column, take the path leading toward the small white building to the right. This is the Deer House, a simple building, looking rather like a shut-down railway station on a branch line in Greece – although, to be sure, that particular classical link is something Lord Burlington would not have known. It was intended to be one of a pair, the second standing at the other end of the path which stretches ahead, but it is now thought that the second one was never built. The name of the Deer House is explained by the fact that the area behind it, now occupied by a lawn and a shrubbery, was once a deer paddock. The animals could be a feature of the grounds if they were not obscured from view by a fence, so a ha-ha was dug out. The ha-ha was an invention of the early 1700s. ('Haha, that's a clever idea' was the origin of the name). It is a simple device, a ditch edged on one side with a vertical wall which the deer cannot jump. It still runs alongside the straight path on which you are now standing.

The Conservatory and The Italian Garden

Take a side trip now, along the path that curves round the back of the Deer House. You pass a doorway to the left, leading to the nurseries and the information centre; turn left, just past it, into the southwest entrance to the Conservatory.

This conservatory, designed by Samuel Ware in 1813, has the wings that were a feature of the time, and an innovative central dome (which was altered somewhat in 1933, and again in 1990). This was a forerunner of Decimus Burton's Palm House at Kew Gardens (*see* page 149), and Joseph Paxton's Crystal Palace (*see* page 90). Paxton is said to have worked at Chiswick House as a boy.

In 1828 the sixth Duke filled the conservatory with an outstanding collection of camellias, and today it is a key British collection, a brilliant sight in early spring. These flowers had become known earlier. At the turn of the 17th century. for example, John Cunningham, a surgeon with the East India Company, had landed at Shanghai in China to find nurseries of them, together with chrysanthemums and peonies in great variety. Before the 1830s, when the use of glass wardian cases made the safe transport of large numbers of living plants possible, cultivating camellias was a hobby for those rich enough to be able to afford a conservatory. Only later, when these shrubs had become common enough for gardeners to take chances with them, were they found to be reasonably hardy plants in the British climate.

Leave the conservatory by the central door. The front walk is lined with catmint, late-flowering wisteria, hydrangeas, and other flowers of subtle colour. Ahead of you is the Italian Garden, bright with red, white and blue flowers on a recent visit. This was originally laid out by the garden designer Lewis Kennedy for the sixth Duke of Devonshire in 1814, when, after some decades of enthusiasm for the natural look, formal planting was again becoming fashionable. 'Italian' was a blanket description; this garden, with its geometrically patterned parterres, its bedding, and its Coade stone urns was, in fact, modelled on a garden designed by the Empress Josephine, wife of Napoleon. Walk along the central path to view the flower beds. Today, the garden is a shadow of its original self, but the carefully trimmed low box hedges, with their unusual patterning, are still splendid. There are plans to restore the original plant lists. Turn right by the maidenhair tree *(Gingko biloba)* at the end of the path, stroll back toward the conservatory.

Leave the Italian Garden by the path to the left. Just to the left is the site of an orangery, made redundant by the conservatory and pulled down, and ahead a little lily pool with its goldfish, which also remain small, for these fish grow only as far as the size of their pond.

The Inigo Jones Gateway

Turn left up the path alongside the ha-ha to view this gateway. It dates to 1625, when it fronted Beaufort House in Chelsea, which became the home of Sir Hans Sloane, Lord Burlington's doctor. Inigo Jones (1573–1652) was the first English architect to build in Palladian style, with his Queen's House, Greenwich *(see* page 84). Knowing of his admiration for the classical architect, Sloane bequeathed this gateway to Lord Burlington in his will; it was reerected on the site of the proposed second Deer House in 1736. In those days it was not unusual to swap and change such features. The original gate piers at the end of the drive in front of Chiswick House, after several moves, have ended up in Green Park.

From the Inigo Jones Gateway, walk along the north front of Chiswick House. Across the lawn to the right runs a broad avenue flanked by cypress and cedar trees and stone urns. This ground was originally a grove of close-set youngish trees, which were, in time, cleared away. About halfway down the lawn is a pair of stone sphinxes, which were placed, one on each side, by 1742. One of them is new, and if you look behind you through the doorway of the Link Building to your left, you can see the original lead sphinx it replaced, now kept there for protection from the elements. In classical times, sphinxes signified wisdom. Those out on the lawn are shaded by two magnificent cedars of Lebanon *(Cedrus libani),* a signpost to a grand house, are first recorded growing in Britain in 1659). Continue walking past the front of the house until you reach the top of the avenue, and look along it. Your eye is directed along the middle alley of the goosefoot to the *faux* temple at the end – another of the surprise vistas that are an essential part of this garden.

If you have to return to the car park, take the avenue leading back to the hub of the goosefoot and follow the straight alley to the right. It leads to the Rustic House, which you can see ahead. Close to, it turns out to be a stone shed of no obvious use. Inside it a copy of a bust of Napoleon looking quite out of place (not quite the hero that Lord Burlington would have chosen), and three other pedestals, all unoccupied. About halfway along the alley, however, turn along a narrow path to the right, which leads to a gate in the wall surrounding the gardens. Go through it, turn left, and walk up the path beside the sports field. Go through the gate at the end and right into the car park. Otherwise, walk around the house to the south front and the main gate, where the walk ends.

Fulham Palace Gardens

Location	About 4½ miles (7 kilometres) west of Charing Cross.
Transport	Putney Bridge Underground Station (District Line) is 10 minutes' walk away. Putney Station (overground trains from Waterloo) is 20 minutes' walk away. Buses 72, 220, C4 stop on Fulham Palace Road, and 14, 22, 85, 93, 265 near Putney Bridge. There is a small car park.
Admission	Open daily from 07:30 hours–dusk. Bishop's Park opens daily from dawn–dusk. Admission to both is free.
Seasonal features	Spring blossom, magnolia walk April–May, herb garden in summer, fruit in October and autumn colour.
Events	Tours of the grounds and the Palace. Plant sales.
Refreshments	Bishop's Park Tea House open daily: winter 10:00-16:00 hours; summer 10:00-19:00 hours.

From the 11th century until 1973, Fulham Palace was the residence of the Bishops of London, and its beautiful gardens were largely the creation of the many keen gardeners among them. They have the atmosphere of very personal gardens – indeed, one Bishop Longfield loved Fulham Palace and its gardens so much that a special Act of Parliament was passed to allow him to live there in retirement. Before that, bishops did not retire, but died in office. Many are buried in All Saints Church by Putney Bridge, which from medieval times was the local parish church.

The site of the Palace, beside the River Thames, is a more ancient settlement, however. Archaeologists have recently discovered traces of Neolithic dwellings and Roman defensive earthworks. The Manor of Fulham was granted to Bishop Waldhere in 704, and from the 11th century the bishops had a country residence on the site. The Palace is at heart a Tudor mansion with later additions and alterations, but beneath the Great Lawn traces have been found of its predecessors. In medieval times, the site was surrounded by a massive defensive moat, the longest in England, which remained until the 1920s. Beyond it stretched Thameside water meadows, and the manorial farms and fields. Today, the buildings and gardens that were enclosed by the moat are classified as an Ancient Protected Monument.

A key figure in the development of the gardens was Henry Compton, Bishop of London 1675–1713, and, incidentally, the only bishop to sign the invitation inviting the Dutch Prince William of Orange and Queen Mary to become King and Queen of England in 1688. The diocese of this bishop included North America. He sent a botanist from Oxford, the Reverend John Banister, to Virginia as a missionary, with instructions to send interesting plants to Fulham. During his bishopric the

Palace gardens were planted with new trees and shrubs from America, the West Indies, India, and Africa. Early stove houses (greenhouses) were built in the gardens and filled with 'exoticks'. People came from all over England to see them.

John Banister went to Virginia in 1680 and collected plants there until his death. In 1688 he sent back to Britain *Magnolia virginiana* (sweet bay), the first magnolia to be grown in England. He also sent the sweet gum *(Liquidambar styraciflua)*, scarlet oak, the box elder or ash-leaved maple *(Acer negundo)* – all trees admired for their foliage. It is almost certain that these were first grown in Britain at Fulham Palace, starting the tradition of fine specimen trees. The original stock has died and been replaced, but some trees in the gardens may date from Bishop Compton's time. The success of his introductions is partly explained by the fact that for some years from 1681 his gardener was George London, who, with his partner Henry Wise, set up the influential Brompton Nurseries (where the South Kensington museums stand today), an important source of exotic plants for British gardeners.

Situated so close to the River Thames, the Palace was often flooded, and when in the 19th century the Bishops presented two water meadows along the riverside to the people of Fulham as a public park, they funded the building of an embankment to prevent further flooding. Steps in the embankment descend to what was then a sandy strand, popular with local children for bathing. The Victorians planted the embankment with a fine avenue of London plane trees.

As London and its population expanded, the bishops commuted less and less frequently to their summer retreat, and during the 20th century the Palace and its gardens fell into disuse. Eventually, in 1973, they leased them to the Borough of Hammersmith and Fulham. In 1976, the gardens were opened to the public. A survey was made of their trees and shrubs and a program of restoration began, in line with plans to restore the gardens' historic layout. In 1992 three rooms on the ground floor were opened as a small museum of the house, its beautiful gardens, and the adjoining Bishop's Park.

Many of the splendid trees in the 41-acre (16-hectare) gardens are name-tagged, but some labels are difficult to see, and they give only the Latin names. Those described on the walk are located on the map on pages 38–9, and a detailed map of the trees in Fulham Palace Gardens is available from the Museum shop, but it is a good idea to take on the walk one of the tree identification guides on page 173.

THE FULHAM PALACE GARDENS WALK
Start and finish The main gate on Bishop's Avenue.
Time Allow 1½ hours.

The walk begins at the old gateway to the Palace on Bishop's Avenue. The stone gateposts date from the early 19th century. As you pass through them you are, in fact, walking onto a bridge across the ancient moat which for centuries surrounded the Palace and its grounds. It was originally dug around a pre-Norman settlement, which occupied the site between the River Thames and the present palace. If you look through the railings on either side you can see the line of the moat, which existed until the 1920s, when it was filled in at the orders of Bishop Winnington-

Ingram. The moat also ran along Moat Gardens beside Fulham Palace Road, and along the boundary between Fulham Palace Gardens and Bishop's Park.

The quaint Coachman's Lodge which marks the end of the bridge just ahead to the left was designed in 1898 in the fashionable neo-Gothic style by the Victorian architect William Butterfield (1814–1900). Opposite is the Chauffeur's House faced with black clapperboard, a rural touch.

At the information board, which you see ahead, take the right fork. Just beyond to the right is a lime tree, perhaps planted to commemorate an avenue of limes planted along this road – the main drive up to the Palace – by Bishop Compton. Walk right up the drive to the red-brick facade of the Palace, and over the cobbles beneath a Tudor archway. Notice the great medieval wooden gates. The archway leads into the intimate West Court, a rare example of a Tudor courtyard, although the central fountain was built in Victorian times on the site of the old well. Vines clad the walls in places, and subtropical plants grow in the borders, while just to the right of the main doorway, opposite the archway, is a shrub that no one has yet been able to identify – not even the experts of a television programme, 'Gardeners' World', when it was being filmed at Fulham Palace.

Leave the courtyard through the Tudor archway, turn right along the outer wall of the palace, then right again onto the path that leads to an open lawn planted with trees. To the left is a fine horse chestnut *(Aesculus hippocastanum)*, and ahead, evergreen oaks *(Quercus ilex)* – the grounds are strong on these. The cedar of Lebanon *(Cedrus libani)* ahead to your left was planted in the late 18th century.

The Great Lawn
Continue past the entrance to the Museum on the right. Ahead of you and to the left, spreading around the Palace, is a gracious open lawn. This is the Great Lawn, dating from the 18th century. Take the path that skirts it on the left. Many of the trees on the lawn were damaged during the hurricane of October 1987, among them the Judas tree *(Cercis siliquastrum)* to your right, which is now regenerating. To your right at the point where the path starts to bend is a statuesque black walnut *(Juglans nigra)*, maybe 150 years old, a tree native to North America which would certainly have been planted by Bishop Compton.

Just ahead, turn onto a small path leading off to the right and turn to look at the garden façade of the Palace. It was added to the Tudor core in 1814 by Bishop Howley (1813–1828), who disliked the 'Gothick' taste of his 18th-century predecessors. Ahead of you is a blue Atlas cedar *(Cedrus atlantica)* from North Africa, with somewhat upgrowing branches, another tree probably planted about 150 years ago. Ahead of you in a coppice just to the right is an ancient sweet chestnut *(Castanea sativa)* with a beard of twigs on a goitred, swollen-looking trunk. It is tree of distinct personality, very likely planted by Bishop Compton.

Return to the main path and continue walking southeast. Across the yew hedge on your left, you catch glimpses of an allotment area. Despite its proximity to the Bishop's Palace, in Tudor days, this area was the site of pleasure grounds. Elizabeth I was a regular visitor, presumably to watch deer being coursed and other sports. The land was made over for use as allotments during World War I, so these are

FULHAM PALACE GARDENS

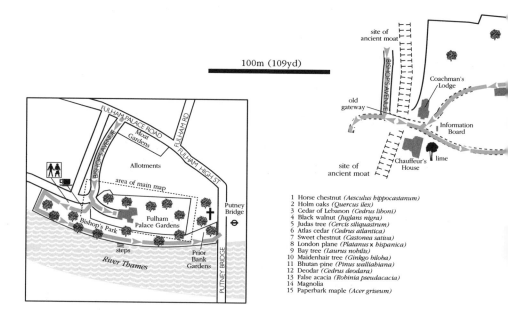

1 Horse chestnut *(Aesculus hippocastanum)*
2 Holm oaks *(Quercus ilex)*
3 Cedar of Lebanon *(Cedrus liboni)*
4 Black walnut *(Juglans nigra)*
5 Judas tree *(Cercis siliquastrum)*
6 Atlas cedar *(Cedrus atlantica)*
7 Sweet chestnut *(Castonea sativa)*
8 London plane *(Platanus x bispanica)*
9 Bay tree *(laurus nobilis)*
10 Maidenhair tree *(Ginkgo biloba)*
11 Bhutan pine *(Pinus walliabiana)*
12 Deodar *(Cedrus deodara)*
13 False acacia *(Robinia pseudacacia)*
14 Magnolia
15 Paperbark maple *(Acer griseum)*

quite early examples of their kind. At the end of the path you come to a dinosaur of a tree trunk with no branches. This is a London plane, seemingly dead a few years ago, the victim of the 1976 drought, but now growing a sturdy young limb.

The Kitchen Garden

In front of the plane the path veers right and you shortly see to the left an isolated length of brick wall. In its situation, this wall reminds the Curator of the Museum, Miranda Polyakoff, of a pine pit — a place where pineapples were grown in pre-Victorian times. It consisted of a cold frame with a brick trench outside, heaped with manure. The heat from fermentation warmed the bricks, which radiated warmth into the cold frame, helping to ripen the fruit.

Beyond the pine pit, pass through the gateway in the wall ahead into the kitchen garden. This large enclosure was probably converted from water meadow to kitchen garden in the 18th century (the area is shown blank on a map of 1745). Bear right along the curved path. To the right is a range of decaying greenhouses, the glass long gone. This was the Palace Vinery, the grape vines still surviving gamely, but the Vinery marvellously tumbledown, romantic in decay. It was already being neglected in the 1970s, but there are plans to restore it. Planted alongside the path are cotton lavender, borage, and other herbs backed by flowering shrubs.

To the left of the path is an oval-shaped knot garden which was laid out in the

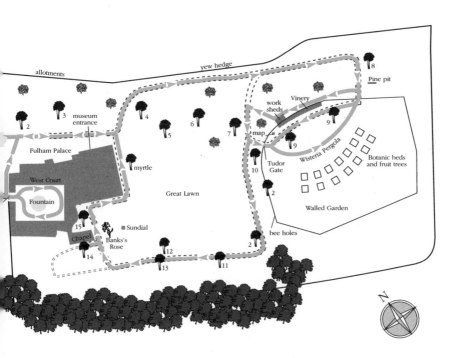

1830s. Its beds, edged with dwarf box, are densely planted with herbs used for culinary, household and medicinal purposes, such as purple sage, sorrel, salad burnet, lavender, and feverfew, many of which scent the air. At each end is a golden bay and a tall green bay tree. At the far end of the knot garden, beside a fine Tudor gateway, is a metal map in Braille of the herbs planted in it. The walk now turns sharp left and takes you back along its crowning glory, the magnificent wisteria pergola which encloses it, bearing cascading lilac flowers in spring. Its age is not known exactly, but it was planted before 1899, since a photograph taken in that year shows it.

When you reach the end of the wisteria pergola, turn to look across the kitchen garden. Its beds once supplied the Palace kitchens with fruit and vegetables. Recently, part of it has been used as a tree nursery, but during the 1970s some new plots were created by Hammersmith and Fulham Borough Council, and planted in the traditional way with families of botanically related plants. Near these botanic beds there are fruit trees; where trees have died the gaps have been replanted with old varieties of fruiting trees. This is policy in any garden which, like this one, has been declared a national monument – the sanction of English Heritage would have to be gained for any drastic change of use. As a result, this kitchen garden has the appearance of a garden that is well used and loved, something that is rather rare today.

Retrace your steps toward the pine pit, then turn left along the rough path leading past the high wall backing the Vinery. To your left, behind a screen of trees and shrubs, you can see once-busy work sheds, and the buildings used by the staff who tended the stoves that heated the greenhouses, which had to be fed day and night. For safety reasons, this part of the garden is closed to the public.

The Tudor Gate

Turn left at the end of the wall and continue straight ahead until you are level with the Tudor Gate at the end of the knot garden in the kitchen garden wall. Facing the Palace across the lawn, this gateway was once the exit from the formal garden to the water meadows. During recent restoration work it was found that the lower brickwork courses were laid in about 1480, and most of the remainder around 1500, with some Victorian additions at the top. The arms at the top are of Bishop Fitzjames, a bishop under Henry VIII.

There are some interesting trees hereabouts. Near the Tudor Gate to the right is a young maidenhair tree *(Ginkgo biloba)*, with leaves like no other coniferous or deciduous tree. These leaves turn a buttery yellow in the autumn and the small fruit (this tree is a female) have a rather unpleasant scent. Further along the wall is a magnificent holm or evergreen oak from the Mediterranean, and just past it there some bee boles in the old brick wall. These semicircular niches held round straw or cane skips, which were the beehives of the age (slatted wooden hives are a Victorian invention). The niches have now been filled in, however.

Toward the river where the path bends right is an evergreen oak with a sculptural contortion of riven trunks which are probably the branching of one tree, its original trunk now dead and rotted away. It is thought to have been planted in Tudor times, perhaps by Bishop Compton. To the left round the bend is a pretty Bhutan pine *(Pinus wallichiana)* from the Himalayas and a little beyond it, a false acacia *(Robinia pseudacacia)*, with attractive bunches of fragrant white flowers in June. Traces of the ancient moat can be seen in the shrubbery to the left, and almost opposite, to the right of the path, is a deodar, a Himalayan cedar *(Cedrus deodora)*.

Carry on up the path until you reach the chapel built onto the east façade of the Palace in the 1860s. It is an example by William Butterfield (1814–1900) of Tudor revival architecture. There is an unidentified magnolia with yellow flowers against its wall, and round the corner, on the lawn front, is a Banks rose *(Rosa banksiae* 'Lutea'), with small yellow flowers. Opposite this, to your right, is the base of an 18th-century sundial (the dial is in the Museum). Around it can be seen traces of the rose garden, which was grassed over in the 1970s. Round the corner ahead is a paper-bark maple *(Acer griseum)*, which originated in China, but is now thought to be extinct in the wild. Its name is derived from its thin, peeling, orange-red bark. The last stop is before the house front, where strong growths of scented myrtle are said to have been grown from cuttings used for Queen Victoria's wedding bouquet.

Return through the car park, once a farmyard and the site of the tithe barn. The building to your left is the old stable block. Follow the drive back to the main gate, where the walk ends – perhaps with thanks to the three gardeners who maintain this magic garden. Outside the gate to the left is the entrance to Bishop's Park, which offers the pleasant prospect of a stroll around its beds and shrubberies, and a delightful walk along the embankment, past All Saints Church to Putney Bridge.

Plate 1: *Osterley Park offers walks among some of the most superb cedars and other estate trees to be seen in London. (see page 16)*

Plate 2: *The Great Conservatory in the gardens surrounding Syon House, erected in 1820–30, is the world's largest and most magnificent conservatory (see page 26).*

Plate 3: *The artist William Kent (1685–1748) planned this amphitheatre and other classical features to be seen in Chiswick House Gardens (see page 28).*

Plate 4: *The Tudor Gate in Fulham Palace gardens overlooks a 19th-century Knot Garden (see page 39). A metal map identifies in Braille the herbs planted within it.*

Plate 5: *The Japanese Kyoto Garden in Holland Park (see page 44) is a favourite haunt of Holland Park's white peacocks. The pool contains Koi carp.*

Plate 6: *A stream flows through the English Woodland Garden in the Kensington Roof Gardens to a pond stocked with carp and a pair of pink flamingoes (see page 48).*

Holland Park

Location	About 3 miles (4.8 kilometres) west of Charing Cross.
Transport	Holland Park Underground Station (Central line) is 10 minutes' walk from the park. Three Underground stations: High Street Kensington (District and Circle lines), Notting Hill Gate (Central line) and Shepherd's Bush (Central and Hammersmith and City lines) are a short bus ride away. Buses along Kensington High Street are 9, 10, 27, 28, 31, 49; along Holland Park Avenue are 12 and 88. There is a car park on the west side of the park.
Admission	The park is open daily from 07:30 hours until half an hour after sunset. Admission is free.
Seasonal features	The Camellia Border and Azalea Walk in spring; The Dutch Garden, Iris Garden and Rose Garden in spring and summer; the Dahlia Garden in summer. Spring blossom and autumn colour in the woodland enclosures.
Events	Open-air theatre, opera and concerts in summer. Art exhibitions and other events in the Orangery April–October, and in the Ice House. Displays and exhibitions in the Ecology Centre.
Refreshments	Holland Park Café open daily 10:00–19:00 hours or later.

This 54-acre park, with white peacocks in the Japanese garden, rabbits in Fox Enclosure, open-air theatre, art exhibitions, and woodland walks can seem like a world of its own. It surrounds what remains of Holland House, a splendid Jacobean mansion built on one of the natural terraces of the River Thames, with views south over what was then open countryside. The house was built on the H-plan, with formal gardens alongside and a wilder area of woodland divided by paths behind.

Holland House was built around 1608 for Sir Walter Cope, Chancellor of the Exchequer to King James 1, and was originally called Cope Castle. After his death it passed to his daughter, whose husband was created Lord Holland in 1624. Under Henry Fox (1773–1840), the third Lord Holland, and his imperious but witty wife it became something of a court in its own right, London's established centre of literary and political society. To Lady Holland's salon came the literary luminaries of her day, such as Byron, Macaulay, Sir Walter Scott, and, when he was fashionable, Charles Dickens, to mingle with politicians such as Melbourne, Palmerston and other Whigs (members of the political party that evolved into the Liberals). In the 1840s, part of the Jacobean stable wing was converted into a Garden Ballroom, and this and the Orangery were linked to the main house by the terraces and arcades which can be seen today.

This fine house was bombed and gutted by fire during World War II, leaving only the east wing worth restoring. The remains of the house and the estate were purchased in 1952 by the London County Council, and ownership passed to the Royal Borough of Kensington and Chelsea in 1986. The east wing, renovated in 1959, now forms part of what must be London's best-sited youth hostel. The Royal Borough has been active in restoring the gardens and creating new interest.

THE HOLLAND PARK WALK

Start and finish The Kensington High Street gate. *Time* Allow 1½ hours.

Fine wrought iron gates dating from the 1840s mark what was the main entrance to Holland House. The flanking stone piers were inspired by a design of Inigo Jones. From this gate, stroll along the handsome avenue of planes and chestnuts leading past the Commonwealth Institute and a public sports field which is very busy in summer. The path swings left to pass the front of the Jacobean house. Parts of it form a backdrop to the Open-Air Theatre, which opened in 1964.

The Ice House

Passing the theatre and the café terrace beside it, walk through the portal on the right. To the left is the Ice House, a round brick building of 1770 with a handsome domed and tiled roof. This ice house is unusual in being above ground – these buildings were usually partly buried to improve their insulation. It was restored in 1979. To the right is a small lawn with a sculpture of a boy with bear cubs by the English animal sculptor, John Swan, erected in 1902. Follow the path past it, to reach the Dutch Garden.

The Dutch or Formal Garden

This garden, stretching westward from the house, was first created in 1812 by one Buonaiuti, Librarian to the Holland family. Originally, and until a souring of Britain's relations with Portugal, it was called the Portuguese garden. The name 'Dutch Garden' does reflect its layout, however: neat, geometric parterre hedging of miniature box separated by paths, although these are probably broader now than they would have been originally. Within the hedging are bedded out two main displays in the course of the year. There is a spring show of overwintering wallflowers and tulips; and a summer one with geraniums and other bedding plants, perhaps yellow calceolarias and scarlet or blue salvias. What are usually called geraniums are really pelargoniums. They came originally from South Africa and were the key to much Victorian and subsequent planting. The first dwarf 'Tom Thumb' variety, ideal for bedding such as this, was available by 1840.

The walk takes you up to the east end of the garden and then along the paths through the centre to the west end, where there is an armillary-sphere (hollow hoop) sundial, one of the donations of the fund-raising Friends of Holland Park. Other donations from this body include £5,000 worth of snowdrops, an engraving

HOLLAND PARK

to High Street Kensington

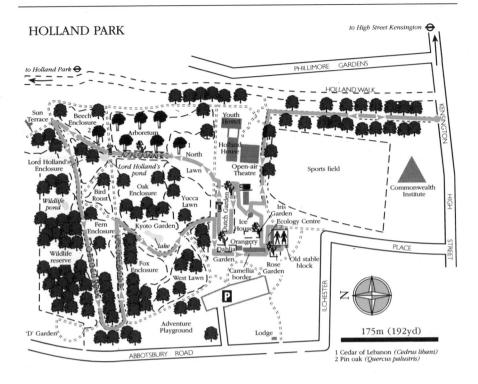

to Holland Park

PHILLIMORE   GARDENS

HOLLAND WALK

Sun Terrace

Beech Enclosure 2

Arboretum

AZALEA WALK

Lord Holland's Enclosure

Lord Holland's pond

Youth Hostel

1

Holland House

North Lawn

Open-air Theatre

Sports field

KENSINGTON

Commonwealth Institute

HIGH

Bird Roost

Oak Enclosure

Yucca Lawn

Iris Garden

Ecology Centre

STREET

Wildlife pond

Fern Enclosure

Kyoto Garden

Dutch Garden

Ice House

Orangery

PLACE

Dahlia Garden

ILCHESTER

Wildlife reserve

Fox Enclosure

lake

West Lawn

Camellia border

Rose Garden

Old stable block

N

CHESTNUT WALK

'D' Garden

Adventure Playground

Lodge

175m (192yd)

P

ABBOTSBURY   ROAD

1 Cedar of Lebanon *(Cedrus libani)*
2 Pin oak *(Quercus palustris)*

machine for labelling trees, bird boxes, and eight hedgehogs. Turn to walk eastward along the warm brick wall, once part of the Jacobean stables, offering shelter on the garden's north side. Turn left up the steps at the end of the path and leave the Dutch Garden through the brick arch.

The North Lawn and Azalea Walk

To the right you can now see remnants of the walls and windows of the house, running toward the Youth Hostel in the restored east wing. Cross the North Lawn, a favourite area for relaxing in the sun in summer; directly ahead is a young Cedar of Lebanon *(Cedrus libani)*, planted in 1996 by the U.K. Alumni Association of the American University of Beirut. Bear right toward what was once a Rose Walk leading off the lawn, but was replanted with azaleas around the turn of the 19th century. Turn left along it; it is usually at its dazzling prime in May when the azalea varieties, many of them scented, are in full flower. To the right is the Arboretum, planted in the 17th and 18th centuries and well known for its many exotic trees cultivated for their scientific interest. It is carpeted with bluebells in spring.

At the end of Azalea Walk you reach a pond and a commemorative statue to the third Lord Holland, the statesman Henry Fox. It was sculpted by G. F. Watts in 1840. Lord Holland sits at ease (note the comforting spats), his head and hands much favoured by perching London pigeons. He was responsible for some of the tree-planting here. There is a fine copper beech nearby, and as an example of the more exotic trees, behind him is a pin oak *(Quercus palustris)* from North America, one of the oaks with handsome red autumn leaves.

The Woodland Enclosures

Continue along the path directly ahead. In this area, behind the North Lawn, are some of the park's ten woodland enclosures in what was originally designated a 'Wildernesse'. To the right is the Beech Enclosure, planted with beech trees and holly as it would if it were natural beech woodland.

At the top of the beech enclosure turn left into a long walk lined with fine horse chestnuts *(Aesculus hippocastanum)* planted in the 19th century. Introduced from the Balkans in the 16th century, these trees are common enough to be taken for granted, but the flowers, which appear in May–June, are as intricate as orchids. They are usually white, but there is a variety with red flowers and one with double flowers which does not produce conkers.

To the right is a Wildlife Reserve. Holland Park has a marvellous wildlife tally for where it is, deep in a city. Sixty different wild bird species have been seen here, 30 of them nesting in this reserve or elsewhere in the park. They include the tawny owl, the sparrowhawk, and the great spotted woodpecker. There are many voles and mice, although they are rarely seen. Halfway along the path is its pond, which was established as recently as 1991 but is now a major feature. It attracts newts, frogs and toads, and is usually busy with dragonflies in summer.

The ground falls away down the line of the path, set with commemorative benches. At the end to the right is the 'D' Garden – so called because of its shape – an open lawn enclosed with bushes.

Take an abrupt left turn into the Lime Tree Walk, originally planted by one Lady Holland in 1876. Many of its trees were lost in the great storm of October 1987, but they have been replaced with new trees. To the right is Fox Enclosure, named not after the bushy-tailed hunter but after Henry Fox. One would hope so, because these woods and enclosures contain a good many tame, fat sassy rabbits.

The Kyoto Garden

A right turn at the end of Fox Enclosure brings you to the Kyoto Garden, a garden sanctuary created and donated in 1991 by the Chamber of Commerce of Kyoto, a city which is the Athens of Japan, its imperial and cultural capital for 1,000 years. Turn left through the gate and follow the winding path paved with smooth stone through the garden. After the natural tangle of the woodland walks, this garden is a sudden dream of order, with smooth, vivid green lawns set with lime and other trees, a small lake with a tumbling clear cascade, bamboo-spouted water fountains – somewhat unusual to Western eyes – and solidly built stone lanterns.

Although the Japanese and the Chinese had the most ornamental of plants in their nurseries – peonies, hydrangeas, azaleas – which astounded the first European plant collectors, the key to such a garden is simplicity and correctness. Everything has its proper place in the scheme: the cascade and the symbolic bridge; the humps of natural stone (symbolizing mountains); the grouped foliage of the trees and shrubs. It is an artistic composition, a kind of three-dimensional picture, where, by the careful use of proportion an impression of great space is created. The emphasis is on foliage rather than bright flowers. In late summer, for example, the only touch of flower colour might be from some discreet hydrangeas or pink water lilies. In autumn, leaf colour might be a feature. A garden like this, epitomizing the Japanese value of order is, in its way, as formal as the Dutch Garden.

Leave the garden via the steps at the far end and follow the path as it bends left. It passes the Yucca Lawn, where there is a stand of these exotic plants, but Peacock Enclosure would be an appropriate name for it. These birds have the unexpected habit of roosting in trees. There are rabbits aplenty on the Yucca Lawn.

The Dahlia Garden
Turn sharp right at the end of the Yucca Lawn, walk down the steps and turn left off the path into the Dahlia Garden at the west end of the Dutch Garden. The Dahlia Garden was planted in 1992. The first dahlia seeds to germinate successfully in England were planted nearby by Lady Holland in 1790. The seed possibly came via Spain, where they were first grown successfully. They are Mexican in origin, but they are named after a Scandinavian botanist, Andreas Dahl. They speedily became popular, partly because they can grow from seed to flower in one summer and partly because they exhibit a great variety of colour and shape, as every seedling is different. However, they do not always produce tubers for future years.

The Orangery
From the Dahlia Garden, turn left along the path leading past the chic Belvedere Restaurant and the lovely old Orangery. Alongside the path is a marvellous tall camellia border. Through the end windows can be seen a pair of bronze figures of boy wrestlers, about 4 feet (1.2 metres) tall. Known as the Herculaneum wrestlers, they are Roman, of the 4th century AD, and were donated by a London County Council chairman. Turn left at the end of the Orangery; to the right is a rose garden, sheltered by the high walls of the old stables, but the walk takes you left again through an open arcade, and right along a covered walkway.

The Iris Garden
On the left side of the walkway, arches open cloister-like onto a charming Iris Garden with a central fountain. Irises are a flower family that excite passions. An iris (maybe the wild yellow flag) was adopted as a royal emblem in the arms of both France and England, and the flowers have been bred to some unexpected colours – the pinks and browns of the artist Sir Cedric Morris (1889–1982), for example.

Continue to the end of the covered walkway. At the end you see the café terrace ahead. In the old stable block to the right, there is an Information Centre and an Ecology Centre which has natural history displays, including live terrapins and freshwater fish. Follow the path ahead along the top of the sports field, and turn right along Holland Walk to the main gate, where the walk ends.

Kensington Roof Gardens

Location	About 4 miles (6 kilometres) west of Charing Cross, above Bhs on Kensington High Street, W8. The entrance is at the bottom of Derry Street, W8, on the right (west) side. You sign yourself in at the reception desk in the foyer, and take the dedicated lift to the roof.
Transport	High Street Kensington Underground Station (District and Circle lines). Bus 9, 10, 27, 28, 31, 49, 52. There is an underground car park beneath Kensington Town Hall on Horton Street, W8.
Admission	Open 09:00–18:00 hours whenever the Club is not in use. Tel: 0171 937 7994 to check. Admission is free.
Seasonal features	The English Woodland Garden in winter and spring; The wisteria in the Tudor Garden in spring; The Spanish garden in summer.
Refreshments	Not available in the Roof Gardens. The Muffin Man tea shop, 12 Wright's Lane, W8. opens Mon–Sat 08.30–18:00 hours.
Events	The Roof Gardens and adjoining Club are privately owned, but can be hired for private events.

These roof gardens are above what was once Derry & Toms department store. Briefly during the 1970s it became the fashionable Biba department store, with an Art Deco-style restaurant overlooking the Roof Gardens The Virgin Group now operates the gardens and the night club and functions complex at the top of the building. At 1.5 acres (0.5 hectares), this is the largest roof garden in Europe. It was planted in 1936-8 and was the brainchild of Trevor Bowen, then head of the Barker's Stores empire (which had taken over Derry & Toms). The garden design was by Ralph Hancock, a leading gardener of the day.

This is a short walk, and afterward you may have time to visit Kensington Square, at the bottom of Derry Street. It was one of the first new developments when the former village of Kensington became invaded by London's fashionable set seeking pure air. Then, when William III and Queen Mary moved to Kensington Palace in the 1690s, the square was taken over by courtiers. Nos. 11 and 12, built in 1683, are probably the best-preserved houses. Among the residents have been the political philosopher John Stuart Mill (1806–73), who lived at No. 18 (there is a statue to him in Temple Place Gardens, *see* page 98) and the actress, Mrs. Patrick Campbell (1865–1940). The square is planted with some fine old London plane trees.

KENSINGTON ROOF GARDENS

1 Windmill palms (*Trachycarpus fortunei*)
2 London planes (*Platanus x hispanica*)

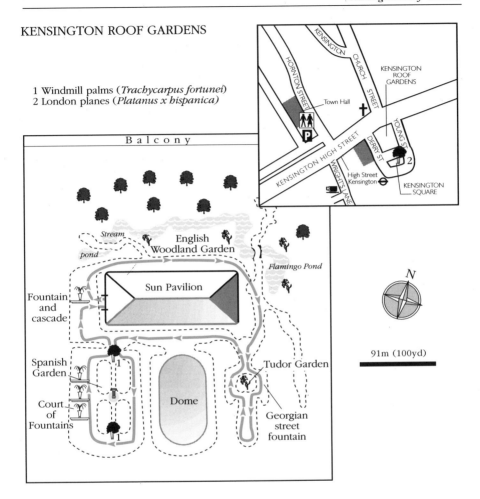

THE KENSINGTON ROOF GARDENS WALK

Start and finish The Sun Pavilion.

Time This very short walk can be completed in under 10 minutes, but allow half an hour or more to really enjoy these gardens.

The lift opens into the Sun Pavilion – originally a roof restaurant and now the Roof Gardens Club. It was designed by Barker's in-house architect, Bernard George. Pause for a moment to admire the polished flagstone floor and other attractive touches, before turning left to walk out through the swing doors. You will immediately hear the unexpected sound of water from the rockwork fountain and cascade now facing you. The water from the cascade flows away as a stream, and you should follow it to the right (if you turn left you arrive at the Spanish garden, which will be the climax of the walk).

The Woodland Garden

The stream winds delightfully with one or two low cascades, in a setting of mainly evergreen shrubbery with a tree or two. It follows the line of the Sun Pavilion; notice its windows – with their metal bars, they are pure 1930s in style. Two bridges cross the stream, leading to bosky recesses with gates which lead out to balconies. These balconies are now closed off, but you can still look out over Kensington to remind yourself that you are six storeys high.

This part of the roof gardens has a vaguely English woodland theme. Many of the shrubs and border plants are exotic, however; there are Corsican hellebores, mahonias, camellias, phormium, with long, swordlike leaves, and a few fatsia shrubs with figlike leaves (fatsia is also called the figleaf palm, although it is not a palm, but related to ivy). There are beds with ferns and foxgloves. This woodland area makes visiting the Roof Gardens delightful even in winter, when the mahonias, especially *Mahonia lomariifolia*, the shrub with sea green foliage and long racemes of pale yellow flowers, the forsythia and the hazel catkins add sparkles of gold.

The Tudor Garden

Pass the flamingo pool and to the left you enter the Tudor garden of walled courtyards with herringbone brick floors. The roughly carved Tudor arches were salvaged, so it is said, from some unidentified stately home. There is a street fountain to the left, which is probably Georgian, while the main arch between the courtyards is backed by a handsome wisteria which is gorgeous in spring. Old-fashioned roses usually occupy some of the beds in summer, but in two corners there are small, latter-day knot garden motifs, with dwarf box edging and a tall, spiral-clipped centrepiece to each. In the second courtyard there is an unusual brick-built fountain.

The Spanish Garden

Leave the Tudor Garden and turn left through more Tudor arches, to reach the Spanish Garden. This has quite a different atmosphere from the other two gardens. 'Spanish convent' sums up its style: an exit gateway is dressed up as a convent gatehouse, with a pantiled roof, white walls with a hanging bell, and a slender tower alongside. The beds are crowded with shrubs and palm trees. The palms in this garden are windmill palms *(Trachycarpus fortunei)*, which are natives of China and tolerant of frost.

This picturesque assembly of gatehouse and planted beds faces a quartet of vivid green lawn plots with kerblike edgings painted white. At their centre is a well with a statue of Venus. This characteristically Italian feature looks somewhat out of place in a Spanish garden. Notice the attractive, colourful Spanish tiles on the insides of the edgings of these plots and surmounting the 'convent' door.

Running down the right side of the Spanish Garden is the Court of Fountains, a lengthy water feature set with fountain spouts - the water was an unexpected, sharp nightclub blue colour on a recent visit. There is an attractive weeping ash in the nearby border.

Leave the Spanish Garden to the left and you arrive back at the cascade and the door leading to the lift, where the walk ends.

Kensington Gardens

Location	About 2½ miles (4 kilometres) west of Charing Cross.
Transport	North side: Lancaster Gate or Queensway Underground stations (Central Line); 12, 94 bus. South side: High Street Kensington Underground Station (District and Circle lines); 9, 10, 52 bus. On foot, 10–15 minutes' walk from the underground car park on Park Lane.
Admission	Open from dawn–dusk daily. Admission is free.
Seasonal features	The Sunken Garden and the Flower Walk in spring and summer. Spring blossom and autumn tree colour.
Events	Thursday evening concerts at the Bandstand, kite-flying, model boat-sailing on the Round Pond, summer puppet shows on weekdays. Events booklet *(see* page 171).
Refreshments	Orangery Café open 10:00–18:00 hours daily.

Kensington Gardens were at first only an extension of Hyde Park, and then in 1689 William III, seeking to ease his asthma with the clean country air of Kensington, commissioned Sir Christopher Wren and Nicholas Hawksmoor to convert the old Nottingham House as a palace-cum-country retreat for himself and his household. It was linked to St. James's Park and his London palaces by the Route du Roi (now Rotten Row, *see* page 56). The Palace, an example of domestic rather than florid state architecture (described by John Evelyn in his diary in 1696 as 'very noble, tho not greate'), had 26 acres (10.5 hectares) of Dutch gardens laid out around it, including parterres. In the 18th century Queen Anne added the red-brick Orangery; Queen Caroline, wife of George II, extended the grounds; and Charles Bridgeman (appointed Royal Gardener in 1738) created long avenues of trees stretching to the distance as they do today, and possibly also the Round Pond. Caroline also had the Serpentine dug out, later extending it as The Long Water.

Under George II, Kensington Gardens was opened to visitors, although Queen Caroline had servants placed at the different entrances 'to prevent persons meanly clad from going into the garden'. When George II died in 1760 the Palace fell out of prime use, although various royals lived and were born there, Queen Victoria among them. The Gardens were opened up, eventually even to the hoi polloi, which caused a certain Princess Lieven to write in 1820 that they had been 'annexed as a middle-class rendezvous and good society no longer goes there, except to drown itself' – an allusion to Harriet Shelley's suicide *(see* page 62). Along with the other Royal Parks, Kensington Gardens passed into public hands in the last century and today almost all is maintained by the Royal Parks Agency.

THE KENSINGTON GARDENS WALK
Start King's Arms Gate. *Finish* Palace Gate. *Time* Allow 1½ hours.

A dramatic introduction to the Gardens is at King's Arms Gate. Cross to the right and walk up Dial Walk toward the magnificent Crowther Gates in front of Kensington Palace. Through them you can see a statue of Prince William of Orange (who later became William III). The drama is created by the tulip trees that line the walk. The tulip tree *(Liriodendron tulipifera)* was one of the first exotic trees to be brought to Britain from America in the 17th century. A close relative was later found growing in China. It has leaves shaped unlike those of any other tree, and yellowish flowers which are cup-shaped but do not look much like tulips.

Turn right at the Crowther Gates, then left into The Broad Walk. This grand alley, part of Bridgeman's original design, is 15.25 metres (50 feet) wide. It was originally lined with elms, but by the 1970s these had died of Dutch elm disease and what remained was felled and replanted with limes and Norway maples.

To the right of the Broad Walk, almost opposite the statue of Prince William, 'The Hump' can be traced – the edge of a great semicircular terrace with the Round Pond at its centre. This feature, with avenues of trees radiating from it, was the crux of Charles Bridgeman's design. In 1988 a double avenue of 160 lime trees was planted around the plateau, reviving another original period feature, The Great Bow. Occasional and impromptu concerts are held at the bandstand to the right.

Walk up The Broad Walk until you come to a statue of Queen Victoria to the left. It was unveiled in 1887 to commemorate 50 years of the queen's reign. It shows a young woman aged 18 years – her age when she took the throne in 1837. It was at Kensington Palace that she was told of the death of William IV, and she held her first Privy Council in the Red Saloon. The statue must have been modelled from a painting, since it was carved by her sixth child, Princess Louise, a respected sculptress. Notice the fine detail in the drapery curls and the thistles and other decoration at the back.

The Sunken Garden
Turn along the next path leading to the left off The Broad Walk, then left again. You are now entering an alley formed by pleached lime trees, which surrounds the Sunken Garden. This is a superb example of a Dutch-style garden of the early 18th century, but it was laid out in 1906–9. You can see into it through squints cut in the limes. It has three tiers of flower beds leading down to a rectangular pond 50 yards (45.7 metres) long with water lilies and a line of three handsomely decorated lead cisterns of the period, two with fountains. The upper bed is devoted to perennial herbaceous flowers; the lower two to seasonal bedding. These display tulips and other bulbs; forget-me-nots; polyanthuses planted in October for flowering in spring; and bedding plants raised in the Hyde Park greenhouses *(see* page 62), which are planted out in May to flower until September. Perennial sword-leaved phormiums with their long, reddish flower spikes in summer add crisp definition to the corners. The design and the focus on pastel shades are the work of Paul Clark, the working gardener in charge.

KENSINGTON GARDENS

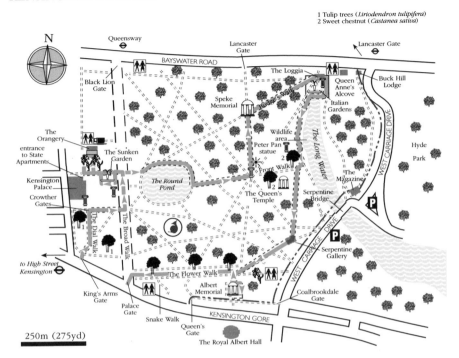

1 Tulip trees (*Liriodendron tulipifera*)
2 Sweet chestnut (*Castanea sativa*)

N

Queensway

Lancaster Gate

Lancaster Gate

BAYSWATER ROAD

Black Lion Gate

The Loggia

Queen Anne's Alcove

Buck Hill Lodge

Speke Memorial

Italian Gardens

The Orangery

Wildlife area

Peter Pan statue

Hyde Park

entrance to State Apartments

The Sunken Garden

Front Walk

The Long Water

Kensington Palace

The Round Pond

The Queen's Temple

The Magazine

Crowther Gates

Serpentine Bridge

The Dial Walk

The Broad Walk

Serpentine Gallery

to High Street Kensington

The Flower Walk

WEST CARRIAGE DRIVE

King's Arms Gate

Albert Memorial

Coalbrookdale Gate

Palace Gate

KENSINGTON GORE

250m (275yd)

Snake Walk

Queen's Gate

The Royal Albert Hall

The Orangery

Walk all the way round the Sunken Garden and you emerge to see directly ahead what the staff call the pepper pots – lines of tall drum topiary with holly and bay trees alternating – marking the path to the Orangery. Follow this path, which is attributed to Sir Christopher Wren (although the topiary is, at a guess, 60 years old). It is not clear whether the Orangery was designed for Queen Anne by Sir Christopher Wren, by Sir John Vanbrugh (1664–1726), or even by Nicholas Hawksmoor (1661–1736), Wren's assistant. It was built in 1704 and has superb brickwork, especially in features such as the rubbed brick columns at the central entrance. It has tall windows coming down to near the paved terrace to let in as much light as possible. Inside is a café-restaurant where you can take tea, as Queen Anne did. The decor is coolly white with good copies of classical busts of the kind favoured in the 18th century, stone urns, and dark green orange bushes. Over the archways at each end are swags by the Dutch woodcarver, Grinling Gibbons (1648–1721), who also carved the tumbles of flowers.

Turn left along the terrace in front, usually set with orange trees in tubs as it would have been when first built. (It may be that orangeries were promoted not wholly because of the exotic bushes but also in deference to William III's title, linked to the French city of Orange, and anti-Catholic politics; his queen, Mary,

51

was the Protestant daughter of James II, and William, who was Europe's Protestant figurehead, was invited in as joint ruler.)

At the end of the terrace turn left again and walk back toward the Palace. Ahead of you is a beautiful Wren doorway and the entrance to the Palace apartments. Many rooms suffered bomb damage in World War II, losing details by Grinling Gibbons and other notables, but fine ceilings and wall-paintings by William Kent (*see* page 9) survive. Victoria's bedroom, where she awoke to find herself queen, is one of the rooms on display.

The Round Pond

Turn left again, walk back to The Broad Walk and take the path ahead which leads to the north bank of the Round Pond. Commanding a grand terrace, with wide views and a vast open sky above, the Pond is an invigorating place, popular for kite-flying. It is not round, but its formal shape is difficult to discern from the ground. It was probably the work of Charles Bridgeman, but perhaps of Henry Wise, the partner of George London, who set the gardening pace in the early 18th century (Bridgeman worked under them for a time). And even though there is no plant cover out on the water, there are always a few water birds swimming on the pond, including swans, coots, and gulls. More action comes from the model yachts which dedicated enthusiasts sail on the Pond; model speed boats are not allowed.

Walk round the pond to the east side and take the path leading due east through the trees. It takes you to the bronze statue of Physical Energy, the creation of the 19th-century Royal Academician, George Frederick Watts, who shows energy as a naked male rider on a rearing horse. The original stands on Table Mountain outside Cape Town in South Africa as a memorial to Cecil Rhodes; this copy was placed at this spot in 1907.

The statue stands on what Gardens staff call Front Walk, one of Bridgeman's key avenues, at the centre of a star of paths. There are splendid vistas across the park from this hub, which Bridgeman crossed with a straight avenue from Lancaster Gate. It was later angled to lead to the Albert Memorial. Some way south of this statue trees still mark the old line. The walk turns left, however, up the straight avenue to the memorial to the 19th-century explorer, John Hanning Speke. It is a pointed column of polished granite inscribed with the terse words: 'In memory of SPEKE. Victoria, Nyanza, The Nile 1864'. Terse, but a cloud hung over his memory: his death may have been not a hunting accident, but suicide; his better-known colleague, David Livingstone, disputed his claim to have discovered the source of the Nile.

The Long Water and the Italian Gardens

From Speke's Monument, turn northeast onto Budge's Walk. A line of sweet chestnuts, planted in 1992, guides you along it to the Italian Gardens at the head of Long Water. This lake had been a series of fishing pools in a natural valley until Queen Caroline had it dug out as an extension of the Serpentine. It is quite shallow, only 4½ feet (1.4 metres) deep on average. The Italian Gardens were designed by James Pennethorne in 1861, with pools and osprey-plumed fountains, urns and balustrades. The path takes you to the Italian Pavilion at the north end, which was perhaps designed by Prince Albert himself, echoing the Petit Trianon at Versailles

The plumbing is Best Victorian. Water from an artesian well on Duck Island in St. James's Park is piped through a 10-inch (254-millimetre) pipe (fitted with valves to fill Buckingham Palace lake) to feed into Long Water and then into the Serpentine. The massive chimney of the Italian Pavilion is a clue to its former role: it contained a steam engine (now replaced by an electric pump) to operate the fountains, but this also fed the Round Pond and created an 18-foot (5.5-metre) head of water on the fountains, so that the royals of the day (on restricted Sunday afternoons) could see them play without the gouts of smoke from the engine. The paved manhole in front of the Pavilion hides a secret, 230-foot (70-metre) deep well shaft of mysterious origin. It is called St. Agnes Well and is so far unused.

Cross to the east side of the Pavilion to see a large, wood-panelled alcove set in brick. It was designed by Wren for Queen Anne and moved brick by brick to this site from near King's Arms Gate. Walk a little further along the path in front of it to Buck Hill Lodge, one of the most attractive of Kensington Garden's lodges, with a secluded, well-hidden pets' cemetery nearby.

Return to the Italian Gardens and turn left along the east side. The Portland stone vases on the balustrades are of five main designs known as swan breast, woman's head, ram's head, dolphin, and oval; in 1990 an English Heritage stone carver recarved one of each, offsetting the ravages of weathering. Halfway down, facing the fountains, is a bronze statue of 1858 of Edward Jenner (1749–1823). In 1798 Jenner perfected vaccination and fought for its use; his discovery is still saving countless lives today.

Peter Pan

Turn right at the southern end of the gardens, pausing to admire the view down Long Water, then left down the path leading south along its bank. Alongside the fence to your left is a wildlife area where the grass grows long for the butterflies, and at the end is an information board with details of some of the diverse waterfowl to be seen swimming on The Long Water.

To the right is the famous statue of Peter Pan by Sir George Frampton. It was commissioned by Sir James Matthew Barrie (1860–1937), the Scottish writer of the children's fantasy play, *Peter Pan*. In 1912 the statue was unveiled unofficially, but once in place it was so popular it could not be moved. It depicts Peter Pan with pipes, and the tortuous design oozes rabbits, mice, squirrels, and bronze fairies clad in what look like Edwardian party frocks. One child remarked that Wendy, who is part of the group, looks puzzled. The ensemble is intended for children, but what today's computer miniboffins make of it is unclear; the rabbits' ears (now shiny from touching) are as likely to be tweaked by Japanese grown-ups.

J.M. Barrie lived in a house overlooking Kensington Gardens and it was while walking in these gardens that he met the sons of an impecunious barrister and unofficially adopted them, sending four to school at Eton and one into a British navy cadetship. Royalties from his play, a fairy tale about a boy who never grew up, still go to Great Ormond Street Hospital for Sick Children.

Behind the statue's enclosure is the Leaf Yard, an ecological innovation of the early 1990s. Autumn leaves collected from Hyde Park and Kensington Gardens are shredded, stored, and shredded again to make a rich mulch for the shrubberies. They used to be taken by barge to be dumped in landfill sites down the Thames.

The Queen's Temple

Take the path that leads directly south, following the right fork leading away from The Long Water toward The Queen's Temple. Between Peter Pan and this temple, by Front Walk, are some ancient gnarled sweet chestnut trees, the only surviving trees from Bridgeman's plantings of the 1730s. The Queen's Temple was designed by William Kent (*see* page 9), who worked at Hyde Park after Bridgeman. He was famous for his 'picture' approach to landscape, designing buildings and the settings for them. This temple had been used as a keeper's lodge, but was restored in 1977. It faces Long Water; a sculpture by the modern British artist, Henry Moore, stood on the opposite bank for many years, but it has now been taken in for repairs.

From The Queen's Temple you can glimpse the Magazine, now the Kensington Gardens' offices and depot, but once a gunpowder store. The storerooms have walls 4 feet (1.2 metres) thick to withstand explosions.

Continue walking south along the path and you come to what was originally a refreshment house designed by Henry Tanner in 1908, when it was decided that 'poorer visitors' might cause trouble if there were no facilities. It remained a tearoom until the 1960s and is now The Serpentine Gallery, a leading art gallery.

The Albert Memorial

From the back of the Serpentine Gallery stroll along the path that leads to the Albert Memorial, a huge monument normally clearly visible to the southwest but clad in protective sheeting since the mid-1990s. The Memorial's long restoration may be complete by the turn of the millennium; meanwhile there is a (free) exhibition in a visitor's centre alongside it. Examples of the Memorial's intricate decoration of inlays of agate, jasper, crystal and other semiprecious stones, usually seen close-up only by pigeons, are on show, with displays of the Great Exhibition of 1851.

Albert, Queen Victoria's cousin and Consort, died from typhoid in 1861. His Memorial, built from money raised by public subscription, was erected between 1864 and 1876. It was designed by Sir George Gilbert Scott (1811–78), architect of the fantasy front of St. Pancras railway station, and built by the Lucas firm, who were also builders of railway stations. They often dined their 80 workmen on beef and plum pudding while suffering them to hear speeches on temperance.

The base of the monument, in neoclassical style, is adorned with statuary groups in marble representing the four continents. They can still be seen: for Europe, Britannia rides a bull surrounded by crowned women. The next stage is a frieze of Great Figures, ranging from William Shakespeare to Sir William Chambers, the designer of the Pagoda in Kew Gardens (*see* page 148). Above them is the statue of Prince Albert, 15 feet (4.5 metres) high, seated and grasping a catalogue of his Great Exhibition of 1851, which was held nearby in Hyde Park (*see* page 62). The monument changes to neoGothic style as it rises above him.

The map on page 51 shows a worthwhile diversion due east along West Carriage Drive to see the Coalbrookdale Gates from the Great Exhibition. They are intricately decorated with metalwork stags and other ornament.

The Flower Walk

Retrace your steps along the path leading north from the Albert Memorial and go through a gate in the railings to the left. Ahead of you is one of London's best and most carefully planned flower walks. The 500-yard (457-metre) path was laid in 1843 and exotic trees planted along it. They are name-tagged: near the Lancaster Walk entrance, for example, is a maidenhair tree *(Gingko biloba)*, a species thought extinct until it was found growing in China in the 18th century; a lucombe oak, with thick, fissured bark; and an enormous ilex (an evergreen oak). There is also the weeping beech where Peter Pan spent a very cold, wet and miserable night.

Today's garden format is a shrubbery of varying depth backing curves of flower beds (50 in all) set in fine green turf. But there are also delightful hollows with evergreen and deciduous azaleas and small, highly colourful Japanese maples.

Planting is programmed to maintain interest through the growing season and to offer a continual element of surprise as you walk slowly along and meet the various colour combinations, both complementary and contrasting. Nick Butler, superintendent of the Gardens, plans the planting himself. The map for the 1997 spring programme near the maidenhair tree, for example, spelled out a bed of 300 ivory white wallflowers, 15 inches (38 centimetres) high, with 250 jasper red tulip 'Bahama', 18 inches (46 centimetres) high; while opposite are 200 12-inch (30-centimetre) orange-red wallflower and 180 18½-inch (47-centimetre) deep yellow tulip 'Ornament'. Other combinations are white aquilegia with pink tulip, orange pansy with red tulip, and crown imperial with pink tulip and deep red pansy. Camellias were also planted.

The colour range of each bed can also be heightened in summer with the greater variety of bedding plants available. In August, for example, you might see beds ranging from mixed multicolour dahlias to one with a cool motif of white and green. There might also be exotics – young banana plants, for example. The thing to do is to choose a bench opposite the bed of your choice and sit and admire.

At the west end of Flower Walk turn left along Snake Walk, a sinuous side path bordered by raised heather beds, camellias, deciduous azaleas and rhododendrons. Turn right at the bottom and left to Palace Gate where the walk ends.

Hyde Park

Location	About 1½ miles (2 kilometres) west of Charing Cross.
Transport	North side: Queensway, Lancaster Gate and Marble Arch Underground stations (Central Line); south side: Knightsbridge and Hyde Park Corner Underground stations (Piccadilly Line). Buses: Bayswater Road 10; 12; 94; Knightsbridge: 9; 10; 19; 22; 52; 137; Park Lane: 2; 36; 137. There is an underground car park on Park Lane.
Admission	Open daily dawn–dusk. Admission is free.
Seasonal features	The Flower Gardens in spring and summer; The Dell in winter and spring; autumn tree colour.
Events	Concerts at the Bandstand on Sundays and Bank Holidays in summer; Speakers' Corner on Sundays. Events booklet *(see page 171)*.
Refreshments	The Dell Restaurant and café open Mon–Fri 10:30–18:00 hours or later; Sat, Sun 10:00–18:00 hours or later. Kiosk café near Marble Arch.

In 1536, Henry VIII purloined land around the manor of Hyde, which belonged to the Abbots of Westminster, fencing it to make a private park for the royal hunt. During the next century, James I permitted his courtiers access to the enclosure, and a circular drive called The Ring became fashionable. It was daily filled with the chaises (light, horse-drawn carriages) of the wealthy. The ground was opened further by Charles I, but after his execution Cromwell sold it off in three lots. The diarist John Evelyn noted on April 11, 1653: 'I went to take aire in Hyde Park, when every coach was made to pay a shilling and horse sixpence by the sordid fellow who purchased it off the state'.

After the monarchy was restored under Charles II, the park was reopened and The Ring became fashionable once again. The diarist Samuel Pepys wrote: 'To Hide Park, where great plenty of gallants. And pleasant it was, only for the dust'. He was wearing his 'painted gloves ... all the mode'. This was just before the park was swamped by refugees fleeing the Great Plague of 1655.

In the 1690s William III renovated Kensington Palace and set up court in it. However, footpads became a danger on the road leading to it along the south side of the park and, as a deterrent, he had it illuminated at night with 300 flickering oil lamps hung from the branches of the trees alongside. They were the first known street lights. This road was called the Route du Roi, a name that became corrupted to Rotten Row. In the mid-18th century Queen Caroline, wife of George II, deprived Hyde Park of as much as 200 acres (80 hectares) to form the grounds of Kensington Palace *(see page 49)*, but she had the southern part landscaped, creating the Serpentine lake. In 1851, Queen Victoria's Great Exhibition was held there.

Hyde Park is 350 acres (142 hectares) in area, and many walks are possible across its wide expanses of grass and trees. The one described here embraces most of the important sights.

THE HYDE PARK WALK
Start and finish: Marble Arch. *Time* Allow 1¼ hours.

Marble Arch was erected at Hyde Park's northeast corner in 1851, as the main gateway to the park, but in 1918 it was severed from the park by traffic, and today it is outside the park boundary, isolated on one of the busiest traffic roundabouts in London. Reach it via subways 4 and 5 from Park Lane or from Marble Arch Underground Station, emerging at Exit 3. A recent scheme for an underpass to bury the traffic extends from Marble Arch to Hyde Park Corner, so creating a piazza to rival St. Mark's Square in Venice, with the Arch as its centrepiece.

The Arch was originally to have been the main gateway to a remodelled Buckingham Palace and a memorial to the victories in the wars against Napoleon, but when finished it was said to be too narrow for the state coach. When Queen Victoria had the front of the palace rebuilt, it was moved to this spot. Designed in 1827 by John Nash, with decoration by artists such as John Flaxman, Marble Arch is a dream of pure white Italian Carrara marble, styled on the triumphal Arch of Constantine in Rome. It originally carried a statue of George IV rising from horseback without the aid of stirrups, which is now in Trafalgar Square. The arch is hollow and housed a tiny reporting police station in the days before radios. And there are gatekeepers' rooms above, unused for many years although there have been recent proposals to let them out as an apartment. They have twisting staircases 2 feet (60 centimetres) wide, vaulted brick ceilings, Regency fireplaces, and portholes as windows.

The early 20th-century bronze gates open onto what is believed may have been the site of the Tyburn Tree, the public gallows for two centuries, until they were moved to Newgate in 1783. There is a memorial stone on the small traffic island at the mouth of the Edgware Road. Condemned prisoners were transported to the gallows by cart, on which they stood for the noose to be put round their necks, then the cart was whipped away. Up to eight unfortunates could be hanged at a time on each of gallows' three sides. Most were not hardened criminals but the poor down on their luck. The laws of the time were a morass: to take fruit from a neighbour's tree was a minor crime, but to steal fruit already picked was a hanging offence. Hanging days were like public holidays, with crowds of spectators avid for morbid entertainment. As a joke, the highwayman Jonathan Wild picked the chaplain's pocket of a corkscrew which he held while dying. This part of London is a haunted place.

Cross to Hyde Park via the subway beside the fountain to the west of the Arch, emerge at Exit 8, and enter the park gate.

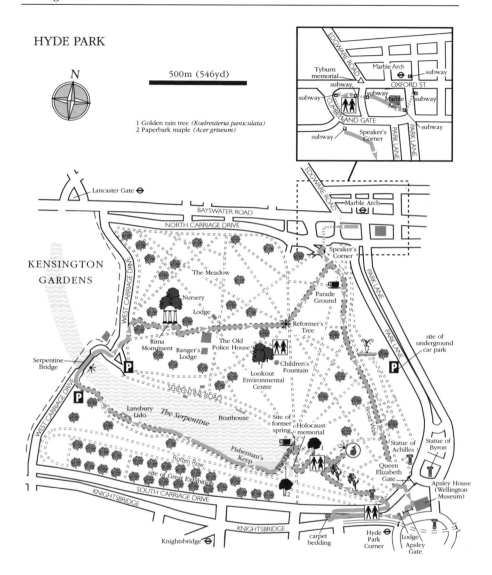

HYDE PARK

N

500m (546yd)

1 Golden rain tree *(Koelreuteria paniculata)*
2 Paperbark maple *(Acer griseum)*

Speakers' Corner

The area in which you are now standing is Speakers' Corner, the traditional spot for anyone to speak on almost any subject to anyone who will listen – at any time, although activity is mainly on Sunday mornings. Some maintain that the tradition originated with the right of the condemned to speak before their execution. However, the legal right of assembly here was only established in 1872 as a result of public demonstrations mounted by the Reform League to campaign for a wider vote, established by Edmund Beales. Speakers' Corner is a showcase for stubborn opinions straight from the mouth – microphones are not allowed – and real audience participation. Topics range from the flatness of the earth to pro-smoking tirades. The ground rules are: no sedition, treason, blasphemy or obscenities; and no incitement of race hatred.

Park Lane

Stroll south along Broad Walk, the footpath leading to Hyde Park Corner, avoiding the marked cycle track for safety. Park Lane, to your left, is hardly a lane any more. Some of the private houses and mansions built along its east side to face the park date were rebuilt as hotels or showrooms, mainly after bombing in World War II, so the façades are now largely 20th century, although one or two old curved bay windows remain. Roughly marking the halfway point between Marble Arch and Hyde Park Corner, just to the left of the path, is The Joy of Life fountain, an enthusiastic 4 tons of bronze sculpture of 1963 by the sculptor T. Huxley-Jones. It has star-shaped pools surmounted by a nude couple holding hands and was donated in 1944 by the Constance Fund.

Hyde Park Corner

Follow the path down a shallow slope to the park's southeast corner, commanded by a bronze statue of a naked Achilles, 18 feet (5.5 metres) high and weighing 33 tons, by the Royal Academician Sir Richard Westmacott. It was erected in 1822 as a memorial, paid for by public subscription 'by the women of England', to the victorious Duke of Wellington, whose home was Apsley House, the large neoclassical building – now the Wellington Museum – ahead of you. The statue was cast from 22 French cannon captured at Salamanca, Waterloo, and other Napoleonic battles. In 1822 there were complaints about the statue's fig leaf, and calls for more substantial cover, but it is obvious that the statue is underendowed and George Cruikshank, Charles Dickens's cartoonist, was quick to make fun of it. The fig leaf has been twice chipped off, in 1870 and 1961. The leaf you see now dates from 1963.

The statue of Achilles occupies a small rise, and round it, to the left, are the ornate Queen Elizabeth Gates, closing South Carriage Drive from Park Lane. They were erected in 1996 in honour of Queen Elizabeth the Queen Mother. Designed by an Italian metalworker, Giuseppe Lund, they are a model of filigree work. From the gates, look out into Park Lane where you can see a statue of the English Romantic poet, Lord Byron, erected in the park in 1880 but now isolated on a road island outside. It was carved by Richard Belt from an eccentric lump of granite donated by the Greek Government, for Byron was active in the Greek War of Independence against the Turks.

Cross South Carriage Drive to the formal gates beside Apsley House to the right. The classical screen of Apsley Gate was designed by the British architect Decimus Burton (1800–81). The horsemen motif is based on the frieze from the Acropolis in Athens, parts of which are in the British Museum. Turn right, at this point, for a good vista down the wide, sandy, tree-shaded Rotten Row, also known as The Mile. The horses ridden along it are hired from stables around the edge of the park, from private riding clubs. The Household Cavalry have their modern barracks on the south side of the park, and you often see detachments riding along South Carriage Drive. Ahead of you, The Friends of Hyde Park Information Centre is in the Lodge just inside the Apsley Gates. Walk through the gate beside it onto Hyde Park Corner.

Carpet Bedding

The southeast corner of Hyde Park has been a hotbed of horticulture for a century and a half. The Victorians delighted in the botanical discoveries being made at the ends of their empire, and enthusiastically grew many of the plants newly introduced by botanists, many of them delicate species native to hotter climates, in greenhouses for bedding out in the warmer months. Turn right and walk along the pavement until you reach a round concrete structure (an air shaft serving Hyde Park Corner Underground Station) in the grassy bank on the right. Planted on the bank beside it is an example of traditional carpet bedding in which, as I write, the plants form the words 'The Royal Parks'.

Carpet bedding uses foliage plants that can be close-clipped to create intricate designs. The plants, tightly positioned with formers (wooden frames) while in the greenhouse, might include fleshy-leaved South African crassulas, and Mexican echeverias. The displays are usually sponsored, and in 1966 the motif of an association for disabled people was featured. In winter these beds are usually planted with wallflowers for spring display.

The Flower Gardens

Re-enter the park via the steps to your right, cross the South Carriage Drive at the crossing and walk through the gate ahead into the flower gardens. The Victorians held display competitions in this area, and it is policy under Jennifer Adams, Superintendent of the central Royal Parks, to reproduce some of their early bedding schemes. An explanatory notice is normally pinned on a board nearby. The path through the beds takes you past two interesting fountains. The first one you come to is a boy with a dolphin, the water jetting unexpectedly not from its mouth but from its nose. It is by a Victorian sculptor, and was erected in 1862 on a site on Park Lane, moved to The Regent's Park, and then to this spot. The second, to your left, has Diana drawing her bow over a bowl supported by four caryatids; this was executed in 1906 by Countess Feodora Gleichen.

On the west side, the Flower Gardens give way to a necklace of small rose gardens, a type of planting very much in tune with current fashion. Follow the path leftward to walk through an impressive new feature, a long, sinuous, metal-framed pergola, planted with a white rambler, 'Gloire de Dijon' and other roses (all name-tagged), and large-flowered hybrid clematis. Teresa Short, the supervisor in charge of the rose garden, is creating a new look for the area, with a sense of enclosure, and is planting it with spring and herbaceous bedding and border plants to give all-year interest. Take a few minutes to wander among the rose beds – the species and varieties are all named. There is more general planting among the roses, with the silvery cotton lavender often prominent.

Before you reach the end of these Rose Gardens, take a diversion via the low gate to the right. Almost directly ahead, across Serpentine Road, is the Victorian bandstand, from where there is a marvellous vista north across open grass to the roofs and towers of Bayswater.

Recross Serpentine Road and turn right. Just past the toilet block to the left is a young, recently planted, golden rain tree *(Koelreuteria paniculata)*, a species from eastern Asia, which carries large, open clusters of yellow flowers in July. Leave the road just past it and wander leftward down a grassy bank planted with some magnificent trees, many of them labelled. There is, for example, a magnificent weeping beech, its contorted branches forming a tent. It is worth penetrating beneath its pendulous branches when it is in leaf, to see the unusual sculpturing of its branches.

About halfway down the slope to the right, a small stand of young silver birch trees surrounds a moving memorial to the Holocaust, composed in 1985 simply of two natural boulders set in raked gravel, ringed by silver birch trees. The inscription is a quotation from The Book of Lamentations: *For these I weep, streams of tears flow from my eyes because of the destruction of my people.*

The Dell

Turn right up the path beside the Holocaust Memorial, which leads back up the slope, You are now walking through The Dell, an attractive hollow with, to your left, a cascade and a pool fed by spillage from the Serpentine lake which lies unseen, banked up behind the bridge-like parapet above. The planting, set in smooth grass, is mainly for foliage effect with, for example, spiky yucca, tall reeds, cypress and other evergreens, and a magnolia. Behind you, at the exit of the stream, is a swamp cypress *(Taxodium distichum, see* page 18*)*, with a stand of gunnera, looking like a giant rhubarb nearby. Other interesting species include a strawberry tree *(Arbutus unedo)* up the bank and a Caucasian elm *(Zelkova carpinifolia)*, with toothed leaves and peeling bark. This is a rich corner, worth a visit in winter when the different shapes of the bare trees create picturesque patterns. In early spring the grass is alight with snowdrops and other bulbs, and the magnolia is in magnificent flower.

The couple of colossal lumps of Cornish granite halfway up the hollow are not prehistoric but are the remains of an 1861 drinking fountain. At the top of the slope to your right is a memorial recording the fact that spring water was once tapped at this spot to serve the monks of Westminster Abbey.

The Serpentine

At the top make a U-turn to the left, past The Dell café-cum-restaurant, marvellously placed with a view up the Serpentine. There are outside tables beside the water for warm days in summer or winter. Walk south across the bridgelike parapet, from where you can look down into The Dell and admire more trees, among them a paper-bark maple *(Acer griseum)*.

The path from the Dell Restaurant bends right to hug the south bank of The Serpentine. This 32-acre (13-hectare) lake was created from the old River Westbourne and a chain of small ponds, probably by the architect and landscape gardener, William Kent *(see* page 9*)* for Queen Caroline, wife of George II. It was extended to form the Long Water of what is now Kensington Gardens, making some 40 acres (16 hectares) of water in all. The spoil dug out was used to build up the banks of The Dell and Fisherman's Keep – the part of the Serpentine now to your right – where people may still fish with a licence from the Park authorities). The depth of The Serpentine is variable but plumbs to 20 feet (6 metres) deep in places. It was opened on May Day 1731, with George II and his family in two yachts, perhaps accompanied by a pair of tortoises sent by the Doge of Genoa to mark the event. The lake was the site of another great gala in 1814, a reenactment of the Battle of Trafalgar of 1805. It was, however, rather a smelly lake for the first part of its life, partly because sewage was carried into it by the River Westbourne. Its murky image was emphasized when it was sometimes chosen as a venue for suicides. Harriet Westbrook, the deserted and pregnant first wife of the poet, Percy Bysshe Shelley, drowned herself in it in December 1816. Today, the lake is much cleaner and usually full of high-prowed boats painted an attractive, dusky aquamarine blue. They are hired from the Boathouse you can see on the opposite side of the lake.

The Great Exhibition
To the south, opposite Rutland Gate, was the site of the Great Exhibition of 1851. It was held in a great hall of glass and iron, like a gigantic greenhouse, big enough for tall trees – and their accompanying birds – to be enclosed within it. When Queen Victoria asked the Duke of Wellington what could be done about the pigeon and sparrow nuisance, he uttered the immortal answer: 'Sparrowhawks, Madam'. When the Great Exhibition was over, the hall was moved to Crystal Palace Park. The entire area south of Rotten Row is now occupied by sports pitches and courts and a children's playground.

The Serpentine Bridge
The path now crosses the Lansbury Lido, a 20th-century creation named after George Lansbury, a pioneer of the Labour Party. Bear left beyond it, then turn right onto the Serpentine Bridge. This was a Regency addition of 1826 by Sir John and George Rennie, sons of the famous John Rennie (1761–1821) who built the first Waterloo Bridge and updated the Southwark and London Bridges that stood at the time (they have since been replaced).

Whatever the weather and at any time of day there is a splendid, nostalgic view from this bridge down the Serpentine across to the towers of Westminster Abbey and the Victoria Tower of the Houses of Parliament framed by trees, with the water in the foreground, maybe broken by those elegant, high-prowed rowing boats.

The Nursery
Cross the bridge, follow the West Carriage Drive past the car park, and then take the first turning to the right, beside what looks like a plantation. This is, in fact, the nursery area, where, hidden away behind the shrubs and trees, 12 great greenhouses produce 500,000 plants a year for bedding out in the Royal Parks and government gardens, and for indoor displays. The tally includes 2,000 varieties of 200 different species (10 different shades of begonia, for example). Along the path to your left,

built into the boundary shrubbery of the Nursery, is the Rima Monument to the Anglo-American naturalist and writer, W. H. Hudson (1841–1922). It takes the shape of a formal pond and an emerald green lawn, at the back of which is a memorial stone carved in 1925 by the American-born sculptor, Jacob Epstein (1880–1959). It shows Rima, a goddess in Hudson's book *Green Mansions*, with an eagle and other symbolic birds. It is difficult now to understand what all the fuss was about, but when the statue was first unveiled there was public outcry, spurred on by some of the newspapers of the day; it was tarred and feathered on two occasions.

The Ranger's Lodge

From the Rima Monument, follow the path eastward and turn left onto a path signposted to the Ranger's House. The path climbs toward a group of buildings. To the left is a quaint house, a typical keeper's lodge, while to the right is the Old Police House, a work yard, and beyond it, the old Ranger's House, now the headquarters of the Royal Parks Management. Outside its wall is a relict, a handsome red double postbox. With many sizeable trees roundabout, this part of the park looks for all the world like a settlement in the New Forest.

In front of the Old Police House is a signpost; follow the sign pointing to The Reformer's Tree. This path leads northeast through ancient woodland. To the north is The Meadow, an area of grass left to grow tall for hay, which, incidentally, encourages many butterflies. In the summer of 1996, shire horses Jim and Gaymer were used to pull the haycart, collecting 250 bales a day for a couple of months. Most of the hay is sold to riding stables, but some goes to the 16 police horses based in Hyde Park. They continue a long tradition, for horses were regularly used by the staff in all the Royal parks until the 1950s.

To your right you see a coppice which is a protected area for birds and conceals the Lookout Environmental Centre for local schools, a joint venture between the Park agencies and the Royal Society for the Protection of Birds. In front of the coppice is The Children's Fountain, erected in 1981, following an enormous party of 180,000 children in celebration of The Year of the Child. A detour to the fountain is great fun for children, since it squirts in unexpected directions.

Continue along the path, keeping the copse concealing the Lookout Centre to your right, and you come to a point where several paths meet. It is called The Reformer's Tree because an oak tree that once grew on this spot was a rallying point for The Reform League and other protest groups – huge crowds used to assemble around it. Today a lamp post marks the point where it grew. There are magnificent open views from this spot across an expanse of treeless ground called The Parade Ground, where Queen Elizabeth I reviewed her troops; during the Civil War this open space was the front line in Cromwell's chain of defence, and bristled with his troops. The path takes you back to Speakers' Corner and Marble Arch, where the walk ends.

The Regent's Park

Location	About 1½ miles (2.5 kilometres) north of Charing Cross.
Transport	Southeast side: Regent's Park Underground Station (Bakerloo Line) and Great Portland Street Underground Station (Hammersmith and City, Metropolitan, and Circle lines). Southwest side: Baker Street Underground Station (Jubilee, Metropolitan, Hammersmith and City, and Circle lines); Marylebone Station (overground terminus). Northeast side and Primrose Hill: Camden Town Underground Station (Northern Line). Buses 18, 27, 30, 74, 274. There is meter parking on Chester Road.
Location	Open from 05:00 hours until dusk. Admission is free.
Seasonal features	Avenue Gardens and Queen Mary's Rose Garden in spring and summer, spring blossom; autumn tree colour.
Events	Open-air theatre. Music on the Bandstand and in Queen Mary's Rose Garden in summer, nirdwatch walks and talks. Events booklet (*see* page 171).
Location	Rose Garden Buffet, Broad Walk Tea House, and Chester Gate Tea House open daily 09:30–17:30 hours.

In the 18th century a relic of the Middlesex Forest, old royal hunting ground to the north of London, was being let out as farmland, but by chance the leases came to an end in 1811, the year when the Prince of Wales (the future King George IV) took the title of Prince Regent. The architect John Nash (1752–1835) seized the opportunity. Until then, he had had a humdrum career, including a spell of bankruptcy following failed property speculation in Bloomsbury Square, and he was nearly 60. There were rumours that his wife was the Prince Regent's mistress, but the two men got on well, sharing an interest in architecture.

Nash proposed a courageous plan to honour the prince – and change the face of London. A triumphal route was to link Whitehall via Regent Street to the farmland, which, renamed The Regent's Park, was to become a 'garden city' of large houses in their own grounds, a foretaste of the Victorian suburb. Terraces, squares and open spaces were designed together, all part of one plan. Nash, working with Decimus Burton and other assistants, based the almost circular park on two ring roads, the outer faced by terraces of breathtaking beauty clad in stucco. The north side of the Park was left open so that people might enjoy 'the many beautiful views toward the villages of Hampstead and Highgate'. The lake was dug by 1830, and the park was opened to the public in 1835. The Prince Regent was delighted: 'It will quite eclipse Napoleon' he said. The grand plan was never completed, however. Apart from the great terraces, there are only fragments, such as Park Crescent with its sweeps of Ionic columns, which was finished by the early 1820s (and is now separated from the Park by traffic). Another is Park Square, with its little doll's-house Greek Doric lodges. Within the Park only eight of the planned twenty-six villas were built, and few of those remain. The Prince Regent's own retreat was never started.

As for the park, although it was laid out on more or less flat ground it is marvellously varied, with vast expanses of open green grass planted with statuesque trees at one extreme, and highly detailed and intricate flower gardens at the other. Water plays an important part, with a lake to match any in London and a splendid complement of waterfowl. To the north of the park is Primrose Hill, a 50-acre (20-hectare) public open space managed by Regent's Park staff. No primroses grow in the grass, but the area is scattered with some stately trees and it is a marvellous place for a brisk walk. There is a panoramic view over London from the brow of the hill 219 feet (65 metres) above sea level.

THE REGENT'S PARK WALK
Start Avenue Gate. *Finish* York Gate. *Time* Allow 1½ hours.

Opposite Avenue Gardens, where the walk begins, are Park Square Gardens, where horse chestnuts are in flower in late spring. As you enter the gate into The Regent's Park, you see the broad Avenue, bordered by hedging, stretching ahead, but instead of proceeding along it, turn right, and then immediately left at the stone fountain you see just ahead of you. Your gaze is immediately arrested by a vista of brilliantly colourful formal gardens and the sight of many fountains playing. On the other side of the garden, a similar scheme of flower beds and fountains is repeated.

These are the Avenue Gardens, perhaps the most handsome formal gardens to be seen anywhere. They were first laid out in 1864 by the great Victorian garden designer William Nesfield *(see* page 10), with strong spring and summer bedding backed by alleys formed by hedging and trees, set with stone vases and shallow tazzas (planters shaped like wine cups) spilling flowers. But little of his original design and even less of its splendour lasted long into the 20th century. Walk up the path ahead to admire the restoration work, which started in 1993. It has involved replacing the original paths and boundaries and major planting, including the four rows of a selected form of small-leaved lime trees *(Tilia cordata* 'Green Spire') on the central avenue of trees and tulip trees on the outer. There are upright conifers *(Juniperus chinensis)* in the outer avenues with hedges of hornbeam and yew. Smaller containment hedges are of box, berberis, euonymus and santolina.

The new scheme includes stonework, as did the original: there were 32 tazzas or vases. You see that some, such as the Lion Tazza, have been restored, but most have needed the casting of new moulds, and some eight have been or are being restored as fountains, not part of the original scheme. Sponsors are invited to finance this stonework. A highlight of these formal gardens was the cable frieze beds halfway up. The name comes from the rope-like pattern of the low evergreen hedges.

The Terraces

The gardens end at Chester Road, from where it is worth a detour to Chester Gate on the right to glimpse Chester Terrace, built in 1825, set back behind its own length of tree-shaded garden. It has its own grand triumphal arch as the north entrance, which carries a bust of Nash.

Cross Chester Road and veer right across the grass to view Cumberland Terrace, built in 1826–8, across the Outer Circle Road. It is 800 feet (244 metres) long, and is adorned with Ionic columns topped with rooftop statues. At the centre is a classical pediment with white Empire females in elaborate poses against a blue background. At the end of World War II, this was damaged, but it had been restored by 1980, and converted into apartments. The leafiness of the trees determines how much of the Terrace you can see, but any glimpse will be rewarding.

London Zoo

Cross the grass northwestward, heading for the line of trees opposite, which flank The Broad Walk. When you reach it, turn right and you soon reach a handsome Victorian Gothic drinking fountain, a gift in 1869 of Sir Cowasjee Jehangir of Bombay. The designer is unknown. To one side there is a sacred humped cow under a palm tree and, as well as a fulsome inscription, a plaque honouring Queen Victoria. Drinking fountains were a popular Victorian commemoration. In the days before cafes, the only alternative to a drink of water was in an inn or a pub, with all the temptations they offered.

Retrace your steps to the edge of the belt of trees around the fountain, and take the first path to the right leading southwestward across a large expanse of open grass. The southern border of London Zoo can be seen to the right. The Zoological Society of London moved in 1828 from the Tower of London into buildings on the northern edge of The Regent's Park. designed by Decimus Burton. Some of the buildings are the originals, the giraffe house, for example, but there are also some startling 20th-century creations to be glimpsed rising above the walls. To the sound of the animals might be added a whiff or two on a hot day. To the north of the Zoo is the Regent's Canal, which formed the edge of the park's grand design.

The park north of the path is given over to facilities for sports, such as football, baseball, and cricket. Several hundred teams might be registered every year, and there are usually golf and tennis schools.

The Lake

As you reach the sports pavilion halfway across, the path divides and you take the right fork. The belt of trees to your left marks the bank of the lake, and the path takes you to its western end. At the head of the lake the path narrows to cross a bridge to the small Duck Island. Ahead, a second bridge leads off the island to the opposite bank, where there is a round children's boating pond with blue-topped pedalos. To the right, beyond a children's playground, you can just glimpse the grounds of Winfield House, built in 1937 for Barbara Hutton, who was then the heir to the Woolworth's stores. When her marriage to film star Cary Grant ended in 1945, she gave the house to the U.S.A. as the American ambassador's residence.

THE REGENT'S PARK

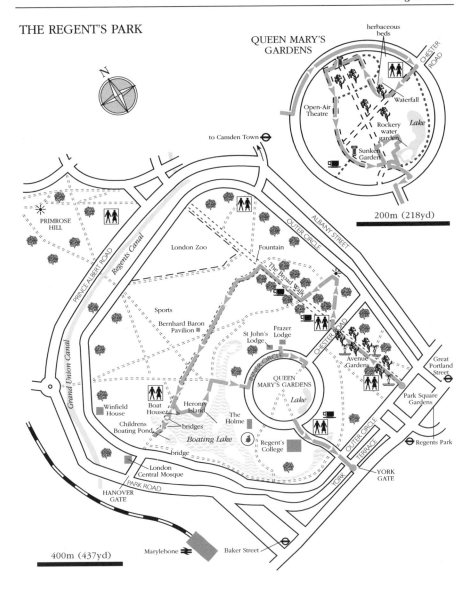

QUEEN MARY'S
GARDENS

herbaceous
beds

CHESTER ROAD

Open-Air
Theatre

Waterfall

Rockery
water
garden

Lake

Sunken
Garden

200m (218yd)

to Camden Town

N

PRIMROSE
HILL

Regents Canal

PRINCE ALBERT ROAD

London Zoo

Fountain

OUTER CIRCLE

ALBANY STREET

The Broad Walk

Sports

Bernhard Baron
Pavilion

St John's
Lodge

Frazer
Lodge

CHESTER ROAD

Avenue
Gardens

Great
Portland
Street

Grand Union Canal

INNER CIRCLE

QUEEN
MARY'S
GARDENS

Lake

Park Square
Gardens

Winfield
House

Boat
House

Heron
Island

The
Holme

Regents Park

Childrens
Boating Pond

bridges

Boating Lake

Regent's
College

OUTER CIRCLE

TERRACE

bridge

London
Central Mosque

PARK ROAD

YORK GATE

HANOVER
GATE

YORK

400m (437yd)

Marylebone

Baker Street

Its garden, which extends into the Park, is one of its few remaining private areas. Above the trees to the west rises the golden roof and minaret of the Central London Mosque, built in the 1980s.

Retrace your route back over the two bridges across the lake and bear right to follow an arm of the Y-shaped lake, 22 acres (9 hectares) in area, one of Nash's creations. In the boatyard to the right, handsome, high-prowed wooden rowing boats are for hire. This lake was the scene of a disaster in January 1867, when 41 skaters drowned after the ice collapsed. Several park lakes were made shallower as a result, and new regulations subsequently forbade skating in London parks on ice less than 5 inches (13 centimetres) thick. Across the water and through the trees you may be able to catch a glimpse of Hanover Terrace, with a pediment of white figures against blue, as they are on Cumberland Terrace. Sussex Place to its south has unusual octagonal domes; it was designed by John Nash in 1822 when he was also designing Brighton Pavilion for the Regent's father, George III.

You pass Heronry Island, the name a reminder that the lake is bursting with waterfowl. By now you will have heard the squeakings and gruntings and clattering of ducks. The Holme can be seen across the water, an essay in cream. Built in 1818, it was the first villa Decimus Burton designed, at the age of 18, for Nash's scheme, and the first of the villas to be built. Its garden is occasionally open to the public; consult the notice boards dotted around the Park.

Cross the water by the next bridge you come to. It is a substantial bridge with stone piers at each end, separating the bird sanctuary to the left from the Boating Lake to the right. On the opposite side of this bridge is a bird identification board. The lake accommodates an outstanding collection of waterfowl, including 45 different duck, some familiar from other parks, others less so – the canvas-backed duck, for example. The bar-headed goose, its white head cut by dark stripes running from the nape of its neck, is among the most handsome of the geese with its elegant, classic plumage. Alongside this board there is usually a handwritten list of recent sightings of wild birds – the spotted flycatcher, the garden warbler, and so on, all summer migrants, perhaps dropping by to rest.

The Secret Garden

Turn left to follow the Inner Circle road, and pass St John's Lodge, originally designed by Decimus Burton, but later extended. The house and grounds together give an idea of how Nash's original settlement could have looked. Lord Bute lived in this house in late Victorian times, describing it as 'terra incognita to a great many Londoners ... almost a country house yet only a shilling cab fare from Piccadilly Circus'. It is now in Government use.

Continue past the low, one-storey Fraser Lodge and turn left down a narrow alley arched with widely spaced iron pergola hoops, with flower beds to each side. This is the entrance to Lodge Garden, a delightful secret garden created for an owner of St. John's Lodge as a garden of meditation. At the end of the alley is a stone urn, brimful of plants, a memorial to a journalist who loved this place. To enter the garden, turn left and you see an immaculate lawn with beds edged with lavender which is busy with bees in summer. The garden curves in quadrants around a pool with a fountain and, at its centre, a statue of a boy and a girl frolicking. If you look closely, however, you see that the girl is a mermaid, with fins growing from her thighs; the boy is Hyras, a favourite of Hercules. The statue was sculpted in 1933 by the Royal Academician, H. A. Pegram. To the left is the impressive façade of St. John's Lodge, fronted by a handsome ironwork screen. On top of the pillars to each side, boys called armorini display the coat of arms of Lord Bute. To the right, an ironwork gateway beckons you on.

This gateway leads to another garden, which some regard as the real hidden delight of this urban haven. It is a secluded, round garden, walled in by a circle of pleached, interlacing lime trees and beds of flowers, such as perfumed roses in summer, edged with lavender, and set with trimmed topiary balls of box. In a recess facing the gateway is a blue-painted seat in memory of Nicholas Baker, who died not so long ago aged 16, and who loved the quiet of these gardens. They are at their most nostalgic when the first falls of autumn leaves drift across the grass.

There is a recent addition, following the original design. A gap in the lime trees to the north leads to a second, new, round garden, its limes only recently planted and still quite thin. To the left, at the end of the alley, is a statue of a shepherdess carrying a lamb, with an inscription reading 'To All Protectors of the Defenceless'. It was sculpted in 1932 by C. A. Howell, and protests against cruelty to animals.

Queen Mary's Gardens

Continue around the Inner Circle and turn right by the 1933 gateway at Chester Road to enter the central gardens. For this area, Nash planned a temple dedicated to British Greats. For nearly 100 years until 1932 the beds were planted by the Royal Botanic Society. Nowadays, however, as you see to your left and ahead, a great deal of the area is occupied by a most marvellous rose garden, where ramblers hang in swags between pillars wreathed in climbers set in beds of large and cluster-flowered varieties. It is named for Queen Mary, the wife of George V and a keen gardener. It has a collection of perhaps 30,000 roses of almost 400 different varieties, including the greatest modern cultivars, and all labelled – an aid for beginners; 'Ice Cream' is vanilla white and 'Greta Garbo' is (of course) a deep, lipstick red. There are some interesting trees to spot, such as the manna ash *(Fraxinus ornus)*, a tree from central Europe, with showy heads of white, scented flowers.

To the right of the Chester Road path, follow the curve of the superbly planted herbaceous border, perhaps the best in London, which leads on past more roses to the Triton Fountain, with a sculpture of the sea god by William McMillan, erected in 1950. The route circles anti-clockwise to the Open-Air Theatre, opened in 1932. Programmes for the summer season are displayed on notice boards, and the theory is that London rain falls mainly in the afternoon, the sky clearing for the evenings.

Toward the central crossing of the garden paths is a small sunken garden with a bedding display surrounding a statue of a boy with a frog. The display changes several times a year. Almost opposite is a rockery water garden with a cascade and island planted with alpines and with a majestic bronze eagle to one side. By the water on its south shore grows a swamp cypress *(Taxodium distichum)*.

Leave the gardens by the massive gilded gateway toward York Gate; it was presented by the artist Sigismund Goetze in 1935. The red brick building on the right, built in 1913 on the site of a Nash villa, was until very recently Bedford College of London University, the first university college for women. It is now called Regent's College and houses various American colleges. Cross York Bridge to see, opposite, York Terrace. This is the longest of the Nash Terraces, with massive Corinthian pillars (with leafy tops to the columns) decorating the centre block and with pavilions at each end. Cross the Outer Circle Road to York Gate, where the walk ends.

Kenwood and Hampstead Heath

Location	About 2⅓ miles (3.7 kilometres) northwest of Charing Cross.
Transport	Highgate Underground Station (Northern Line) is half an hour's walk; the 210 bus from South Grove, Highgate Village, stops near West Gate. Hampstead Underground Station (Northern Line) is three-quarters of an hour's walk away. The 210 bus from Jack Straw's Castle pub, Heath Street, reaches Kenwood via Spaniards Road. There is a car park alongside the West Gate.
Admission	Open daily from 08:00 hours–dusk. Admission is free.
Seasonal features	The Lime Walk in June and July, spring blossom and autumn tree colour.
Events	Summer concerts beside Concert Lake. Monthly walks on the Estate, regular talks.
Refreshments	Brew House Restaurant open daily 10:00-18:00 hours.

Most Londoners regard Kenwood as part of Hampstead Heath, and at one time the Kenwood Estate extended from Kentish Town in the south to Highgate, covering an area of 1,600 acres (650 hectares). For almost two centuries, however, the house and some 200 acres (80 hectares) of surrounding parkland were the private property of the Earls of Mansfield, closed off from the surrounding heath and common. The mansion we see today we owe to William Murray, Chief Justice to George III and the first Earl of Mansfield, who bought an older house on the site in 1754 for its fresh air and magnificent views south across London, and ten years later called in Robert Adam to improve it. William Murray started to landscape the grounds, but in the 1790s his successor called in Humphry Repton for further improvements.

Between 1889 and 1928, most of the former grazing lands of the larger estate were gradually broken up. In 1922 the sixth earl sold off 120 acres (49 hectares) for public use – and these were added to the open space of Hampstead Heath. In 1927, Lord Iveagh (one of the Guinness clan) bought the then derelict Kenwood House and restored it in the 18th-century manner, filling it with paintings by Gainsborough, Turner, Rembrandt, and other great English and Dutch artists. On his death in 1927 he left house, contents, and the remaining 75 acres (30 hectares) of its surrounding land to the public through London County Council, stipulating that 'the atmosphere of a gentleman's private park should be preserved'. It has remained in public ownership since – next with the Greater London Council and, when that was abolished, with English Heritage.

Since 1986, English Heritage has financed extensive careful restoration of the estate. In the future, they plan to restore the old Dairy and the Kitchen Garden, and to create new gardens, including a woodland and a flower garden.

Today, Adam's remodelled Kenwood House and its surrounding gardens and woods occupy 112 acres (45 hectares) at the northeastern edge of Hampstead Heath. From the terrace on the south side of the house, wide lawns sweep down to the lakes, where the Sham Bridge perfectly complements the landscape. Originally devised either by William Murray or by Robert Adam, it was, however, despised by Humphry Repton, but survived to be rebuilt many times. It makes a perfect setting for the summer concerts, which began in 1951 and are performed on the stage behind the Concert lake.

This short walk focuses on the landscaped gardens, the lakes, and the woods behind them. About one-third of these grounds are officially designated a Site of Special Scientific Interest, and large areas are dedicated to conservation. They contain ancient woodlands with many rare and exceptionally old trees, and areas of wetland with rare wild flowers, ferns and mosses.

On the southern side the landscaped grounds merge with the wilder acres of Hampstead Heath. Strictly speaking, the Heath is outside the scope of this book's walks – it isn't a park! But the two are so closely linked that it seems almost *de rigueur* to extend the Kenwood walk into a trek across the Heath's wider expanses. The map on page 73 gives two ideas for walks of about 2 miles (3 kilometres).

The first walk extends the route from Hampstead Station, across the Heath and through South Wood to Kenwood House. Keeping to the leftward paths after you enter Ken Wood (South Wood) will take you past the old farmhouse and dairy of the Home Farm to the west gate, where the Kenwood walk begins.

This route gives a good view of the Heath's prized up-and-down natural wilderness of open grass, scrub and woodland, set with pools and ponds, perched above London and with some magnificent views across the city to the Surrey Hills. It was rescued from builders in the 19th century (Highgate Common, which ran alongside, disappeared completely) and since then has always had a forceful protection society, heavy with well-known local residents. Their predecessors pushed to extend the Heath and as a result, Parliament Hill, then occupied by farmland, was bought in 1886 and Golders Hill was added in 1899. The Kenwood Estate was the last addition, in the 1920s.

The second continues the walk through the gate to the east of Kenwood House terrace, then southward, across the newly planted Wild Flower Meadow and around Highgate Ponds – the string of lakes along the Heath's eastern edge – and across Parliament Hill to Hampstead. Each pond has a different use and atmosphere: the Men's and Ladies' ponds are for bathing; and there is a pond for model boats and a bird sanctuary pond to the south of it. From Parliament Hill, 320 feet (97.6 metres) high, there is a good view of the roof line of Highgate and out across London (there is a view board on the spot).

Together, Kenwood and the Heath cover a vast area with much to do and discover, and rich possibilities for many alternative future walks – including formal monthly walks and talks led by the Head Ranger.

THE KENWOOD WALK
Start and finish West Gate. *Time* Allow ¾ hour.

The walk begins at the West Gate to what was once the main carriage drive to Kenwood House. There is another gate on the eastern side of the house, and each is overlooked by its charming octagonal Lodge designed by Humphry Repton. Walk down the long, curving gravel path. The trees to the left mark the boundary of North Wood, and the house is screened by the shrubbery on the right. There are some splendid oaks in the wood and on a knoll (reached via the path leaving the car park to the left of the drive) a quartet of superb beech trees which miraculously escaped damage in the great storms of 1987 and 1989.

The front entrance of the house comes suddenly into view as you round the last bend in the path. The second Earl of Mansfield diverted Hampstead Lane away from the front of the house, around North Wood and laid the drives to give visitors this surprise view of the impressive north front, with its simple Ionic portico of giant columns, with a single medallion in the triangular pediment above. The Half Moon lawn in front was laid over the old road.

The Ivy Tunnel
Take a sharp right turn along the path leading into the shrubbery. To the left of the path is a monument to peace: a metal column impressed with Japanese characters reading 'May Peace Prevail on Earth' – a legacy from the Greater London Council. A short distance ahead you pass through a hooped tunnel clad with ivy – quite low (perhaps Lord Mansfield was a bit short), and popular with children. When you emerge, look to the right for a young paper-bark maple *(Acer griseum)*, a tree from China with orangey bark that peels off in patches. Just ahead to the right is a raised recess with seating, overlooked by a huge old oak. This is the spot where there stood a 'humble little summer house of rough wood', in which Dr. Johnson used to sit and talk with Mrs. Thrale. It was moved from her Streatham house in 1968, but was burned down by vandals in 1993.

The area to the left is called the Flower Garden – oddly, it seems, since rhododendrons in island beds are the only flowers to be seen. However, this was the site of a fenced flower garden, created by Humphry Repton, which was grassed over in the 1960s. Follow the path around the end of the lawn and leftward, passing a couple of rhododendron roundels and a sculpture by Barbara Hepworth entitled *Monolith-Empyrean (The Heavens)*, and turn left. A shingle path leads through an avenue of limes, which perfume the air in June and July, to the terrace running along the south front of the house, and is generously provided with commemorative seats.

The 'Oyster Shell'
The South Front of the house is a perfect Adam composition, enhanced by the Orangery to the left and the Library to the right. The Orangery was already built in Adam's day, but he remodelled it and built the Library on the other side of the house, to match. As you reach the terrace, your eye will be attracted to the magnificent vista to the south – as typical of the 18th century as is the house. This

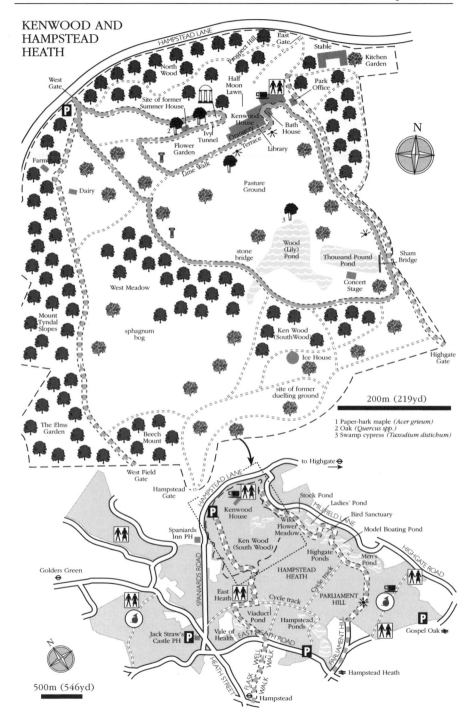

KENWOOD AND
HAMPSTEAD
HEATH

HAMPSTEAD LANE

East
Gate

Prospect Hill

Stable

Kitchen
Garden

North
Wood

West
Gate

P

Half
Moon
Lawn

Park
Office

Site of former
Summer House

2

Kenwood
House

Bath
House

Ivy
Tunnel

Orangery

Library

Flower
Garden

Terrace

Farm

Lime Walk

Dairy

Pasture
Ground

3

stone
bridge

Wood
(Lily)
Pond

Thousand Pound
Pond

Sham
Bridge

West Meadow

Concert
Stage

Mount
Tyndal
Slopes

sphagnum
bog

Ken Wood
(SouthWood)

Highgate
Gate

Ice House

site of former
duelling ground

200m (219yd)

The Elms
Garden

Beech
Mount

1 Paper-bark maple *(Acer grieum)*
2 Oak *(Quercus spp.)*
3 Swamp cypress *(Taxodium distichum)*

West Field
Gate

N

to Highgate

Hampstead
Gate

HAMPSTEAD LANE

Stock Pond

Ladies' Pond

P

Kenwood
House

Bird Sanctuary

Wild
Flower
Meadow

MILLFIELD LANE

Spaniards
Inn PH

Model Boating Pond

Ken Wood
(South Wood)

Highgate
Ponds

Men's
Pond

Golders Green

HAMPSTEAD
HEATH

HIGHGATE ROAD

SPANIARDS ROAD

East
Heath

Cycle track

PARLIAMENT
HILL

Cycle track

P

Viaduct
Pond

Hampstead
Ponds

Jack Straw's
Castle PH

P

Vale of
Health

EAST HEATH ROAD

P

Gospel Oak

N

HEATH STREET

FLASK WALK

WELL WALK

PARLIAMENT HILL

Hampstead Heath

500m (546yd)

Hampstead

sweeps down the steep bank in the foreground, past a splendid magnolia tree, across lawns to two lakes planted with fine trees, with glimpses through the foliage of the London skyline beyond. This landscaped area between house and water has been described as 'a gigantic oyster shell beside a lake'. It is a man-made view, the trees originally placed and planted to a tight plan. It is easy to forget that although landscape designers like Humphry Repton could plant sizeable trees while designing their idealized paradise, they would never see the results in their full-grown glory.

Stroll along the terrace. In the past, the path was surfaced with cork preparation to deaden the noise of footsteps when concerts are held in the Orangery. The handsome white bridge at the left edge of the left-hand lake catches the eye. It is, in fact, a fake, only about 2 feet (61 centimetres) wide, a trompe l'œil of flat, painted wood, placed to add a focus to the view. It is a typical 18th-century conceit, possibly added by William Murray himself.

Walk on past the library (the inside is counted the best Adam room to be seen anywhere), and look for a small white door labelled 'Bath House'. If it is open, turn through it and walk down the narrow steps (if it is locked, walk further on and down the steps on the left to the café, turn left at the bottom, and walk to the end of the yard). The steps from the terrace door lead down to the 18th-century Bath House, a small, round building housing a chilly-looking white marble plunge bath. The buried bath at Greenwich Park *(see page 89)* must have been rather like this.

The Lakes

Walk through the yard, full of café tables in summer, which is overlooked by outbuildings that were once stables and other service areas. Return to the terrace via the steps to the right, walk on past the Information Office and turn along the path to the right, leading along the eastern edge of the oyster shell. You pass some magnificent old oaks and a chestnut tree planted in Repton's time.

As you approach the lake, the Sham Bridge can now be seen for what it is. Look back, as you reach it, for a magnificent view of the house proud at the top of the slope. Such views were part of Repton's original concept. Woods, water and lawns, paths and drives were arranged in a composition whose aim was to show the house to its best advantage from every point of view.

The lake ahead of you has several names. It was originally called Thousand Pound Pond – a name apparently inspired by the cost of building it when it was created as a reservoir in the 18th century. Today, however, it is most often referred to as the Concert Pond, since on summer evenings open-air concerts are held on the staging behind this lake, the audience dotting themselves down the grassy slopes behind you. It is well populated with carp and rudd. Its partner is traditionally called Wood Pond, but has come to be known as Lily Pond after the water lilies that flower on its surface in summer. It was formed from a number of medieval ponds in the mid-18th century, and later enlarged. It has an island which has become a refuge for wildlife, and amphibians and all manner of invertebrate life thrives in it because it has no predatory fish. Along its north bank, a stately swamp cypress *(Taxodium distichum)* with feathery leaves grows. This North American tree was very popular a couple of centuries ago.

Ken Wood

Cross the causeway–dam behind the bridge and bear right along the path through Ken Wood (also called South Wood). In the past, these ancient woodlands were set out in 'quarters': islands of trees separated by paths to give quiet and secluded walks. This was an 18th-century idea, whose purpose was to give visitors an opportunity to stroll through safe, idealized wilderness. A similar idea was realized in the enclosures behind Holland House *(see* page 44). Ken Wood is a marvellous wildlife wood, the oaks and beeches statuesque and among them, plenty of trunks and boughs lying rotting, which attract beetles and other insects, and after them, birds. Ken Wood is a breeding area for 40 bird species, and an important resting point for migrant birds.

Keep right along the paths through the wood and you skirt the southern banks of the lakes. Look right now and again to catch glimpses of the house through the trees. Eventually, the paths lead to a short bridge at the west end of Wood (Lily) Pond. Walk up the rise. The sculpture to the right, by Henry Moore, is entitled *Two-Piece Reclining Figure*. When you reach the west end of the terrace across the front of the house, take a left-hand path back to the West Gate, where the walk ends.

Bloomsbury Squares

Location	About ⅔ of a mile (1 kilometre) north of Charing Cross.
Transport	Russell Square Underground Station (Piccadilly Line). Holborn Underground Station (Piccadilly and Central lines). Tottenham Court Road Underground Station (Central Line). Buses along New Oxford Street/ Tottenham Court Road: 19, 24, 29, 38, 73. There is a car park beneath Bloomsbury Square.
Admission	Bloomsbury Square, Russell Square, Tavistock Square and Gordon Square gardens are open daily 08:00 hours– dusk. Admission is free. Bedford Square gardens are closed to the public.
Seasonal features	Spring blossom. Autumn tree colour.
Refreshments	Russell Square Café open daily 08:00–18:30 hours.

London's squares with their central gardens identify London, no other city has so many. The oldest squares were laid out nearly four centuries ago, speculative developments of the mid-17th century built as wealthy people began to reside outside the City. Until the 1600s, most of the population of London lived mainly within the City's protective walls, while the King and court resided in and around the Palace of Whitehall, near Westminster Abbey, and monasteries owned vast acres of the area covered by London today. In the 16th century when the monasteries were dissolved, their lands were sold into private ownership. During the 17th century, some of the landowners granted leases to speculative builders, who erected squares, streets and terraces. These they hoped to let to aristocratic and wealthy tenants seeking more spacious and salubrious surroundings.

The first such development was Covent Garden, originally the site of an abbey, whose land after the dissolution of the monasteries was granted to the Earls of Bedford. In 1627, the fourth Earl commissioned the English Renaissance architect Inigo Jones to design a number of houses on the site. Jones's scheme for St. Paul's Church, and tall houses surrounding a piazza was inspired by the Italian architect, Andrea Palladio (1508–80), and it seemed very foreign. As it became fashionable for the aristocracy to live outside the City, and the builders expanded further west to Soho, and later to Mayfair and Belgravia, squares ornamented with statuary became very fashionable.

Bloomsbury – roughly the area between New Oxford Street and Euston Road, Tottenham Court Road and Gray's Inn Road – is on the land of an ancient manor, recorded in the Domesday Book. After the dissolution of the monasteries, the manor was granted to Sir Thomas Wriothesley, Lord Chancellor under Henry VIII. In 1660 his descendant, the 4th Earl of Southampton, built a square 'at the bottom of the Long Field' and called it Southampton Square (now Bloomsbury Square). It became a model for other squares as the area developed in the 18th century.

Today, what were originally the bare centres of these squares are fenced with iron railings, grassed over, and planted with shrubs and the stately plane trees that have become a signature of London. The tall trunks of these fine trees are dappled with attractively scaling bark, the leaves are sharply lobed, and the fruit is a distinctive, hanging bobble. These trees are as handsome in winter as in summer, tracing beautiful silhouettes of arching branches against the surrounding buildings. In the days before smoke control, the London plane tree was famous for its tolerance of the city's grime. The poisonous soot was shed with the bark. Frances Partridge, one of the literary Bloomsbury set, describes living in Bedford Square around 1910, with the plane trees thick with soot. She had to scrape the evergreen laurel leaves to see that they were indeed green. The parentage of the London plane is obscure. It is probably a hybrid between the 'Oriental' plane (which grows in the Balkans, as well as in Asia) and the American plane, which resulted in the 17th century when they grew near each other in the Oxford Botanic Garden. The cross-bred offspring, whose Latin name is *Platanus x hispanica* proved highly vigorous, quick-growing and fertile. It regularly grows as high as 99–115 feet (30–35 metres).

This walk tours four of the most interesting of Bloomsbury's many garden squares, each with its own personality.

BLOOMSBURY SQUARES WALK
Start Holborn Station. ***Finish*** Tottenham Court Road Station.
Time Allow 1 hour.

From High Holborn Underground Station, cross Kingsway and High Holborn at the traffic lights and walk north up Southampton Row – named after the first Earl of Southampton, who bought Bloomsbury from the Crown in the 16th century. Just before you reach the top you pass on the left the pretty Sicilian Avenue, a shopping street paved with Sicilian marble, planned by W.S. Wortley and built in 1905.

Bloomsbury Square
Cross Bloomsbury Way at the traffic lights, turn left, and walk along until you come to Bloomsbury Square. Enter the gardens through the southeast gate and follow the path to the left. The name Bloomsbury comes from Blemund's Burgh, the name of the medieval manor which occupied this site until the Reformation. Bloomsbury Square originated around 1660, when the fourth Earl of Southampton built a mansion on its north side – the opposite side of the square from where you are now standing – set back in a railed courtyard. Along the other three sides of the square, building plots were let out at peppercorn rents. This was good business acumen, for there was a valuable reversion when their leases fell due.

This new square was typical of the developments that sprang up in what later became known as London's West End. They had a self-contained feel about them,

BLOOMSBURY SQUARES

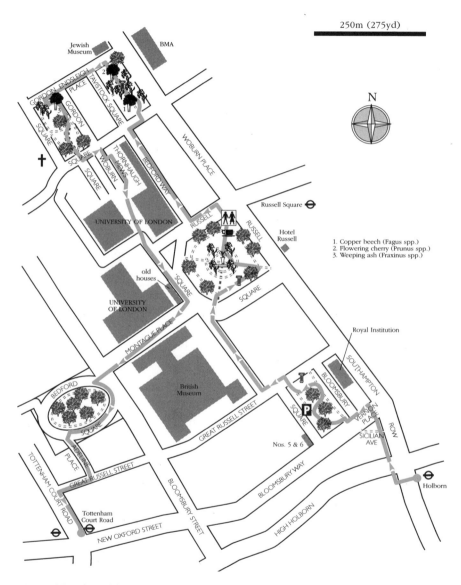

250m (275yd)

N

1. Copper beech (Fagus spp.)
2. Flowering cherry (Prunus spp.)
3. Weeping ash (Fraxinus spp.)

quite unlike the rabbit warren of jumbled streets and alleyways of the old City of London. Bloomsbury Square, when completed, led the diarist John Evelyn to write with approval of 'a noble square or Piazza, a little Towne' – an interesting comment, because when he saw it, the square was probably standing out alone among fields and kitchen gardens. None of the 17th-century houses survive, but Nos. 5 and 6 in the square's southwest corner, which you can see over the railings at the end of the path, were built in the mid-18th century.

Turn right and follow the path toward the centre of the gardens. There is a small. hedged-off plot with a swing for children just ahead of you on the west side, but the square is no longer residential. The gigantic insurance company building on the east side was put up in 1928, and since then all the houses on the other three sides have been converted to commercial uses.

When you reach the centre of the gardens, you see that it is paved and bare, although surrounded by benches. However, a print of 1787 shows that the whole area now occupied by grass and trees was then merely bare gravel. Gardens were not unknown in London at that time. Indeed, a Swedish visitor of 1748 was struck by the number of flowers growing (despite the soot) in private gardens, for whereas in 1700 most houses had paved back yards, by 1800 these had largely been replaced by gardens. Nurseries of the time listed plants which are still mainstays: privet, box, holly, ivy, lilac, white lily, perennial sunflower, sweet william, poppy, lupin, and even the scarlet runner bean as an ornamental climber. By 1760 there were around 30 commercial plant nurseries feeding the capital.

'I think some sort of wilderness work will do much better' complained the writer Thomas Fairchild in his *City Gardener*, which he wrote in 1722. But the reason why squares of the time were usually barren was that provision was not usually made to pay for any improvements. It was not until the 1760s that residents began to obtain private Acts of Parliament to pay for planting and upkeep with money from a local rate in order to improve the outlook from their windows. The change was dramatic: the squares were now usually grassed, with shrubs and trees planted as screens. A Danish visitor in 1809 enthused that the 'squares afforded very sensible relief, the eye being wearied of the sameness of colossal piles of bricks and mortar'.

Follow the path as it meanders along the quieter east side of the gardens, shaded by handsome plane trees underplanted with a scattering of evergreens, and an occasional flowering shrub for seasonal interest. In the original garden design there may have been flower beds, as Humphry Repton *(see* page 10) had a hand in its planning.

The path turns left along the north end of the gardens, where there is a statue of the statesman Charles James Fox (1749–1806) facing out of the gardens onto the square. Statues have been features of London squares since the 1600s, but this one, by the Royal Academician Richard Westmacott was erected around 1812. Fox was a son of the first Lord Holland *(see* page 41) and he died in Chiswick House *(see* page 28). A Whig (the Whigs were the predecessors of the English Liberal Party) and a rake, he was also passionately in favour of personal liberty, counting among those who had hailed the French Revolution in 1789. He is dressed as a Roman senator, with a copy of Magna Carta in his hand.

Leave the gardens through the gate to the left (west) of Fox's statue, cross the road and turn left. In 1800 this square underwent a major change when the Duke of Bedford, who by then owned the land, demolished the mansion that had stood for 140 years at the north end and commissioned the architect James Burton to replace it with the terraces and streets which lead north to Russell Square. It was part of a massive family development of much of this part of London – Tavistock,

Woburn, Russell, and Montague are all names linked with the Bedford family. The new development was very profitable, but note that John Nash (see page 64) was bankrupted speculating in property in this area.

Now turn right, up Montague Street. To your left is the British Museum, with its wonderfully elegant façade. It was built between 1823 and 1838 on the site of Montague House, one of several grand mansions built for the Bedford clan.

Russell Square

At the top of Montague Street is Russell Square, built around 1800, one of the largest of the London squares. Cross the road at the traffic lights and look along the west side where some of the houses are the originals built by James Burton in 1800.

Enter the gardens through the southwest gate. These gardens were originally laid out by Humphry Repton. Although he is best known as the natural heir to 'Capability' Brown (*see* page 10), and a believer in natural landscaping, he also designed garden areas, scaling down his plans near the house. He would have advised clients that flower beds set in grass and edged with a low basketwork trellis were fashionable and that they might be planted with lupins, hollyhocks, roses, and mignonette, which had recently arrived from Egypt. At that time, the fashion in grand design in country estates was evolving from 'Capability' Brown's concept of the grand vista into what was later called the gardenesque. The area near the house came to be seen as a setting for imported plants and flowers from warmer climates reared in greenhouses. With the current surge of interest in the exotic and the new, both were ideal for town squares.

Turn right along the southern side of the gardens and pause to admire the statue of the fifth Duke of Bedford (1765–1805) by the Royal Academician Richard Westmacott. The curly-haired Duke, the owner of a large slice of Bloomsbury, was also a keen farmer – which explains the sheep appearing below his feet. Continue walking on, and when you reach the southwest corner, turn left along the path leading into the centre of the gardens, passing an air-monitoring station on the right. You are shaded by the canopies of some fine plane trees.

Around the perimeter of the gardens and around the centre there is a handful of flower beds planted with roses and seasonal successions of bedding plants, but these represent little more than the spirit of the gardenesque. These gardens were redesigned during the 1960s, when the three fountains (now dormant for some time) were installed at their centre and surrounded by honeycomb concrete paving. The Russell Square Café, ahead of you in the northeast corner of the gardens, is intrusive, but the café tables overlooking the flower beds, make Russell Square a pleasant lunchtime retreat for people who work in hotels and offices roundabout.

Turn right in front of the café and walk to the path running along the east side of the gardens. The terrace of houses that originally overlooked this side of the square was demolished a century ago to build the Russell Hotel, which faces you on the left. It was designed by Charles Doll and opened in 1900, and it is perhaps the best of the remaining Victorian grand hotels. Its style, which embraces red terracotta and red brick, colonnaded balconies and prancing cherubs, is based (loosely) on a French château.

Turn back along the path and leave the gardens by the gate in the north corner. Cross the road at the traffic lights, turn left, and then right up Bedford Way. Bloomsbury is London's University quarter, and institutions of the University of London line this and the surrounding streets.

Tavistock Square

At the top of Bedford Way is Tavistock Square, which was begun in 1803 by James Burton shortly after Russell Square. The east side was rebuilt in the first half of the 20th century. Tavistock House, where the novelist Charles Dickens lived in 1851–60, was replaced in 1938 by the present British Medical Association building designed by Edwin Lutyens (1869–1944). The west side, built between 1820 and 1826 by Thomas Cubitt (builder of the streets surrounding Battersea Park, see page 122), is well preserved. Cross the road, enter the gardens by the south gate, and turn right along the perimeter path, which is shaded by some magnificent, tall plane trees. In the southeast corner is a statue of one of the first women surgeons, Louisa Brandreth Aldrich-Blake, Dean of the Royal Free Hospital School of Medicine for Women until her death in 1925.

Turn left and follow the path into the centre. To the left of the path is a handsome copper beech, planted in 1963 by the Indian President, Jawaharlal Nehru (1889–1964). This restful garden square, its benches much appreciated by students from nearby colleges seeking a tranquil place to read in summer, could just as well be called Peace Square, for it shelters several monuments to peace. In the centre of the gardens is a statue of the Indian pacifist Mahatma Gandhi (1869–1948), who led the struggle for independence. It was erected in 1968. Commemorative candles and incense are often lit beneath the statue, giving the gardens a particularly meditative atmosphere at dusk.

Colourful flower beds surrounding Gandhi's statue fan out to green lawns. Follow the path leading to the north end of the gardens, but pause to admire a cherry tree on the left, planted in 1967 to commemorate the victims of Hiroshima. On the grass in the northwest corner is a large rock honouring the conscientious objectors – men who refused to fight during World War II.

Leave the gardens by the north gate. Adler House, opposite, the Court of the Chief Rabbi, houses the Jewish Museum. Turn left, cross the road and walk along Endsleigh Place, to arrive at Gordon Square.

Gordon Square

These days, Bloomsbury is most closely associated in most people's minds not with the Dukes of Bedford but with the Bloomsbury Group. This was an association mainly of artists and writers who were active in the early years of the 20th century, many of whom lived in Bloomsbury. The Hogarth Press, founded early in the 20th century by Leonard and Virginia Woolf, was at No. 52 Tavistock Square. Another prominent member, the economist, John Maynard Keynes lived on the east side of Gordon Square, at No. 54; several members of the group lived at No. 46; and the biographer, Lytton Strachey lived at No. 51. These houses replaced the Georgian houses erected by the builder Thomas Cubitt in the 1820s.

Cross the square – which was named after Lady Georgiana Gordon, the second wife of the sixth Duke of Bedford – and enter the gardens on the north side. With its verdant lawns and mix of fine evergreen and deciduous trees, this is perhaps the most beautiful of Bloomsbury's garden squares. Turn left just inside the gate and walk toward the northeast corner to admire a venerable weeping ash, its weighty branches stooping to ground level, and a seat spanning its wide trunk. The path meanders into the centre of the gardens, planted with rose beds and with benches placed invitingly here and there – there are roses everywhere in summer.

Leave Gordon Square by the south gate, cross the road and walk southeast through Woburn Square and along Thornhaugh Mews, and back along the west side of Russell Square to Montague Place. Turn right and cross Bloomsbury Street to stand in Bedford Square.

Bedford Square

This, London's only complete surviving Georgian square, was designed by Thomas Leverton in 1775, a century later than Bloomsbury Square. Each side is a dignified composition in brick, but notice the decorative use of white Coade stone in the round-headed doorways: it was an artificial stone made in Fulham to a secret formula (*see* page 153).

The square was once gated, and some of this sense of privacy remains, at least at weekends. In the words of the artist John Piper, on a quiet Sunday it is an 'almost hallucinatory piece of preservation of late 18th-century London'. This privacy still extends to the central garden, a central, luxuriant oval – so unfortunately you can do no more than peer over the railings on the south side to see the carefully contrived setting of grass, elegant trees, and shrubs, dappled in light and shade. It makes a perfect foil for the elegant house façades.

Cross Bedford Square on the west side and head south down Adeline Place to Great Russell Street. Turn right for Tottenham Court Road and the Underground Station, where the walk ends.

Greenwich Park

Location	About 6 miles (9.5 kilometres) east of Charing Cross.
Transport	Greenwich, Maze Hill or Blackheath stations (overground trains from London Bridge; 15 minutes' walk from Blackheath Station). Island Garden DLR on the Isle of Dogs, then to the south bank via the foot tunnel. Buses 53, 177, 180, 286. Boats (about 45 minutes) from Charing Cross Pier. There is a car park in the Park.
Admission	Open daily dawn–dusk. Admission is free.
Seasonal features	The Flower Garden has azaleas in spring, bedding plants and perennials in summer and autumn.
Events	Band concerts, children's workshops in summer; cricket and rugby and hockey to watch in season.
Refreshments	Tea House open 10:00–17:30 hours.

Greenwich Park, beside the River Thames, is one of the most dramatic open spaces in London; and with Palladian and English Baroque buildings by two of the most notable British architects, Inigo Jones (1573–1652) and Christopher Wren (1632–1723) on its riverside, it is a masterpiece. There is a good view of the architecture from a small garden (created in the 1890s) on the Isle of Dogs near Island Gardens DLR station. This viewpoint, favoured by Wren, can be reached by foot tunnel under the river from the Greenwich side; its entrance is near Greenwich Pier and the Cutty Sark tea clipper.

In 1433 the Duke of Gloucester, uncle of Henry VI, fenced in 88 hectares (200 acres) and built a lodge, Bella Court, on the banks of the Thames. The Tudors felt at home there and rebuilt the lodge as a favourite palace. Henry VIII and his daughters Mary and Elizabeth were all born there, and Henry married two of his wives there. Elizabeth used the palace when she became queen, arriving on her gilded royal barge (it was at Greenwich that Sir Walter Raleigh flung his cloak over a puddle in her path). Around 1620, James I surrounded Bella Court park with a brick wall, some of which remains. Greenwich Park occupies the area within this enclosure.

James I did not much like Bella Court, however, and settled it on his queen, Anne of Denmark. And it was for Anne that in 1616 Inigo Jones began to build Queen's House (also known then as the House of Delights) behind the palace; it was England's first Palladian villa, although it was not to be finished for some years. It is worth making a diversion, before or after exploring the Park, to admire this jewel of a building. If you stand between the buildings of the Royal Naval College (entered from King William Walk) you have a framed view of it with the Old Royal Observatory on the brow of the hill behind. In 1614 Inigo Jones wrote of this unaffected Palladian style: 'Ye outward ornaments oft to be solid, proporsionable according to the rulles, masculine and unaffected...'.

The old palace was vandalized by Cromwell's Roundhead soldiers, and when the monarchy was restored in 1660 Charles II ordered it to be demolished and a new palace built to complement the Queen's House. However, the project stalled when the money ran out, and, as William and Mary preferred the then country setting of Kensington Palace *(see* page 49) when they took the throne, the site was turned over to a Royal Naval Hospital (to match Chelsea's military hospital) and Wren given the job of designing it. He worked without fees, so it is said; and the English Baroque architect, Sir John Vanbrugh, who lived nearby, later also played a role. The need to keep the view of the river from Queen's House explains why Wren's design for the hospital was essentially two buildings. In 1873 they became the Royal Naval College; and they are now about to change hands again, perhaps welcoming the new Greenwich University as core tenant. The ornately painted interiors can be visited in the afternoons.

The Queen's House has also had changes of tenants. In the early 19th century two side blocks were added, joined by colonnades, to make a school for naval orphans. Today the whole assemblage houses the National Maritime Museum.

The Park has seen many changes since it was laid out. Cromwell's troops cut down many of the park trees, but Charles II energetically set about restoring them. The French landscape designer, André Le Nôtre, famous for his work at the Palace of Versailles outside Paris, which combined Italian influences in the way of terraces with Dutch influence in the way of formal avenues and canals, was invited in. Large numbers of trees were planted − 300 elms in 1664, for example − to surround a formal terrace at the brow of the hill. Avenues of sweet (edible) chestnut were also planted and some of these trees are still alive. The buildings of the Royal Observatory, founded in 1675 by Charles II, are also in the Park.

THE GREENWICH PARK WALK
Start and finish St Mary's Gate. ***Time*** *Allow 2 hours.*

Before beginning the walk, stop to admire the nicely gilded ironwork of St Mary's Gate, and, to the left inside it, the statue of William IV, king for seven years before Victoria, holding a jutting telescope. He had a naval background, serving at the first Battle of Cape St Vincent, Portugal, in 1780 when he was only 15, and later in the West Indies. He was known as The Sailor King. Turn right just inside the gate onto a path leading off the tarmac road called The Avenue to see the small scented herb garden, past St Mary's Lodge. It is at its fragrant peak in June and July. Ahead of you the ground rises, but the flat ground before the rise was the scene of tilting, archery and midsummer bonfires in Tudor days. Later, it became the setting for riotous May Day and October fairs (described by Charles Dickens in *Sketches by Boz)* until they were banned in 1857. Broad, grassy steps are cut into the slope − there seem to have been a dozen originally and they may well have been terracing, part of Le Nôtre's scheme. Running up and down them was part of the fun for children at those fairs.

Return across the grass and follow The Avenue up the steep hill ahead toward the dome of the Old Observatory which rises above the treetops. Halfway up, you may glimpse through the foliage a bronze by the sculptor Henry Moore (1898–1986) on the brow of the rise to your right. When you reach the top, walk over to the statue of General James Wolfe (1727–1759), which commands the highest point of the Park, 50 metres (165 feet) above sea level. It was donated by the Canadian government in 1930 and commemorates his 1759 victory against the French at the Heights of Abraham in Quebec, which won Canada for the British. Wolfe lived in Macartney House *(see* page 89). Parts of the statue's pedestal remain holed and chipped by shrapnel from World War II – there were anti-aircraft gun emplacements in the Flower Garden *(see* page 88). The statue faces a superb view north, across the river to the City and East London, and a panorama board identifies what you can see, including the ever-visible Canary Wharf Tower, the dome of Wren's St Paul's Cathedral, and Tower Bridge.

The Royal Observatory

From the Wolfe statue cross to the complex of linked buildings surrounding a courtyard which lie just to the west (left). Charles II encouraged science, and in Greenwich Park, because of its position clear of the 'Great Smoake' of London, he set up his Royal Observatory in Flamsteed House. A fortified tower called Greenwich Castle had long stood on the site, acting at various times in Tudor days as a prison, a wine store, and a lodge. Henry VIII penned some doggerel there: *Within this towre/There lieth a flowre/That hath my hart ...* Flamsteed House was built in place of the tower, in 1675, by Wren 'for the Observator's habitation and a little for pompe'. The red-brick building is charming but not all it seems: what look like stone dressings are, in fact, wood.

John Flamsteed (1646–1719), the first Observator, or Astronomer Royal, was convinced that astronomy and the mapping of the stars would enable longitude to be determined, and hence make proper navigation possible (in the days before radar). Armed with a sextant, two clocks, a 16-metre (52-foot) telescope, and a quadrant, he went to work. The calculation of longitude requires a base line to represent zero, and through the iron gates that close off the courtyard can be seen the Greenwich Meridian: a metal strip set into cobbles and continuing up the wall of the Meridian building adjoining it to the left. This is the Prime Meridian of the World.

To the right of the courtyard gate, a Shepherd 24-hour clock – one of the first electric clocks – keeps Greenwich Mean Time, based on the zero meridian. Set into the wall there are also yardsticks, the official compensated metal measures of 1 yard and 1 foot, and an Ordnance Survey benchmark. This is the height above mean sea level at Newlyn in Cornwall (of all places).

You can go into the courtyard to see these historic measuring devices, but only via the Meridian Building, where you must buy a ticket (it is good value, because it enables you to be photographed astride the Meridian – with one foot in the east and one in the west) and to explore Flamsteed House, part of it decorated and furnished much as it was three centuries ago. The Octagon Room by Wren is a rare unspoilt interior. Atop the eastern turret is a red time ball on a pole (erected in 1833) which is raised half way at 12:55 and to the top at 12:58, to drop at 1 p.m. (13:00 hours) precisely. It once enabled departing ships to set their clocks accurately for their long voyages across the oceans of the world. In the courtyard there is also a camera obscura, a device for viewing the scenery in miniature from within a dark room, a precursor of the camera. From the courtyard you can also visit the elegant Altazimuth pavilion, built in brick with handsome carriage-style lamps at the corners, which houses a refracting telescope, and the Planetarium, both to the south.

The Formal Avenues

From the Planetarium, cross Blackheath Avenue to the east (right) and walk toward the Tea House. It is a typical 1930s building, white-walled with blue woodwork, a restored dovecot on top, and a pleasant lawned garden for fine weather. As the map shows, it is almost at the hub of the park's original formal avenues. By some accounts these reflect Le Nôtre's hand – and by rights they should have converged on Queen's House (as Lover's Walk does), but there is little sign of this. The truth is that Le Nôtre did his designs by letter; he may never have seen the park and was never told that the ground dropped away. His Grand Avenue (the Blackheath Avenue), for example, ends at the Wolfe Statue alongside Flamsteed House.

Make a diversion past the Tea House into Great Cross Avenue. Although the elms that were planted in the park succumbed to old age and the Dutch elm disease epidemic of the 1960s, many of the original sweet chestnut trees planted in these avenues in the 1660s still survive, and a few can be seen along this avenue. Their massive trunks often have curiously netted bark with a spiral twist.

The Queen's Oak

Some of these ancient chestnuts are also to be seen on the way to the Queen's Oak. Return to the Tea House and follow the path beyond it that leads east (to the right). Eventually you come to a huge, dead tree, surrounded by railings. With its iron grey wood and prostrate form it looks a real dinosaur, and in tree terms it is primeval; it is thought to have grown from an acorn in the 12th century. Elizabeth I often picnicked near it, it is said, and Henry VIII danced around it with Anne Boleyn. It was hollow, nearly 6 feet (1.8 metres) across inside, and in its time had been used as a lockup for offenders against park rules (apparently a doorway and windows were cut in it), but it last bore leaves over a century ago and it tottered over in a storm in the early 1990s. A replacement sapling has been planted alongside.

Vanbrugh Castle

Take the switchback path running northeast toward Maze Hill Gate, passing on the left a stone drinking fountain and the steep Lover's Walk, planted with planes and other trees. From the open ground approaching the Park wall there is a marvellous view of the watery reach of the Thames. The brick wall was probably built in the 1620s, although the simple ironwork of Maze Hill Gate probably dates to 1699. Leave the park through the gate to view the Vanbrugh Castle. Sir John Vanbrugh

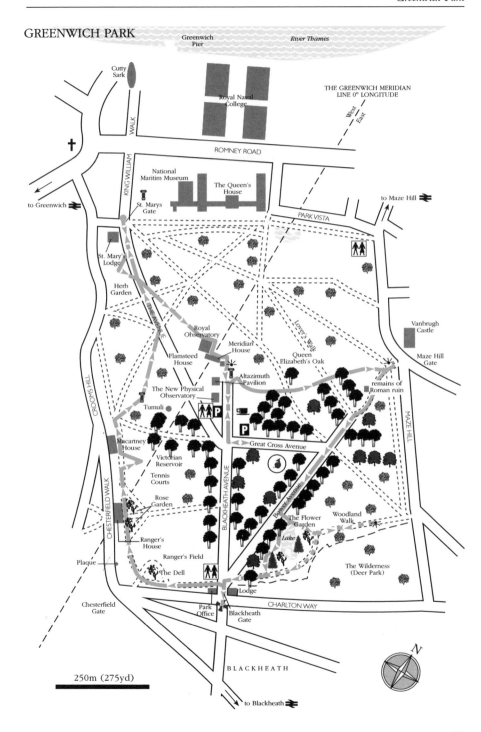

GREENWICH PARK

250m (275yd)

(1664–1726) built it for his own use, finishing it in the 1720s. He had an eccentric career as a soldier (he was imprisoned in the Paris Bastille for a time), a playwright, and finally as an architect. Although he was untrained, he became a foremost architect of his age. In 1716 he succeeded Wren as Surveyor of Greenwich Hospital. This house was quite unlike anything else he designed. It was an early folly, a brick building with turrets and battlements in places, possibly modelled on the Bastille in Paris. Vanbrugh has the quaint (but perhaps just) epitaph in St Stephen's Church, Walbrook: *Lie heavy on him, Earth! for he/Laid many heavy loads on thee.*

Reenter the Park and take the path running south; to the right, inside metal rails, is a boss of tiled flooring, marking the site of a Roman temple. Coins were found when it was excavated in the 1800s.

The Flower Garden

Follow the southward path until you reach Bower Avenue. To the right, near Great Cross Avenue, is a bandstand erected in 1891. To the left you see a gate leading into the Flower Garden, which also dates from Victorian days. These large, triangular gardens are visually striking, with smooth turf planted with cedars and other ornamental conifers. There are one or two ancient chestnuts to be seen, and notable examples of exotic trees which became popular last century – the tulip tree *(Liriodendron tulipifera),* for example, the paper-bark birch *(Betula papyrifera),* with papery peeling bark; and the pride of India or bead tree, introduced in 1763, which carries dense clusters of orange berries that were once used for necklaces and rosaries. Some trees show truncated tops – they were lopped in World War II to give clear lines of fire for the anti-aircraft gun batteries in the park.

As well as banks of azaleas and a variety of magnolias, there are more than 30 flower beds in these gardens, notable for their spring displays of bulbs and later the dahlias. That there is imagination at work is evidenced by an autumn bed tight with mingled white, ochre and yellow chrysanthemums, for example. But every year, indeed every season, sees its own changes in planting.

It will be rewarding to take detours along the paths through the beds and curving round the sunken lake. Duck nest around the lake, offering visitors the odd experience of being chased by pochard. There are identification boards to the birds on the railings. Alternatively, wander along the diversion to the Deer Enclosure, marked on the map. It lies hidden in the Wilderness, originally planted in the 1660s, just prior to the chestnut avenues, by Sir William Boreman, keeper of the Park at the time. The open deer lawn is hidden by a belt of shrubbery; the best viewpoint is down the path nearest Vanbrugh Gate. The herd is about 30 strong mixed red and fallow deer.

Blackheath Gate

From the Flower Garden or the Deer Enclosure make your way southwest to the Blackheath Gate, passing, to the left, a fine ancient chestnut with a girth of about 34 feet (10.5 metres) growing on the edge of the flower gardens. Through Blackheath Gate can be seen the open expanse of Blackheath; it was an assembly point for those marching on London: invading Danes; Wat Tyler and Jack Straw

Plate 7: *You cannot enter the Sunken Garden in Kensington Gardens (see page 51), but you can look into it through squints cut into the surrounding wall of lime trees.*

Plate 8: *Hyde Park (see page 56) offers glorious long walks in the fresh air, vistas along wide avenues of trees, and some interesting horticulture to see.*

Plate 9: *The palatial façade of Cumberland Terrace rising above the trees of The Regent's Park (see page 68), counts as one of Europe's most elegant townscapes.*

Plate 10: *The hidden garden of St. John's Lodge in Regent's Park (see page 68) is one of the most enjoyable public corners in London, at its most romantic in high summer.*

Plate 11: *The Sham Chinese bridge beside the lake at Kenwood (see page 74) is a typical 18th-century conceit added by the first Earl of Mansfield, who landscaped the grounds.*

Plate 12: *Beautiful cedars, ornamental conifers and colourful bedding plants in The Flower Garden (see page 88) in Greenwich Park, create an attractive area for a walk.*

Plate 13: *Charles II encouraged science, and in the 1670s set up the Royal Observatory on Greenwich Hill, well away from the 'great smoake' of London (see page 85).*

with their throng of 100,000 peasants in revolt. This was where Henry V was greeted on his return from the Battle of Agincourt in France, and John Wesley, the founder of Methodism, preached at this gate in the 1800s. In recent years it has disgorged runners at the start of London Marathon, held in April.

Turn round again to face into the Park. Blackheath Avenue, ahead of you, is lined by young horse chestnut trees replacing the original 1700s planting. Walk along it past the Park Office and turn left along the path in front of the toilets. The Ranger's Field to the right is dedicated to cricket, hockey or rugby by the season. Follow the path to Chesterfield Gate in the southwest corner past The Dell, an enclosed and sunken rhododendron and azalea garden, noted for its nesting birds and its spring colour. An enormously tall beech tree looms to one side.

The Ranger's House

Turn northward (right) and walk toward The Ranger's House. Look left when you are about half way there. A plaque on the park wall records that below the paving lies a sunken cold bath, all that remains of Montague House, once the home of Caroline, Queen to George IV while she was Princess of Wales. The house was demolished in 1815, the bath was discovered in 1890, but in 1983 it was filled in.

The Ranger's House overlooks a large rose garden, resplendent with delicate scent and colour all through the summer. Pass through the gate in the railing surrounding it and follow the path past the house front. The Ranger's House was built in red brick, mainly in the 18th century. The Park Ranger was often one of the Royal family, the title and the house being a kind of perk. The house has been restored and it is now a museum open to the public, with a collection of portraits of the 17th and 18th centuries, and musical instruments.

Leave the rose garden by the gate on the far side and follow the path ahead. To the right, across the grass you see a giant, grassed mound skirted by bushes and trees. This is the Victorian Reservoir, built to feed water via conduits to drinking fountains and elsewhere. There is a subterranean network of these conduits, some quite wide and paved, but closed to the public.

Almost opposite the reservoir, to the left of the path, is the elegant Macartney House, the home of James Wolfe during the years 1727–69, from where he departed for Quebec in 1759. Just beyond it, at Croomshill Gate, take a detour eastward along the path that leads to a cluster of tumuli or burial mounds, low humps in turf. Some were dug in 1784 and glass beads, wool and hair were found. They may be Danish, for a Danish army camped on Blackheath in 1011. Northwest of these, right on the brow of the ridge, is *Standing Figure – Knife Edge,* a dramatic bronze sculpture by Henry Moore. Continue walking down the slope back to St Mary's Gate, where the walk ends.

Crystal Palace Park

Location	About 6 miles (9.5 kilometres) south southeast of Charing Cross.
Transport	South side: Crystal Palace Station, buses 2, 3, 63, 78, 122, 137, 154, 157, 202, 249, 358. East side: Penge West Station (overground trains from London Bridge) is 5 minutes' walk away; buses 176, 227, 351. West side: Gypsy Hill Station (overground trains from London Bridge and Clapham Junction) is 10 minutes' walk away. There is a free car park.
Admission	Open daily 07:00 hours-dusk. Admission is free.
Seasonal features	Flower beds at Boundaries Gate in spring and summer; autumn tree colour.
Events	Guided tours in summer; sporting events at the National Sports Centre; open air concerts at the Concert Bowl.
Refreshments	Crystal Park cafés open daily approximately 09:30–17.30 hours.

Crystal Palace Park is magnificently sited on the southern slopes of Sydenham Heights, with views south toward the county of Kent. It was until 1960 an open space of 106 acres (43 hectares), but part is now occupied by the buildings and pitches of the National Sports Centre. The Crystal Palace, which gives the Park its name, was the gigantic glass and ironwork exhibition hall designed by Sir Joseph Paxton (1801–65) for Queen Victoria's Great Exhibition of 1851, and built in Hyde Park *(see* page 62) in the centre of London. Paxton was one of the great Victorian engineers – a gardener, architect, Member of Parliament, editor and railway magnate, who had ambitious ideas. As garden superintendent to the Duke of Devonshire at Chatsworth House in Derbyshire he had developed an enthusiasm for iron and glass architecture and an interest in the design and mechanics of water gardens; and he had been involved in the creation of the first Victorian city park at Birkenhead, and these interests culminated in the design of The Crystal Palace.

After the Great Exhibition was over, the Crystal Palace was dismantled and reerected at the brow of Sydenham Heights. It was an ideal site, in the centre of the spreading Victorian suburbs of south London, and from its promontory the gigantic domed glass building could be seen for miles around. Below it, magnificent terraces to match any found in Europe were constructed under the direction of Joseph Paxton, and the park was ornamented with features such as statues, enormous, vividly coloured flower beds, magnificent fountains, and a wooded lake.

The Crystal Palace opened again on its new site in 1854 as a kind of museum and celebration centre, a Palace of the People, handily placed 'near a population weary of labour yet thirsting for knowledge', as the persuasive Victorian writer, John Ruskin (1819–1900) fervently hoped. People certainly thirsted for the spectacles, for each year, two million people came to watch the fireworks and archery contests or cricket, to shoot at the rifle range, listen to the music festivals, or take a trip in a hot air balloon (filled with gas from the gas works at Sydenham) at a cost of £5 per trip. During World War I, the park around the Palace was used as a naval barracks – the ship's bell remains. But after the resumption of peace, it became used for recreation once again. In 1920 the Imperial War Museum opened in the Palace.

All came to an end, however, on November 30th, 1936 when a fire started inside the Crystal Palace, and flames 300 feet (92 metres) high engulfed the magnificent glass structure. The site was cleared, but, bereft of finances, the upkeep of the park could not continue. During World War II, rubble from blitzed houses was dumped in it. The grounds were more or less left to decay until 1960, when the construction of the new National and Youth Sports Centre began in the park, giving it a new lease of life. It was opened in 1964, covering an area of 36 acres (14.5 hectares), with a stadium and swimming and diving pools. Since then, some features of the Victorian park have been restored to make a magnificent and in many ways a unique visit. For the future, Bromley Council plan to continue their careful restoration of the park and to redevelop the Palace site, perhaps with facilities such as cinemas and restaurants.

THE CRYSTAL PALACE WALK

Start and finish Boundaries Gate. *Time* Allow 1¼ hours.

Enter the park through Boundaries Gate. Facing you is a small, somewhat formal garden displaying the brightly coloured bedding typical of municipal parks, with geraniums and calceolarias as part of the seasonal planting programme. Bedding of this kind was popular in Victorian times, when the park was noted for its summer flower displays. The statue of a nymph at the end was rescued from the Crystal Palace fire of 1936. Past her extends the site of the Crystal Palace, used only by travelling fairs from time to time – until recently, perhaps. Just as this book went to press, discussions were being held on the idea of building a new Crystal Palace on the site as part of the millennium celebrations.

Take the short flight of steps down to the right, to a small terrace with a handsome, red-painted, cast-iron signpost. To the right is a round brick structure which was once the base of a water tower, one of two towers, 284 feet (85 metres) high, built by the Victorian engineer Isambard Kingdom Brunel (1806–59). The other was at the opposite end of the Crystal Palace site near the modern BBC transmitter. Each tower carried about 1,500 tons of water, pumped from an artesian well in the bedrock beneath the park, which was forced by gravity to power the water for the fountains in the Victorian park. In its heyday there were 11,788 active spouts. There were two enormous jets at the foot of the slope in the area occupied by the Sports Centre, which reached 250 feet (76 metres). The air was 'filled with a roar-

CRYSTAL PALACE PARK

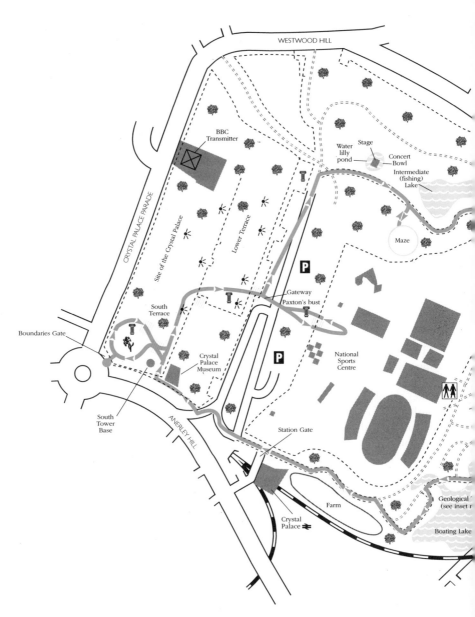

ing sound and as cool as a grotto', the spray dyed with rainbows. At the end of each day, the Park's turncocks had to walk round turning off the spouts individually. To the south of the tower is a small museum of the Crystal Palace.

Follow the route marked 'Terraces' on the red signpost and you arrive at the

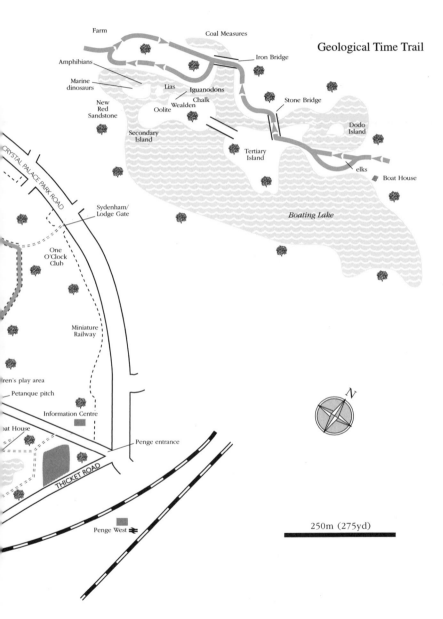

Geological Time Trail

Farm
Coal Measures
Iron Bridge
Amphibians
Marine dinosaurs
Lias
Iguanodons
Stone Bridge
New Red Sandstone
Oolite
Wealden
Chalk
Dodo Island
Secondary Island
Tertiary Island
elks
Boat House
CRYSTAL PALACE PARK ROAD
Sydenham/ Lodge Gate
Boating Lake
One O'Clock Club
Miniature Railway
ren's play area
Petanque pitch
Information Centre
oat House
Penge entrance
THICKET ROAD
N
Penge West
250m (275yd)

upper grand terrace, which once spread below the Crystal Palace. There are some giant sphinxes at this end, copies of an ancient Egyptian sphinx in the Louvre Museum in Paris, which once adorned the Victorian gardens but are now somewhat dilapidated. This terrace gives a marvellous view south toward Kent, and you realize the enormous scale of the landscaping. It was originally planted with berberis and ornamented with statuary and urns. On the plinths along the balustrade were statues wearing national dress, representing the countries of the British Empire. Only one survives intact and parts of one or two others remain, with rusting iron rods protruding. And there are piles of broken sculptured stone, all overgrown. These terraces were once the scene of spectacular firework displays, but if you like ruins, this terrace makes a rather atmospheric walk.

The Italian Gardens
Walk about halfway along the upper terrace and take the steps down to the vast lower terrace. This was once occupied by the Italian Gardens. In Victorian times, 'Italian' was a blanket description, implying some formality, with intricate flower beds set with ornamental tazzas (shallow ornamental bowls) and urns. The beds, with their massed, coloured bedding plants, beloved of the Victorians, were simple in design and rather crude, the choice of plants aimed more at stunning the crowds than at horticultural innovation. Nearly two-thirds of the plants were scarlet geraniums and yellow calceolaria, together with some verbenas and petunias. These beds and other details have all vanished, however, leaving a desert of gravel and skimpy grass with a scatter of stone pedestals with topknots – the feet of tazzas.

In 1854, *The Cottage Gardener* magazine complained that blue and white had been left out because, it was claimed, these were colours that would be supplied by the sky and the foaming water from the fountains. In the early 1900s a notable plant hunter, Kingdon Ward, wrote a spoof about plant-hunting in the Crystal Palace grounds. 'Suddenly I looked up and there, like a blue panel dropped from heaven – a stream of blue poppies dazzling as sapphires in the pale light...' was how he described his first sighting of the blue Mecanopsis poppy from southern Tibet in 1926. In his view, the Crystal Palace did not match up to that. However, in 1875, six carpet or tapestry beds were planted in the style then recently popularized by the Director of Battersea Park (*see* page 128). The beds, in the shape of butterflies, were densely planted with dwarf foliage plants mimicking the insects' wing markings. Similar bedding can be seen today in Hyde Park (*see* page 60).

The National Sports Centre
Leave the Italian Gardens by the main grand steps on the opposite side of the lower terrace. Continue straight across the car park, down some small steps and past an area of seating, and beyond you see a massive bust of Joseph Paxton. When it was unveiled in 1873 he looked uphill toward his great glass creation towering over all. Continue past the bust and along the raised walk to view the Sports Centre. Its 36 acres (15 hectares) include a stadium, swimming and diving pools, artificial grass pitches for football and hockey, and games courts. It was laid out on the site of cascades and two grand fountains, 250 feet (76 metres) high.

The Concert Bowl
Retrace your route to the foot of the steps down from the lower terrace and turn right to follow the terrace wall. At the end is a statue of the Italian poet Dante

(1265–1321), rescued from the fire which destroyed the Palace. There is a small café stall a short way ahead, and the Concert Bowl to the right. This area of the Park is very attractive, with the stone terrace, Turkey oaks, planes and other trees, and open grass sweeping down to a water lily pool at the bottom of the bowl. The lie of land gives good acoustics. The yellow water lilies in the pool *(Nuphar lutea)* are native British flowers, although it is hard to find them growing wild these days. There are dragonflies to be seen in summer. Concerts take place on the staging at the far side of the pool.

The Maze
Leave the path that runs down past the Concert Bowl and walk to the right, over the grass to the Maze, which is signposted by a curve of tall Lombardy poplars *(Populus nigra* cv. 'Italica'). It is a replica of a maze that fell into disuse during World War II, and, at 160 feet (49 metres) in diameter it is one of the largest mazes to be found in Britain. Its hedges are hornbeam, which, like young beech trees, keep their dead leaves to give concealment in winter.

From the Maze, return to the Concert Bowl path and continue down it past the first intersection of paths (almost opposite the corner of the Sports Centre) and on to the next intersection, where you turn right and walk past the children's One o'Clock Club. Look out for a wooden structure, oriental in style, on the right. It contains a ship's bell, a relic of the time during World War I when Crystal Palace Park was a naval barracks, HMS *Crystal Palace*. The bell was originally on the barracks' quarterdeck – the lower terrace with the Italian Gardens.

Now walk straight on to cross the main avenue which once ran from the Penge entrance up to the terrace staircases and to the Palace on the top of the hill, but is now interrupted by the Sports Centre. At its foot, near the Penge Gate, there is a café and an Information Centre.

The Boating Lake
Follow the path across the main avenue and you pass on your right a pitch where the addictive French game of petanque (boules) is played every Sunday. The path curves to the left; take the second path on the right, which leads to the boating lake. This lake was originally a reservoir for the waterworks: when Paxton's system was in full flow, the level of the lake fell to feed the fountains – it was known as the Tidal Lake. Today, visitors explore it on pedalos.

Near the new boat house, you can see life-size models of a family of extinct Irish elks, a sign that you are approaching the extraordinary prehistoric park built by the Victorians. To the right is a small lake with an island, but continue along the path and over a stone bridge, and on the right you see models of extinct, tapir-like animals, early ancestors of elephants. Continue, and you cross a rustic iron bridge designed by Paxton.

In Victorian times this area, which was opened in 1854, was a walk-through, teach-yourself geology exhibition. It was a tribute to the Victorian love of education, for it was almost ahead of its time, scientific geology being a new area of study, understood only by specialists. Tons of stone were carted to the site from all over

Britain to produce replicas of geological formations. For example, from the bridge on which you now stand, you can see to the right a reconstructed cliff of coal seams, sandstone and other strata, or geological layers of around 300 million years ago, complete with faults, where the strata have fractured and slipped against each other.

Prehistoric Monsters

From Paxton's bridge, take the left-hand path along the lake shore. Close offshore are three interlinked islands made of real rocks from different geological periods. On the rocks are models of the animals that had been found as fossils within them. These life-size models of prehistoric animals were made by the sculptor Waterhouse Hawkins under the supervision of Professor Sir Richard Owen, Director of the Natural History Museum in London who, in 1841, coined the word 'dinosaur' from Greek words meaning 'terrible lizard'. The models are now preserved as Grade I listed structures.

As the path passes the first island, two massive iguanodons soon come into view. They are 30 feet (9 metres) long, made of iron columns, 600 bricks, 1,500 tiles, and broken stone. On New Year's Eve 1853, when the monsters were only half-finished, some members of the Royal Society sat down to dinner inside one, protected from the weather by a tent. The models show what Victorian paleontologists thought iguanodons looked like. Now, these prehistoric beasts are known to have been slimmer and to have stood on their hind legs like kangaroos; and their nose horn is known to have been a kind of thumbnail. Perched above them on an outcrop of 120-million-year-old sandstone are two pterodactyls, winged reptiles related to dinosaurs, and there is a fierce, meat-eating megalosaurus nearby.

Continue along the path past the next island, which takes you back in time to 200 million years ago, when bluish lias clay, found today in the coastal cliffs of West Dorset and Whitby in Yorkshire, was laid down. Marine dinosaurs wallow in the shallows at its foot. Some are like crocodiles, while others include the long-necked plesiosaurs and remarkably accurate models of ichthyosaurs or fish lizards, with a long snout full of teeth, and lacking only their back fin.

The path rounds a third island, composed of New Red sandstone 230 million years old, where early, toadlike amphibians and creatures that look rather like turtles wade. The fossils of these creatures were, in fact, wrongly interpreted by Professor Owen. Paleontologists now know that those he thought were prehistoric ancestors of toads were, in fact, more like giant newts; and the fossils that looked like turtles did not have shells, but were rather similar to large dogs.

Work to restore the 1854 landscape has included removing dwarf conifers and other inappropriate planting, and revealing and restoring the original rock strata.

The Zoo

The path now forks; take the right-hand path and explore the Children's Zoo – which is really an urban farm, with goats and sheep, plus deer, monkeys, and a flamingo pool. Follow the path left to Station Gate, and leave the park. Turn right out of the gate and walk up to Boundary Gate, where the walk ends.

Victoria Embankment Gardens

Location	About a quarter of a mile (400 metres) either side of Charing Cross Station.
Transport	Charing Cross Station (overground rail terminus). Embankment Underground Station (Bakerloo, District and Circle Lines). Bus 176. There is parking in the South Bank complex on the opposite side of the river.
Admission	Open daily 07:30 hours to dusk.
Seasonal features	Spring and summer bedding; autumn tree colour.
Events	Occasional recitals of music, poetry and dance
Refreshments	Café open daily 07:30-19:00 hours.

Victoria Embankment Gardens spread along the north bank of the River Thames from Westminster Bridge. This narrow strip of land is beautifully landscaped with curving borders planted with shrubs and fine trees and close-clipped, verdant lawns pierced by formal flower beds, and ornamented with pools, fountains, and statuary. The gardens provide a contemplative atmosphere, colour, visual interest, and a respite from the noisy road outside. They were laid out in 1870, as the finishing touch after the completion of The Victoria, Albert, and Chelsea Embankments along 3½ miles (5.6 kilometres) of the Thames. In fact, as long ago as 1666, after the Great Fire of London, Christopher Wren first suggested narrowing the River Thames and so gaining extra space for the new city he was proposing. But his plan fell by the wayside, partly because the required engineering skills were not available in his day.

The Victoria Embankment is a magnificent feat, and most of its engineering skill lies hidden – indeed, a major reason for its construction was the building of a sewer. The work was controlled by Joseph Bazalgette, and started in 1864 in the face of opposition from wharfingers (wharf owners) and other interests, taking over six years to complete. It is 1½ miles (2.4 kilometres) long and 37 acres (15 hectares) in area, with a variable width. The tidal mud flats were drained and a wall built against flooding, speeding the flow of the water, which partly explains why the Thames no longer ices over in winter. The area behind the wall was filled in to carry a road, which was then lined with plane trees. Then the Embankment Gardens were laid over 20 acres (8 hectares). They were designed by one Alexander Mackenzie 'to avoid the need for expensive gardening'. Presumably that meant not much in the way of flower beds, for they were criticized by the architectural press of the time for being too rural. But they do have striking flower beds today.

The gardens are crowded with statues and memorials to a mixed bunch of people, ranging from dignitaries of the London County Council to military high-ups and figures from the literary and musical worlds. There are memorials outside the gardens, as well as in – among several facing the river is one commemorating Samuel Plimsoll who died in 1881 and is famed not for the sports shoe (that name was first coined in 1927) but for the safety-loading line and associated shipping law.

These gardens fall into four main sections, each of which has a different character and atmosphere. At the entrance gates, a Westminster City Council notice board outlines the history of the building of the Embankment and of that part of the gardens. With a few exceptions, however, the trees, shrubs and flowers are not labelled, and since the gardens contain some exceptionally fine trees and the borders are planted with unusual foliage and flowering plants, it will make the walk more rewarding to take one of the pocket tree recognition guides listed on page 173.

The walk concentrates on the gardens west of Waterloo Bridge, but an interesting diversion can be made to the east of it. Temple Place Gardens are lushly planted with trees, flowers and shrubs, and they shelter a statue of the philosopher, John Stuart Mill (1806–1873). Beside them you can see the magnificent spread of Inner Temple Gardens, the private property of Inner and Middle Temple, two of the Inns of Court having the exclusive right to license English barristers. The public are not, strictly speaking, permitted to enter the Inner Temple Garden, which is open only to members and their guests. You can see into it, however, from the Embankment pavement. This Inner Temple garden, the 'Great Garden' as it is also called, has an important collection of trees, which are you can see from the Embankment. And on working days between 09:00 and 17:00 hours you can walk into the Temple through the Embankment gate and wander through some of the delightful courts and fountains of this legal enclave. Middle Temple Gardens are open to the public at lunch-times from 12:00 to 15:00 hours.

The Temple Gardens are the oldest in London. They originally stretched from the Knights Templars' compound to the river (and were regularly flooded by it until the Embankment was raised). There was once a water gate at the riverside. They played an important part in garden history. Interest in individual flowers grew through the centuries, until the art of bringing flowers to a perfect state of bloom, often by artificial means, was perfected. It was a passion of the Calvinist Huguenot refugees in the 17th century; the Paisley weavers specialized in pinks, others in auriculas. In 1827 the first horticultural fête was held in these gardens and in 1912, the fêtes were moved to Chelsea and were called the Chelsea Flower Show.

THE VICTORIA EMBANKMENT GARDENS WALK
Start Embankment Underground Station. **Finish** Westminster Underground Station. **Time** Allow half an hour.

Take the south exit from Embankment Underground station and cross the Victoria Embankment road to the riverside alongside Hungerford Bridge. Just to the right from the bridge is a memorial erected in 1899 to Joseph Bazalgette, Chief Engineer in charge of building the Embankment. Turn back beneath the bridge and walk toward Waterloo Bridge, passing a memorial to the 19th-century librettist, W.S. Gilbert, who collaborated with the composer, Arthur Sullivan on the Savoy operettas.

The Riverside

The serried lines of stately London plane trees, planted in the 1860s by the Victorians and stoically resistant to pollution from the heavy traffic, are one of the most striking features of the Embankment. However, it is also well provided with intriguing Victorian street furniture, such as Timothy Butler's lamps along the balustrade, with two dolphins entwined around each other, head down, at the base. The benches on this river side of the road have wrought iron armrests in the form of an Egyptian figure. They are a sign that you are approaching Cleopatra's Needle. This 86–foot (26–metre) high ancient Egyptian obelisk was presented to the U.K. by the Viceroy of Egypt in 1819. It is dated to 1450 BC, and most of the inscription on its sides commemorates Pharaoh Rameses the Great, so it is unconnected with Cleopatra, who ruled at a much later date – the name comes from the barge that ferried the memorial to the U.K. It is flanked by two sphinxes, which, by rights, should face outward.

The eye is inevitably drawn to the view across the Thames to the South Bank entertainment complex, begun for the Festival of Britain in the early 1950s. Along the riverside you pass Charing Cross Pier, from where boats take visitors on trips up and down the Thames; and three interesting ships: the *Tattershall Castle,* a paddle steamer, now a floating pub and music venue; the *Hispaniola,* now a floating restaurant; and the *Queen Mary,* which, as this book went to press, was being refurbished and converted into another restaurant ship.

Continue ahead toward Waterloo Bridge. Its elegant concrete curves are little over half a century old, completed by Giles Gilbert Scott in 1945, but it replaced a span bridge designed by the Scottish civil engineer, John Rennie, and built 1811–17, soon after the end of the Napoleonic wars. Cross to the north side of the Embankment at the crossing a few yards short of the bridge, which takes you to the entrance to the gardens.

The Gardens

From the gate, the path winds left between borders planted with shrubs and trees, to reveal an exciting vista of vivid green lawns bordered by beds full of interesting colour and texture, interspersed with statues of a dark, almost blackened bronze, standing on pedestals of pure white stone. The trees along the approach to this garden are planes and a few exotics. In spring, look out for a pretty Judas tree *(Cercis siliquastrum)*, with brilliant pink blossoms in spring, on the left, planted at the point where the gardens widen.

Follow the path as it meanders through the gardens, bordered by strips of emerald green lawn and curvaceous borders. Those to the to your right rise slightly and are planted with shrubs and small trees. By contrast, those on the south side contain modern planting schemes, composed of hostas and other foliage plants with decorative leaves, clumps of festuca and other low-growing grasses interspersed with tall fritillaries, and backed by clematis and other climbers.

You soon come across a bust to the left, erected in 1903, of the composer of hymns such as *Onward Christian Soldiers* (1873) and many popular light operas: Arthur Sullivan (1842–1900) by William Goscombe John. His plinth is accosted by a lamenting half-naked woman representing music (this was added at the sculptor's

VICTORIA EMBANKMENT GARDENS

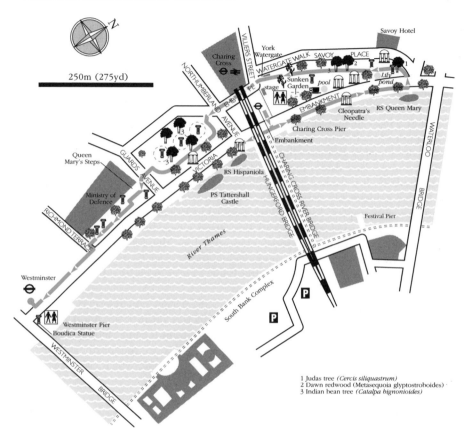

1 Judas tree *(Cercis siliquastrum)*
2 Dawn redwood *(Metasequoia glyptostroboides)*
3 Indian bean tree *(Catalpa bignonioides)*

own expense); while to one side are a music score, a mask of Pan, and a guitar – all in a heap. The monument to his librettist, W.S. Gilbert, is beside Hungerford Bridge, a short way upriver. The riverside entrance to the Savoy Hotel is almost opposite this memorial, to the right. In a small, hedged garden enclosure beside it, a hooped armillary sundial rests on a metal casque commemorating Gilbert and Sullivan's Savoy operas, written mainly between 1871 and 1890. They were staged in the Savoy Theatre by the D'Oyly Carte company (Richard D'Oyly Carte of the Savoy Hotel was the impresario).

There is no escaping the noise of the traffic along the Embankment outside these gardens, yet they have a serenity, and they are full of pleasant surprises. For example, further along on the left is a lily pond with a little fountain, its surrounding beds planted with dwarf azaleas for spring colour, followed by bedding plants. It was installed in 1915 and is planted with handsome emergent marginal plants, such as flags. With its air of intimate seclusion, this is perhaps the finest garden pond in London. Benches are ranged along the gardens on which to sit and admire such gems.

A short distance on, the path is crossed by another leading to gates on either side of the gardens. Guarding the right-hand gate is a statue dated 1880 by Sir Thomas Brock of Robert Raikes. A century before, Raikes had founded the first church Sunday Schools. As if to commend the sanctity of this action, a spotlight illuminates this statue after dark.

The central point of the gardens is marked by two commemorative trees. One is a rather leafy conifer, a dawn redwood *(Metasequoia glyptostroboides)*, called a fossil tree because until its discovery in China in 1941 it was only known from fossils. It was planted in 1971 as first prize in the Britain in Bloom competition. Beside it is an Indian bean tree *(Catalpa bignonioides)*, planted to commemorate the coronation of Queen Elizabeth I in 1953. The sculpted beds beyond these trees are bright, in spring, with vivid blue irises. Almost opposite these trees, on the garden wall, is a medallion to the memory of Henry Fawcett (1838–1884), a blind Cambridge professor and Postmaster General under Gladstone, who was also an advocate of votes for women. From 'his grateful countrywomen' the inscription reads. It is flanked by banks of bedding plants, such as wallflowers, and the walls are planted with shrubs and climbers, including some magnificent roses.

A formal pool is the next feature on the southern side of the gardens. Waterlilies float on its surface and flags decorate its margins. It is surrounded by hostas, planted in spreading groups, and ferns grow to one side. Behind it is a memorial by Edwin Lutyens (who designed the Cenotaph in Whitehall, nearby) to a military man, Major General Cheylesmore, who was chairman of the London County Council 1912–13. Opposite is a 1909 bronze statue of Sir Wilfrid Lawson, an advocate of temperance in Victorian times.

Toward the Hungerford Bridge end of this garden is a terrace, occupied by tables from the streetside café in summer. It overlooks a small, sunken garden with an interesting – if rather thin – piece of topiary of an early aeroplane. Opposite is one of the more impressive of the garden's memorials, a massive bronze statue to the Scottish poet, Robert Burns (1759-96) on a granite plinth. It is by Sir John Steel, a Scottish sculptor of note, and was unveiled in 1844. Burns died in 1796, having written *Auld Lang Syne*, among other familiar poems and ballads, but there is often an aged wreath lying in front of this memorial, dating from the last Burns' Night.

The Water Gate
A small Australian war memorial marks the point where the paths divide and the gardens open out, edged on the river side with a wide border magnificently planted with bedding plants and even banana palms *(Musa spp.)* in summer. On the west side, beneath steps that ascend to a gate at street level, is the York Water gate. This was built in 1626 by master mason Nicholas Stone, but some believe that it was designed by Inigo Jones, or his assistant, Balthasar Gerbier. It marks the line of the old river bank – when it was built it stood at the edge of the Thames. In those days, travel by boat rowed by watermen was the usual way of journeying between the City of London and Westminster, Chelsea and other such places, and this water gate was the landing stage for York House, one of the mansions that used to line the Strand behind. This house was owned by George Villiers (1592–1628), the handsome

first Duke of Buckingham, a favourite of Charles I. The mansion site was sold off for building plots in 1672, but the gate remained. It is decorated with lions, and the family coat of arms is on the landward side. The motto in Latin translates as 'The Cross is the Touchstone of Faith'.

Opposite the watergate, surrounded by a hedge and topiary in tubs, is a small stage for dance, poetry readings, and music during summer lunchtimes and evenings, with seats for spectators. Leave these gardens by the gate to the right of this enclosure.

The Embankment Gardens Extensions

Hungerford Bridge dates from 1863, but now carries trains to and from Terry Farrell's 1990 soaring Charing Cross Station. Cross beneath, by Embankment Place, to reach Northumberland Avenue, and go through the wrought iron gate into the central extension of the Embankment Gardens.

This part of the gardens is very different in style, wider and more open, with more formal plantings and large areas of grass pierced by flower beds. From the gate, follow the path that encircles the river side of the garden. The centrepiece of the first circular lawn is a statue of General Sir James Outram (1808–63). As you move on to the next circular lawn, pause to admire two particularly fine Indian bean trees *(Catalpa bignonioides)*. A second bean tree graces the next lawn, and opposite it, on the right, is a young silver birch, the millionth tree planted after the great storm of 1987. Make your way past the statue of William Tyndale, who completed the first translation of the Bible into English in 1525, through the gate and across Horse Guards Avenue to the western extension of the gardens.

This third part of the gardens has no surrounding wall or hedge and so is completely open to the traffic on the river side; on the north side, the white face of the Ministry of Defence forms a backdrop. The style is entirely different from the gardens you have just visited: ahead of you spreads a smooth lawn from which rise handsome plane trees – no beds, borders, shrubs or flowers, but with two or three statues on plinths. The first, on the northern side, is of General Gordon, who was killed in the siege of Khartoum in Egypt in 1885.

Beyond this statue to the right, an ancient terrace shows the line of the old river bank. It is flanked by curving steps, onto which Tudor royalty once stepped from the Royal Barge. This terrace was designed in 1691 by Christopher Wren for Queen Mary, wife of William III. The wall behind it is the old river wall of the Whitehall Palace, built by the Tudor King, Henry VIII.

The statues in the central lawn are of two 20th-century lords: Trenchard and Portal of the RAF. At the upstream end of these gardens is a memorial consisting of an oriental mythological beast on top of a plinth. The beast is a fabled lion called a *chinthe* in Burmese, the symbol of the Chindits, who fought behind Japanese lines in Burma in World War II. You might very well see someone standing here in memory; it is still relatively recent history.

The Chindit monument faces the Whitehall Police headquarters, with a quaint Victorian POLICE blue lamp standard in front. Past that is Westminster Bridge, adorned with a statue of Boudicca (Boadicea) and her daughters, and, on the right, Westminster Underground Station, where the walk ends.

Victoria Tower Gardens and the Tradescant Garden

Location	About two-thirds of a mile (1.1 kilometres) south of Charing Cross. Victoria Tower Gardens lie alongside Millbank next to the House of Lords. The Tradescant Garden is in the Museum of Garden History on the opposite bank of the river.
Transport	Westminster Underground Station (District and Circle lines) is 5 minutes' walk from Victoria Tower Gardens. Lambeth North Underground Station (Bakerloo Line), and Vauxhall Station (Underground trains on the Victoria Line and overground trains from Waterloo) are 10 minutes' walk from The Museum of Garden History. Bus 77a passes Victoria Tower Gardens; 3, 77, 159, 344, 507, C10 stop south of Lambeth Bridge. There is a 24-hour underground car park off Great College Street, opposite Victoria Tower Garden
Admission	The Victoria Tower Gardens open daily 09:30 hours–dusk. The Museum of Garden History opens Mar–Dec, Mon–Fri 10:30–16:00 hours; Sun 10:30–17:00 hours. Admission to both is free.
Seasonal Features	Spring bulbs and crown fritillaries, and summer colour in The Tradescant Garden.
Events	Exhibitions, lectures and courses in The Museum of Garden History.
Refreshments	Café in the Museum of Garden History, open when the Museum is open.

Victoria Tower Gardens spread along the Thames Embankment, from Victoria Tower on the south side of the Houses of Parliament to Lambeth Bridge. These riverside gardens have little in the way of colourful flower beds, but they offer pleasant views across the river, a shady haven from stuffy offices on hot days, and benches for visitors to London wanting somewhere to rest after seeing the sights.

These gardens have an apparent link with Embankment Gardens *(see* page 97), but they are older, having been laid out shortly after the rebuilding of the Houses of Parliament after the fire of 1834. Parliament's Victoria Tower does, indeed, tower over these gardens.

This walk is unusual in that it crosses the River Thames, spanning two boroughs to visit the small Church of St. Mary-at-Lambeth, beside Lambeth Palace. This church, rebuilt several times since its foundation, looks much younger than its pre-Domesday Survey birth date. In the churchyard are buried John Tradescant (1570–1638), gardener to Charles I, and his plant-collector son (1608–1662), and in the church, now deconsecrated, is the Museum of Garden History. In 1979 the present building was saved from demolition by the Tradescant Trust.

The gardens of Lambeth Palace, the official residence of the Archbishop of Canterbury, spread eastward from Lambeth Palace, whose entrance is beside St. Mary's. They are occasionally open to the public *(see* page 172), so a walk of even greater interest might be devised by combining this short walk with an official tour of the Palace grounds. When, as is usual, they are not open, an alternative is to extend the walk with an enjoyable stroll around the pretty Archbishop's Park, whose entrance is on Lambeth Road, on the south side of the Museum of Garden History. This little park was part of the Lambeth Palace gardens until late in the 19th century, when the archbishops presented it to the Borough Council for the use of the people of Lambeth, especially children, who had traditionally been allowed to play in their gardens.

THE VICTORIA TOWER GARDENS WALK

Start Victoria Tower gate. **Finish** Westminster Bridge.
Time Allow 1 hour.

The walk begins at the gateway in the northwest of the gardens, beside the Victoria Tower, but if you approach the gardens from Parliament Square, Abingdon Street or the underground car park, look out for an interesting sculpture in College Gardens, directly opposite the gateway into Victoria Tower Gardens: *Two Knife Edge Bronze* by Henry Moore (1898–1986).

Ahead of you as you enter the gardens is a memorial to Emmeline Pankhurst (1857– 1928), a leading member of the suffragette movement, who in 1918, after a long struggle, gained women aged over 30 the right to vote in general elections to the British Parliament. She fought for women's suffrage by forceful means, and after one skirmish in 1902 she became the last person to be held in the cell at the foot of Big Ben. The memorial, by A. Walker R.A., was erected in 1930. Beside it there is a plaque to her daughter, Dame Christabel Pankhurst (1880–1956), who was among the approximately 1,000 women who were imprisoned for the cause.

Turn right and follow the path leftward round the shrubbery to reach a replica of Rodin's heroic sculpture, *The Burghers of Calais*, of 1915. In 1347, after the English King Edward III, determined to subjugate Calais, had unsuccessfully besieged the city for eight months, six citizens of the town offered him their lives if he would spare their fellows. Edward's Flemish Queen, Philippa of Hainault, argued their cause and their lives were spared. The reason why this sculpture is here is not entirely clear, however.

From this memorial, turn right and right again, and walk along the riverside path. There are some handsome plane trees along the river, and shaded benches beneath them, with a view across the water to St. Thomas's Hospital and Lambeth Palace. The bench nearest the Rodin sculpture has a coin-operated telescope beside it.

Plate 14: *These Victorian life-size models of prehistoric animals were built beside the lake in Crystal Palace Park (see page 96) for the Great Exhibition of 1851.*

Plate 15: *The Victoria Embankment Gardens (see page 99) contain some exceptionally fine trees and the borders are planted with unusual foliage plants and flowers.*

Plate 16: *This memorial to the fight against slavery in Victoria Tower Gardens (see page 103) takes the form of a small edifice, a complete essay in the ornate neo-Gothic style.*

Plate 17: *The Knot Garden in the Tradescant Garden (see page 107).*

Plate 18: *The Constance Fund Fountain in Green Park (see page 114).*

Plate 19: *The quaint Duck Island Cottage in St. James's Park was built in 1837 by the Ornithological Society of London to house a birdkeeper (see page 118).*

Plate 20: *Battersea Park's Peace Pagoda, erected in 1985, a gift from Japanese Buddhist monks, is based on ancient Indian and Japanese temple architecture (see page 125).*

Plate 21: *Above the beds of apothecaries' plants in the 17th-century Chelsea Physic Garden (see page 129) rises this statue of Sir Hans Sloane in the centre of the garden.*

Toward the southern end of the lawn is the extraordinary Buxton Memorial by S. Teolon, first erected in 1865 in Parliament Square by Charles Buxton M.P., in memory of those, including his father, who had been active in the fight against slavery. It was moved to this spot in 1957. It takes the form of a small edifice, a complete essay in the ornate neo-Gothic style. It is round, with bunches of red granite pillars supporting intricately carved, gargoyle-like figures. Above them rises a bizarrely patterned and coloured conical cap. Parts of it are highlighted in rather faded yellow, as if gilt had been voted for, but the money ran out. Notice also the mosaic patterns set into the white stone. Within the shelter of the pillars, four lion or leopard heads once spouted water into stone basins.

Lambeth Bridge

From the gardens there is a fine view of Lambeth Bridge, built in 1932, with nice curves, handsomely painted red and grey, and set at intervals with ornamental street lights. It replaced a Victorian suspension bridge. Lambeth Pier juts out on the opposite bank. In the late 17th century, the diarist John Evelyn was able to walk across the ice from at this point to dine at Lambeth Palace. There seem to have been ice-age winters three or four centuries ago, and the freeze-up was aided when the giant bastions of old London Bridge impeded the river's flow. That was also before the Embankment had been reclaimed (*see* page 97). The narrowing of the river as a result of this engineering speeded the flow of the water.

At the Lambeth Bridge end of the gardens is a small children's playground, overlooked by two guardian rams carved in stone on top of the encircling wall. Beside it, steps lead up to an ornate gate, opening onto the bridge. Leave the gardens by this gate, and cross the bridge.

Opposite is Lambeth Palace, the official residence of the Archbishops of Canterbury. You can admire the brick Tudor gatehouse of the Palace, dated 1501. Alongside stands the Church of St. Mary-at-Lambeth. Most of this building dates from the 1850s, but the tower was built in the 14th century and the foundations reach back to 1032. The church and its small churchyard house the Museum of Garden History. Cross Lambeth Palace Road with care (there is no pedestrian crossing on this south side of the bridge) and enter the churchyard between pillars appropriately capped with delicate wrought-iron ivy leaves. Turn left into the church porch.

The Tradescants and the Museum of Garden History

The Museum honours the two John Tradescants, father and son, gardeners and plant collectors. The elder John was gardener to several aristocratic families, such as the earls and marquesses of Salisbury at Hatfield House in Hertfordshire, and George Villiers, Duke of Buckingham. He was the first of a line of men who were both garden designers and horticulturists. He went on expeditions to Europe in search of plants that were new to Britain or unusual, introducing pomegranates, oleanders, figs, and brooms. In 1618 he joined an expedition to Muscovy (Russia) and some claim that he brought back to Britain the European larch (*Larix decidua*), which came to be grown for its timber and for medicinal turpentine. Two years later

VICTORIA TOWER GARDEN

N

250m (275yd)

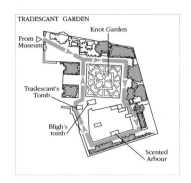

TRADESCANT GARDEN

Knot Garden

From ▷
Museum

Tradescant's
Tomb

Bligh's
tomb

Scented
Arbour

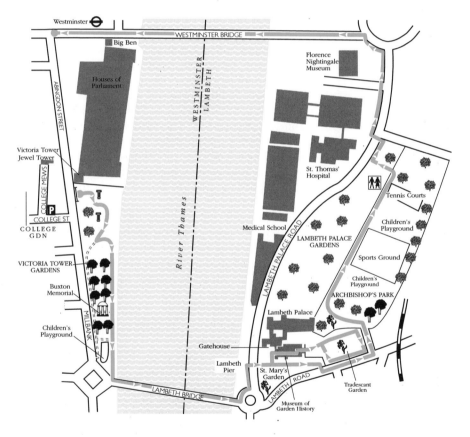

Westminster

WESTMINSTER BRIDGE

Big Ben

Houses of
Parliament

WESTMINSTER
LAMBETH

Florence
Nightingale
Museum

ABINGDON STREET

Victoria Tower
Jewel Tower

COLLEGE MEWS

St. Thomas'
Hospital

P

COLLEGE ST

COLLEGE
GDN

Tennis Courts

Children's
Playground

VICTORIA TOWER
GARDENS

Medical School

River Thames

LAMBETH PALACE ROAD

LAMBETH PALACE
GARDENS

Sports Ground

Buxton
Memorial

Children's
Playground

ARCHBISHOP'S PARK

Children's
Playground

MILLBANK

Lambeth Palace

Gatehouse

Lambeth
Pier

LAMBETH BRIDGE

St. Mary's
Garden

LAMBETH ROAD

Tradescant
Garden

Museum of
Garden History

he sailed for Algiers as a volunteer 'shott' on an expedition to quell pirates, but also
in search of the small, delicious Algiers apricot, which he brought back, with lilacs.

John Tradescant the elder became so famous in the field that he was sent plants
from the new colonies. In 1617 he became a member of the Virginia Trading
Company, a source of exotic plants new to Britain. Through routes such as this,

plants such as tradescantia *(Tradescantia virginiana),* Virginia creeper *(Parthenocissus quinquefolia),* and the black walnut *(Juglans nigra)* reached Britain from North America, and the scarlet runner bean from the West Indies. He never visited America, but in 1637 he sent his son John on the first of three trips. After his death, his son returned from Virginia with 200 new species, including the swamp cypress *(Taxodium distichum),* a tree now seen in many parks. He made two other journeys in 1642 and 1657, from which he brought back the tulip tree *(Liriodendron tulipifera)* and rock bells *(Aquilegia canadensis),* which grow in the knot garden behind this church.

Father and son lived nearby, where they collected curiosities and opened what was virtually the first public museum, known as the Ark, which became the kernel of the Ashmolean Museum in Oxford. They are buried in the churchyard, and although some elements of their work, at Hatfield House, for example, remain or have been restored, this church was the obvious base for the first museum of garden history, which was formally opened in 1983. The museum has displays on the history and development of gardens and on the lives of the Tradescants. Among the exhibits is a fine collection of garden tools, ranging from a 17th-century watering pot to early lawn mowers, one dated 1832. Six archbishops of Canterbury are buried in the church (look for their memorials).

The Tradescant Garden

Leave the church through the door at the back, which leads into the living part of the Museum – the garden. Late-flowering plants were less usual in the Tradescants' day, so the flowering season of this period garden is concentrated in early summer. The plants here all have name-tags and there is a map available in the museum.

The highlight of this garden is the knot garden, ahead of you on the right. It is about 33 feet (10 metres) square and was laid out by the Marchioness of Salisbury to a traditional 17th-century geometric design, with the flower beds marked by low clipped hedges of miniature box *(Buxus sempervivens* 'Suffruticosa'). At the centre there is a sculptured, striped holly *(Ilex aquifolium* 'Golden King').

A knot garden would probably have had only a few different favourite plants growing, perhaps just one type in each bed, but in this garden the beds (and the beds surrounding the knot garden) are full of plants the Tradescants would have known or themselves grown. Some are native species they found growing wild in the countryside; others were brought to Britain from abroad, although some of these had already been familiar for centuries. The striped holly, for example, is said to have been first recorded growing in Britain in AD 995, Mediterranean lavender *(Lavandula angustifolia)* in 1265, and hollyhocks *(Alcea rosea),* which originate in China, in 1300; the apothecary's rose *(Rosa gallica officinalis)* from southern Europe is first recorded in AD 900, and the crown fritillary *(Fritillaria imperialis)* came from Turkey in 1590 – in the knot there are four groups of this majestic plant in flower early in the season.

In a bed by the fountain ahead of you is a strawberry tree *(Arbutus unedo),* native to the mild Irish coasts and the Mediterranean; it was recorded growing in England before 1548. Before moving on, turn left to admire the service tree *(Sorbus domestica),* a member of the rowan family, against the garden's north wall.

Turn right and right again at the end of the path, and walk along the scented arbour. Near one of the bower seats is the attractive smoke bush *(Cotinus coggyria)* brought from southern Europe in 1629, and so called because its feathery white fronds give it a misty appearance. The false acacia or locust *(Robinia pseudacacia)*, with dense, hanging strands of fragrant flowers, is another of the 17th-century introductions from North America.

The Tombs
Turn right at the end of the scented arbour. Facing you is the fine tomb of the two Tradescants, a feature of this unusual garden. It was erected in 1638, and is decorated with scenes showing the dangers they met on their travels. Nearby is the tomb of Captain William Bligh *(c.* 1754–*c.*1817), who also lived nearby and was Captain of *The Bounty* in 1787. This ill-starred expedition set out to collect breadfruit seedlings from islands in the Pacific to grow in the young British colonies in the Caribbean. After the ship's crew mutinied, Bligh was cast adrift in an open boat with 17 men, and navigated 3,618 miles (5,822 kilometres) to Timor, near Java.

This being a London church, think of the many others buried here. If you sit on the seat on the opposite side of the knot from these tombs, you rest your feet on a memorial slab to the Evans family, whose youngest members were John, aged 3, and his sister Ann, aged 16 months. They were the victims of diseases that were rampant in the days before modern medicine, which has a debt to many of the plants that the Tradescants and others of their kind so enthusiastically collected.

Archbishop's Park
Return through the church and turn left into Lambeth Palace Road. About 2–3 minutes' walk, just before the railway bridge, turn left along a cutting leading into Archbishop's Park. There are many fine trees in this park, which was for a long time part of Lambeth Palace Gardens – for example, facing you as you enter the park are two Indian bean trees *(Catalpa bignonioides)*, two or three fine copper beeches dominate the plantings to the left, and the northern end of the park is shaded by the spreading canopies of immensely tall London planes. Following the park's tradition as a recreation area for local children, there are children's playgrounds at either end, and sports pitches in the centre.

Turn left along a path heavily shaded by overhanging limes and a variety of other trees, which circumnavigates a cluster of rose beds. As the path bends right, the walls and towers of historic Lambeth Palace appear. The Archbishops of Canterbury have had a residence on this site since about 1200, but the present palace is largely the result of rebuilding in 1828–34 in neo-Gothic style. Past it appears the red-brick tower of St. Thomas's Hospital Medical School, built in 1871.

Follow the path along the shrubbery and past a small flower garden at the north end of the park, and turn left onto Lambeth Palace Road. Turn right after crossing the road and walk along by St. Thomas's Hospital, eventually turning left onto Westminster Bridge, where the walk ends.

Green Park

Location	About two-thirds of a mile (1.1 kilometres) west of Charing Cross.
Transport	Green Park Underground Station (Jubilee, Piccadilly, and Victoria lines) and Hyde Park Corner Underground Station (Piccadilly Line). Victoria Station (overground rail terminus, underground trains on the Victoria, District and Circle lines, and bus terminus) is 10 minutes' walk away. Buses along Piccadilly are: 19, 14, 22, 38.
Admission	Open daily from 05:00-12:00 hours. Admission is free.
Seasonal features	Spring bulbs, autumn colour.
Events	Gun salutes on special occasions, such as the Trooping of the Colour.
Refreshments	Kiosk beside Canada Gate open daily approximately 09:30-17:30 hours. Café in St. James's Park (see page 118). There are coffee shops and restaurants in the hotels along Piccadilly and around Hyde Park Corner.

Green Park's name is descriptive, for apart from deep drifts of colourful springtime bulbs, and the autumn golds and russets of its closely planted trees, the greens of leaves and grass are its dominant colours. Although it has no flower beds, it is an attractive park all year round, much loved for its tranquillity, despite its location between the traffic lanes of Piccadilly and Constitution Hill.

The peaceful atmosphere of Green Park today makes it hard to believe its hidden history of violence and raucous revelry. Before the 1660s, the area covered by the park was meadowland, rather swampy in places – the Tyburn stream, which arose in Hampstead, flowed south to St. James's Park lake, via Marble Arch, Piccadilly and Green Park. The meadows were acquired by Henry VIII, along with the land on which he established the Court of St. James's Palace in Westminster, and it was enclosed for grazing and hunting. After the king's death it was fortified by forces loyal to Mary I, who clashed with opponents of the Queen's marriage to Philip II of Spain. And during the Civil War it was fortified again by Parliamentarians intent on threatening Charles I, in residence in the Palace of St. James.

In 1667 Charles II turned some 36 acres (16 hectares) of this land into a formal park. A network of paths was laid across it, trees were planted, and a deer enclosure was built near Hyde Park Corner. At that time it was called Upper St James's Park.

Situated on the edge of London as it then was, close to what is now Piccadilly, then the main route west, the park attracted highwaymen and became a convenient venue for duelling. In 1771 a duel between a Viscount Ligonier and a Count Alfieri ended with the latter wounded, but staggering off to the theatre, muttering darkly.

In the 18th century Green Park was handy for military parades – and fireworks. It was here that George II staged his Royal Fireworks of 1749, celebrating the peace treaty which ended the War of the Austrian Succession, the last war to be led by an English monarch. George Frederick Handel (1685-1759), composed music especially for the occasion, employing 40 trumpets and 20 French horns, plus oboes, bassoons and drums, augmented by 100 cannon. A magnificently decorated Temple of Peace – a pastiche of a Doric temple – was built of wood, 410 feet (125.5 metres) long and 114 feet (35 metres) high, with a stage for the 100 musicians (a print of the time shows it standing in a virtually treeless park). But at 8.30pm (20:30 hours) on 27th April, when the first of the rockets were set off and the cannons roared, the building caught fire. Two arches collapsed and a girl in flames had to be stripped to her stays. However, the display continued and the king stayed until midnight.

Later, in 1814, a Temple of Concord in the form of a great, revolving 'Gothick' fort was built there to celebrate a centenary of Hanoverian rule and victory over Napoleon – but the temple was mysteriously burned down one night, and the park severely vandalized the next day by a crowd cheated of its entertainment.

In the 19th century, the park became a popular ballooning ground. A balloon ascent marked the coronation of George IV in 1821. There were inevitably disasters, however. On another occasion a man attempted a lift while mounted on his horse; the balloons failed, and horse and rider fell to the ground. The coronation of Queen Victoria in 1838 was marked by firework displays all over London, including a brilliant one in Green Park.

Today, Green Park is more popular as a venue for quiet walks and lunching. The charm of this small park lies in its trees, of which there are more about 950 in its 53 acres (21.5 hectares). When the park was first laid out, the trees in the water-logged dip, toward the Mall, were mainly willows and poplars. On the higher ground, toward Hyde Park Corner and Piccadilly, oak and ash predominated. Over the centuries, a greater variety of trees has been planted. Although rarities are lacking among the Green Park trees, there are many venerable London planes, and fine forest trees, such as chestnut, lime, poplar, and oak. They are not name-tagged, however, so it is advisable to take with you on this walk one of the tree identification guides listed on page 173.

THE GREEN PARK WALK

Start The Ritz entrance. **Finish** Hyde Park Corner.
Time Allow 1 hour.

The gate beside the entrance to the underpass to Green Park Underground Station, beneath Piccadilly, is overshadowed by the Ritz Hotel, built in 1906. It was the first steel-framed building and a precursor of today's skyscrapers, but it was disguised as a grand French château. Some of its rooms have a restful view onto the park. Proceed through the gate and take the path to the left, parallel with Piccadilly, heading west.

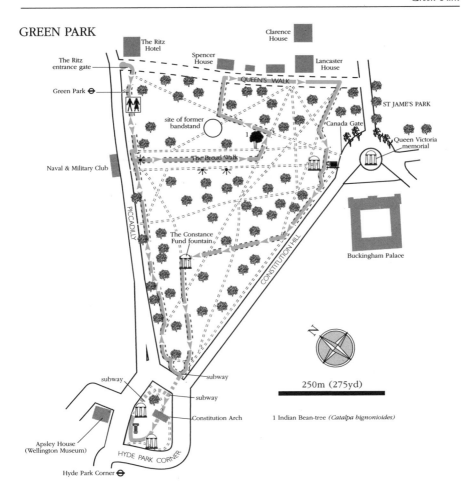

GREEN PARK

The Ritz Hotel

The Ritz entrance gate

Green Park ⊖

site of former bandstand

Naval & Military Club

PICCADILLY

The Broad Walk

Clarence House

Spencer House

Lancaster House

QUEEN'S WALK

Canada Gate

ST JAME'S PARK

Queen Victoria memorial

1

The Constance Fund fountain

CONSTITUTION HILL

Buckingham Palace

N

250m (275yd)

subway

subway

subway

Constitution Arch

1 Indian Bean-tree *(Catalpa bignonioides)*

Apsley House (Wellington Museum)

HYDE PARK CORNER

Hyde Park Corner ⊖

The ground swells away to the west, rolling grassland set with trees. They are plane trees *(Platanus x hybrida)* in the main *(see* page 77), with limes *(Tilia* spp.) and smaller hawthorns *(Crataegus monogyna)*, planted in loose groups. But there is a scatter of others, such as the unusual black poplar *(Populus nigra)*, its trunk often carrying burrs, or warts, of bark. Although it is a very different shape, this tree is a close relative of the familiar tall, thin Lombardy poplar. There are also silver maples *(Acer saccharinum)*, with finely cut leaves, silvery below - in North America this tree is a source of maple syrup; and silver lime *(Tilia tomentosa)*, so called because the undersides of the leaves are silvery white. Young walnuts *(Juglans regia)* and other trees have also been planted out in some of the open spaces.

There is usually little to see in the way of flowers in this part of the park for most of the year, but in spring, flares of naturalized daffodils and other bulbs bloom in the grass along the Piccadilly railings and beside Queen's Walk in the east. Some of the trees bear blossom in spring, and there is red and gold leaf colour in autumn. And the park remains attractive in winter after the leaves have gone, when the spidery branches of the empty trees pattern themselves against the sky.

The Devonshire Gate

Follow the path running parallel to Piccadilly for a short way. There is a street market along Piccadilly at the weekends, when artists and other stallholders sell pictures and crafts from pitches along the railings. After a short stroll, you come to a fine, ornate gate on the right, with no road in front of it on the park side, only rough grass. This is the Devonshire Gate. Its stone pillars have vermiculate rustication (that is, a 'worm-eaten', antique look), and are still etched black, a legacy of pre-smokeless zone years. This gateway was moved here in 1921 after a stay at Devonshire House, the Devonshire family mansion in Piccadilly (by the corner of Berkeley Street), which is now demolished. Before that it was at Chiswick House – the sphinxes that surmount the pillars are a Chiswick motif *(see* page 34). Notice that the ironwork is touched with gilt, and that the coat of arms (three stags' heads) is inscribed with the royal motto.

Through the railings you can see a splendid house on the north side of Piccadilly. This is the Naval and Military Club – known as 'the In and Out' from the traffic notices posted prominently at the entrance to its driveway. In Victorian times this was the residence of Lord Palmerston (1784–1865), the Prime Minister. Green Park was first opened to the public in 1826, and at that time visitors were confined to walking on the paths only, as they still are in the countryside. Lord Palmerston – at that time still to become Prime Minister – was among those who argued against legal trespass, and in favour of allowing people to walk on the grass. He argued that the grass should be 'walked on freely and without restraint by the people young and old for whose enjoyment the parks are maintained'. From this gateway, the Broad Walk stretches south. At this point, either exercise your right to walk down it on the grass, or take one of the paths that border it to left and right.

The grassy Broad Walk is the main avenue descending gently north-south through the centre of the park, lined by a double row of youngish plane trees. It was created to provide a vista from Piccadilly to the Victoria Memorial in front of Buckingham Palace. As you walk down it, however, look to the right (west), to contemplate a magnificent vista of trees.

Queen's Walk

About two-thirds of the way down, The Broad Walk is crossed by a path; turn left along it. A little way ahead, just on the left at the next junction of paths, there is an Indian bean tree *(Catalpa bignonioides)*, its trunk and main branch supported on poles. These trees have large pale green leaves and carry upright panicles of white flowers in summer; in autumn they produce long brown pods, which look like beans, and remain all through the winter.

Follow the cross-path to the eastern border of the park, and turn left along Queen's Walk. This walk, leading from Ritz Corner in the north to The Mall, opposite St. James's Park in the south, was laid out in 1730. It was the creation of

Charles Bridgeman *(see* page 9) for Queen Caroline, wife of George II, for the Queen to walk there with the royal family in spring. The Queen's Library, a small summer house for resting and reading, stood just off the walk until it was burned down during the celebrations of 1749.

In 1790, Queen's Walk became a fashionable promenade, competing with St James's Park. From the Ritz down to Lancaster House, it was lined with fine mansions, some of which you can still see to your right. When you reach Spencer House – the fourth grand house up from the Mall, recognizable by the sculptured figures standing on the pediment - stop to admire it. It was the private residence of the Spencers, the family of Diana, Princess of Wales, until 1927. It was designed in Palladian style in 1752-54 by John Vardy, assistant to William Kent (see page 9), and is the finest building in this area. Its main façade, which faces the Park, is so designed that the shadows strengthen its features. Notice the odd wings decorating the central round window. The house is open to the public on Sundays.

Turn about and stroll down to the southern end of Queen's Walk. Behind the railings on the right, great drifts of daffodils bloom in spring. To your left, as you reach The Mall, is Lancaster House, built in warm Bath stone. It was begun in 1825 by Benjamin Dean Wyatt, and completed by the Greek Revival architect, Sir Robert Smirke in 1841. Queen Victoria was often a guest in this magnificent house, owned by the dukes of Sutherland.

By comparison with St. James's Park, which you can see across The Mall, Green Park is abruptly rural, with none of the sophistication of man-made lakes and water birds of its neighbour. It has its remote spots where people scarcely ever walk. And it also has handsome, old-fashioned lamp standards and benches – and even rubbish bins, as you have seen along Queen's Walk.

Turn right at the bottom of Queen's Walk along the path leading westward. A pool of water once collected in this dip, and trees grow more thickly. You can see across to Buckingham Palace, and through the stone balustrade to the left you glimpse the flower beds surrounding the Queen Victoria Memorial (see pages 120–1). No house existed here when Green Park was first laid out; Charles II resided in St. James's Palace, part of which still stands in the Mall. Buckingham House, the core of the present Palace, was built in 1702–5 for the first Duke of Buckingham. In the 1820s, George IV, having rejected a proposal by Sir John Soane to build a palace in Green Park, commissioned the architect John Nash, who rebuilt part of Buckingham House as the present palace.

Constitution Hill

Continue past the ornate Canada Gate. Across the grass to the right (northwest) is a stone memorial set in the grass. It is the modern Canadian memorial, unveiled in 1994, an unusual and impressive creation taking the form of a pair of smooth, polished red granite wedges, angled one to the other, with maple leaves etched into the stone, their veins glinting with brass. On occasions, water is set to flow gently down their upper surfaces.

Continue walking west. To your left, across a horse ride, is Constitution Hill. The name is said to originate with Charles II's frequent and perhaps rather dangerous constitutionals among his subjects, accompanied by his favourite spaniels. The wall on the opposite side of the road surrounds the gardens of Buckingham Palace. There have been one or two incidents along this route. Sir Robert Peel, twice Prime Minister, was thrown from his horse along this road in 1850 and died soon after. And Queen Victoria was shot at here in 1840, and again in 1842 and 1849. A different assailant was identified each time; all three were arrested and found guilty but insane.

From this side of the park, instead of following a path, head off across north-westward across the grass and through the trees toward the Constance Fund Fountain, which is marked on the map on page 111. In this park, the paths are really for navigating from; it is far more pleasant to walk across the grass. There are, however, restrictions in force (the Park Regulations are posted on an information board at Ritz Corner), and you might pass something slightly bizarre: two notices on posts about a cricket pitch apart (22 yards or 20.1 metres), each radiating to the other the message NO BALL GAMES. Then there is a wooden keeper's hut keeping itself to itself in the centre of an open space. You can have this part of the park almost to yourself; it feels as remote as anywhere can be in London. Few people walk here since it is not on the way to anywhere.

Close to Hyde Park Corner, you come across The Constance Fund Fountain. It looks like an ornamental fountain, but is, in fact, a drinking fountain (now dry) with ornate twisting ironwork branches below, supporting a curvaceous nymph with a leash in her hand and a greyhound bounding across her feet. Created by E. J.Clack in 1954, it is a gift of the Constance Fund, a private charity commemorating the wife of Sigismund Goetze, an artist who was quite well known in inter-war London, and who died in 1939.

Hyde Park Corner

From the Constance Fund Fountain, take the path that leads to the top of Constitution Hill, where there is an underpass leading to the Hyde Park Corner traffic island. The underpass is entertainingly decorated with individual paintings of nearby sights, and of The Green Park's history, such as the 150,000-gallon (6,825,000-litre) reservoir that once existed around the Ritz Gate, an area of seasonal springs, and of a ballooning disaster that took place there.

Hyde Park Corner is at the top of a slight rise. It was fortified as a gun battery in the Civil War of 1642. In 1750 it was described as 'one of the finest eminences in nature, commanding a vast extent of variegated country bounded by distant hills'; one such hill was Wimbledon. Attempts in the past to make this spot a ceremonial western entry to the heart of London failed. The Regency architect Robert Adam was one of several notable people who had grand plans for the area.

The island reached via the underpass now houses a handful of notable military monuments, however. To the left as you emerge from the underpass is Constitution Arch (also called Wellington Arch). Designed in 1828 by Decimus Burton, it was intended as a gateway to Hyde Park. It had on top a colossal equestrian statue of the Duke of Wellington, victor of the Battle of Waterloo of 1815 against the French army under Napoleon, but in 1883 the arch was moved to its present position to ease traffic congestion and the statue of Wellington was sent to the military at Aldershot. In 1912 the Arch was crowned with its statue of Victory riding a quadriga, a four-horse chariot, by Adrian Jones.

Walk through the Arch and follow the path to the right, passing a memorial to Royal Artillery soldiers who fought in the world wars, and circling the island until you reach, to the left, another – a naked David resting on a gigantic sword, a symbol of the machine gun slaying its ten thousands during World War I, against Saul's thousands.

Between the two memorials, to the right of the path, is a statue of the Duke of Wellington, Britain's hero after his defeat of Napoleon at the Battle of Waterloo in 1815. At the corners of the plinth are detailed figures wearing the regalia of four regiments of his time. Wellington is astride his famous horse Copenhagen (which lived 1808-36). They face Apsley House, isolated by traffic since its neighbour was destroyed by the building of the access road into Park Lane. Its address is Number 1, London. It was built in the 1770s, and was later enlarged and encased with stone when it became the Duke of Wellington's residence. Here, close to the underpass, the walk ends.

St. James's Park

Location	About a quarter of a mile (0.4 kilometres) southwest of Charing Cross.
Transport	St James's Park Underground Station (District and Circle Lines) is 5 minutes' walk from the Park on the south side; Westminster Underground Station (District and Circle Line) is about 5 minutes' walk from the Park's southeastern corner. Charing Cross Station (Northern, Bakerloo and Jubilee Underground Lines and overground rail terminus) is about 15 minutes' walk from the northeast corner; and Victoria Station (Victoria and District and Circle Underground Lines and overground rail terminus) is about 15 minutes walk from the southwest corner. Many bus routes pass along Victoria Street and Whitehall, to the south and west. Parking in the area is difficult.
Admission	Open 05:00 hours–midnight. Admission is free.
Seasonal features	Rose beds and Nash flower beds in summer. Spring blossom and autumn tree colour.
Events	Bands give concerts on the band stand between the end of May and the end of August.
Refreshments	Cake House café open daily 09:30–17:30 hours.

St. James's is a magnificent park, strong on birds and strong on people. It is only a few minutes' walk from the Houses of Parliament, and the Chancellor of the Exchequer takes his customary stroll here before his Budget speeches. There is always a good chance of seeing a famous political face taking the air among the civil servants. This park has also long been highly popular with English and foreign visitors to London. During the 20th century it has also been the setting for spy stories involving envelopes containing secrets left on benches, and similar plots.

St. James's is the oldest of the eight Royal Parks. It came into being in the 1530s, when Henry VIII enclosed a park for deer coursing and other palace amusements on marshy land attached to the leper hospice of St. James. It was a convenient distance from his three palaces: Whitehall (burnt down in 1698); Westminster (where the Houses of Parliament now stand); and St. James (part of which remains).

Charles II (1660–1685) put dramatic changes in hand, creating a more formal park between Whitehall and St. James. He had admired the Palace of Versailles, outside Paris during his exile in France, and the name of the French landscape designer André Le Nôtre (1613–1700) has been linked with St. James. But a contemporary visitor from Switzerland wrote that Le Nôtre 'was of the opinion that the natural simplicity and in some places wild character had something more grand than he could impart to it, and persuaded the King not to touch it'. However, free radiating alleys were planted, and a straight canal 100 feet (30 metres) broad, was dug, with an island for water birds. On July 15th, 1666, Samuel Pepys wrote in his diary that he 'lay down upon the grass by the canalle and slept awhile'.

The Park was then a fashionable venue, but was less so by the start of the 18th century. Queen Anne, in an attempt to restore its cachet, introduced stricter regulations: no walking on the grass; no clogs; nothing to be sold (in those days milk was often sold directly from a cow grazing on whatever grass was available); and no linen dried. Later in the century, Queen Caroline, wife of George II, asked the Prime Minister, Sir Robert Walpole, how much it would cost to restrict its use to royals. 'Only three crowns, Madam' he replied. A crown was a coin (there were four crowns to £1), but Walpole meant the kingdoms of England, Ireland and Scotland. Later in the century, the Park had its own breed of muggers, called mohocks; and it had become a haunt of prostitutes, as James Boswell discovered and recorded.

The original formal layout of the Park was undone when John Nash (1752–1835), who had upgraded Buckingham House into Buckingham Palace in the 1820s, redesigned St James's Park, turning the canal into a more natural-looking lake surrounded by the winding paths and lawns skilfully broken by clumps of trees, which is its style today.

THE ST. JAMES'S PARK WALK
Start and finish Storey's Gate Lodge.
Time Allow 1 hour.

The walk begins at the headquarters of the Parks Police, but as I write, the building is invisible behind boarding, since the emergency exits of the new underground Jubilee Line extension are to surface here. Follow the path leading northward to the lake. Either side of this path and elsewhere in this park there are some magnificent plane trees, almost cathedral-like in scale and with massive, buttressed trunks, almost like rainforest trees. They are numbered, since there are Tree Protection Orders on them, and named as London planes, *Platanus x hispanica*. When you reach the lakeside, notice the great, sprawling fig tree. The grass alongside it (so reads the notice) is for the enjoyment of wildlife, so keep off!

The Lake
Follow the path around the eastern edge of the lake. Nash's water feature is very different from the original formal canal, although the map shows that the north bank retains something of the original straight edge. In fact, this wing of the lake was once a 'decoy' – a set of rectangular pools amid swampy ground, dug to attract wild duck, which could be netted for the table. The lake is on average 5 feet (1.5 metres) deep, which was shallow enough to drain and erect huts for government staff during World War II.

117

St. James's Park is famous for its pelicans. They have resided in the park for centuries, the first having been given to Charles II in 1684 by the Russian ambassador. They like this first bay and they can often be seen camped out, collapsed on the rocks in the middle of the water, looking like piles of washing awaiting laundering. They are fed at this spot with whole fish at about 4pm every afternoon.

This Park has always been a home for birds, some of them exotic. Apart from the pelicans, the diarist, John Evelyn (1620-1706) noted storks, swans, geese, and cranes. James I had a menagerie complete with crocodiles and an 'ellefant' which was fed with a gallon of wine a day; and he kept 'outlandish fowl' and had an aviary.

Walk on until you see a rustic cottage to the left. Nash's new lake embraced Duck Island, which is now narrowly joined to the bank. Hidden away on it are artesian wells that feed St. James's Park, including the pumps for the fountains and for aerating the lakes of this park and Kensington Gardens. In 1837 the Ornithological Society of London built a house on the island for a birdkeeper – the quaint Duck Island Cottage, its cottagey garden bright with flowers (they are name-tagged). This is now the address of the London Historic Parks and Gardens Trust, an organization that is active in restoration, but also arranges lectures and entertaining visits for members. Duck Island is normally out of bounds; however since 1996 one or two tours have been organized every month. The dates and times of these are posted on the notice boards in the Park.

Horse Guards Parade

Follow the path past the top of the lake toward the Guards Memorial – prominent to your left – its figures cast in metal from German guns captured in World War I. To the right, you look across Horse Guards Parade, a large military parade ground. The buildings surrounding it make it one of the most dramatic open spaces in London. The ceremony of the Trooping of the Colour is held on a Saturday early in June. For most of the year, however, the parade ground is in daily use as a car park for civil servants working nearby. There are continual proposals to put the cars underground and extend the use of Horse Guards Parade, with (for example) open-air music and opera.

The Cake House

The path from the Guards Memorial runs left past flower beds and an unusual rock garden feature and cascade; it is unusual because the plants growing on it are not the conventional alpine and rockery flowers but ordinary garden flowers. There is a fountain jet in the lake off Duck Island to the left – although it is not always switched on – while the path is lined with benches, where civil servants munch sandwiches at lunch-times, and at weekends tourists from all over the world sit and rest. This is a place to hear languages you have never heard before.

The path passes The Cake House, a self-service cafeteria built in 1970, with a striking pointed hat of a roof and (for sunny days) tables outside with a view out over the water to the sprawling willows of Duck Island. It is the latest of a number of cafés on this spot; the first was established at the end of the 17th century, during the reign of William and Mary.

ST JAMES'S PARK

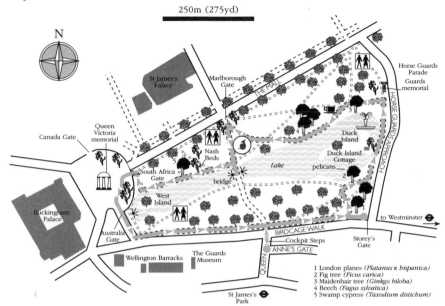

250m (275yd)

1 London planes *(Platanus x hispanica)*
2 Fig tree *(Ficus carica)*
3 Maidenhair tree *(Ginkgo biloba)*
4 Beech *(Fagus sylvatica)*
5 Swamp cypress *(Taxodium distichum)*

The Mall

Continue along the lakeside. To the right at the point where the path diverts from the water is a picturesque beech tree with a twisted trunk. And there are more of those statuesque plane trees.

Leave the waterside path where it forks to the right for Marlborough gate, opposite St. James's Palace, to view The Mall. The walk passes a circle of flagstones where, in summer, an awning is erected for daily concerts by military guards' bands. Concerts are held at lunchtimes and in the evenings. By the gate scatters of mauve autumn crocuses appear at the end of the summer; they are not strictly crocuses but colchicums (they flower without leaves appearing).

St. James's Park is bounded along its north side by The Mall. It was a fashionable walk in the days of Charles II, and people played Paille Maille or Pell Mell. This was a game which seems to have resembled croquet in some ways: a ball was hit down an alley floored with crushed cockle shells, the aim being to drive it through a goal (maybe an iron ring hung at the end of the alley). Hence today's name. Today's wide Mall, however, lined by young plane trees, was laid down in the early 20th century and was designed by Sir Aston Webb as a ceremonial route between Admiralty Arch and the Victoria Memorial in front of Buckingham Palace. The old line of the walk runs parallel to it on the northern side. Notice the unusual design of the lamp standards – eggs held by iron banding – rather Art Deco in style, and the ceremonial flagpoles. The tarmac is not the usual black, but red, composed of chippings of Northumberland granite.

119

The Bridge

Return along the path to the northern lakeside and onto the bridge that crosses the lake. This is a blue, slim-line 1950s replacement of a Victorian iron suspension bridge which, in turn in 1857, replaced John Nash's original bridge. It offers a marvellous view back down the lake to Duck Island, with the roofs and domes of the official buildings beyond looking more Moscow than London. Return to the lake shore and turn left. On this western side of the bridge there are identification boards for the waterfowl to be seen: crested duck; great crested grebe; shelduck; teals of many kinds; Bahama and other pintails; chiloe wigeon; and many others, including ten different types of geese, and black and white (mute) swans. There are usually about 1,000 birds which are forcibly resident because they have had their flight feathers clipped, plus wild birds.

The Nash Beds

Continue walking west along the lake path until you see three flower beds to the right. Take a detour to them. Although they are relatively new, they are of key interest because they are based on garden principles set out by John Nash in 1826. They contain small trees, shrubs, climbers, flowers, and bulbs, all ranked and planted so that they have a natural look, and the edges of the beds are made to curve against the grass. The flower colours and foliage are carefully positioned. The flowers planted include sweet pea, wild geraniums, dwarf chrysanthemums, hollyhocks, and various flowers of the daisy family. Many are pleasantly scented. These Nash beds are, in fact, semi-formal in appearance, but planted with a cottage-garden mixture of flowers.

Continue up the side path running to the right (north) of these beds, passing a number of rose beds to the right. These were dedicated in 1980 to Queen Elizabeth the Queen Mother on her 80th birthday. Her personal choice of roses included 'Korrasia', 'Congratulations', 'Just Joey', 'Blessings', and 'Young Venturer'.

The Horseshoe Fountain

Return along the path to the northern lake shore and continue walking west toward the end of the lake. Water aeration devices can be seen in one or two places; this lake is quite shallow and keeping it from becoming stagnant is something of a problem. At the end of the Park, in front of Buckingham Palace, is a high wall looking like a quay with a fountain at its centre. Apparently, the lake did extend up to it at one time. There is some attractive bedding, with various hostas (foliage plants) and a tall variety of the cottage garden flower, London pride.

Queen Victoria Memorial

If you have never looked closely at the Victoria Memorial facing Buckingham Palace, it is worth a short detour. It is a good, solid, sentimental edifice, exhibiting some highly skilled work. It consists of a colossal white marble statue of Queen Victoria carved from a single block of stone by Thomas Brock. The Queen faces down The Mall toward Admiralty Arch, and is accompanied by female allegories of Charity, Truth, and Justice; below her, around the edge of the Memorial, there are bronze groups representing peace, agriculture, architecture, and other achievements of her reign. Fountains spout below figures, while at the pinnacle of it all is a golden gilded Victory.

As for Buckingham Palace, George IV in 1829 employed John Nash to improve it, but in fact, he rebuilt what had been Buckingham House as a royal palace. St. James's Palace was set aside for use for court ceremonies. Queen Victoria made the Palace her main home. Almost all you see from the front, however, is of a later date, for the front was added in 1912. The palace's real front faces its gardens. Before leaving the Memorial, stop to admire the handsome gates encircling it – Canada Gate (1906) leading into Green Park, bearing the coats of arms of various Canadian provinces, and the gates leading into the Mall. There are usually pigeons roosting on them.

Birdcage Walk

Now return to the lake to complete the circuit along its south side, or along Birdcage Walk with its lines of plane trees. James I and Charles II had aviaries here, and the diarist John Evelyn, noted many 'curious kinds of poultry'. The late Regency barracks of the Brigade of Guards (the body guard) can be seen on the opposite side of Birdcage Walk. Further along, you see the statue of 1883 opposite Queen Anne's Gate. It is known as 'The Greek Boy' for reasons now forgotten. It is also worth taking a detour from the walk by climbing Cockpit Steps to explore Queen Anne's Gate, with its rows of what are probably the best-preserved early-18th-century houses in London. They are built in mellow, dark brick, with porches and torch extinguishers. There was once a cockpit here; cock fights (called 'mains') were very popular. The biographer, James Boswell (1740-95) wrote: 'I then went to the Cockpit, which is a circular room in the middle of which the cocks fight ... nicely cut and armed with silver heels (spurs) ... one pair fought three quarters of an hour ... the uproar and noise of the betting is prodigious...' From Queen Anne's Gate, return to Birdcage Walk and follow it east to Storey's Gate, where the walk ends.

Battersea Park

Location	About 2⅓ miles (3.7 kilometres) west of Charing Cross.
Transport	East and southeast sides: Sloane Square Underground Station (District and Circle lines) is about 20 minutes' walk away; Battersea Park Station (overground trains from Clapham Junction and Victoria) and Queenstown Road Station (overground trains from Clapham Junction and Waterloo) are 5 minutes' walk away; 137 and 137a buses stop on Queenstown Road. West side: 19, 39, 44, 45, and 49 buses stop on Battersea Bridge Road. South side: 44 and 344 buses stop on Battersea Park Road. There are car parks with metered parking in the Park.
Admission	Open daily from 08:00 hours until dusk. Admission is free.
Seasonal features	The Old English Garden, the Herb Garden and the Subtropical Garden in spring and summer. Autumn tree colour.
Events	Weekend events *(see* pages 170–3). Easter Parade. Regular sporting events.
Refreshments	Battersea Park Cafe open daily 10:00–18:00 hours or 22:30 hours for sporting events.

Battersea Park is quite a recent park, created in Victorian days. Before that, the land occupied by the Park and its surrounding streets was an area commonly flooded by the River Thames. There were market gardening plots in places. 'Battersea bunches' were bunches of asparagus grown there. Otherwise, Battersea Fields had a reputation as an unruly playground, with a weekly fair and, on Sundays, donkey-racing, fortune tellers, drinking booths, and much besides. It was often a place of violence. In 1829, the Duke of Wellington rode out of town over wooden Battersea Bridge to fight a duel with the Earl of Winchilsea on this open land. A 19th-century city missionary described it as, '... a place out of Hell that surpassed Sodom and Gomorrah in ungodliness and abomination'.

Eventually, in the mid–1800s, the Victorian authorities decided to do something about Battersea Fields, and made plans to build a park there, and purchased 320 acres (130 hectares) of land. Regulations were drawn up: '...all persons found trespassing with Horses, Donkeys, Cockshies, Barrows on a Sunday will be taken into custody'. The land was drained, and earth was brought from the excavations of the Victoria Docks at Canning Town to raise the level, of which 198 acres (80 hectares) were to become the park, and 120 acres (49 hectares) were sold to a builder, Thomas Cubitt, to erect mansion blocks overlooking the park along the roads south and west of it. To an original plan by James Pennethorne, who had worked at Regent's Park under John Nash *(see* page 64), the ground was landscaped. There were plans to hold the Great Exhibition of 1851 in this park, but it could not be finished in time. Eventually opened as a public open space in 1858. In 1860, the lake was dug out, and its waters made to cascade spectacularly down huge, artificial rocks positioned at the lakeside. This was followed by the building of great banks of earth on the south side to make a subtropical garden. When it was planted in 1864 it was considered the horticultural wonder of Europe. There was much planting of the planes and other trees there today. Toward the end of the 19th century, the park became very fashionable and the drives were filled with carriages and bicycles.

The Festival of Britain was held in 1951, six years after the end of World War II, to perk up people's spirits. The main exhibition celebrating Britain's achievements and expectations was held at the South Bank. The Royal Festival Hall remains. The fun side was located in Battersea Park, and consisted of the Grand Vista with its waterworks, a funfair, shops and stalls, restaurants and beer gardens, and even The Far Tottering and Oyster Creek Railway, after cartoons by Ronald Searle (1920-). There was plenty of bright paint – red, blue, white and gold. Among thousands of bulbs to be planted were 20,000 yellow tulips, as one example.

Since its creation, Battersea Park has always been a local authority park. In 1889, the Metropolitan Board of Works, which had been responsible for building it, handed it over to the new London County Council; the Greater London Council assumed responsibility for it in 1965, and Wandsworth Borough Council in 1986. Today, the park is maintained and run with considerable care and (one could also say, in these days of council cash cutbacks) devotion and love.

On Battersea Park's 200 acres (81 hectares), an extraordinary number of events takes place – from sports and children's events to circuses, ballet, and theatre, regular classic and custom car meetings, numerous festivals, and the annual Easter Parade and fairs. Yet it remains a place where you can get away from crowds and enjoy the greenery, the flowers, and the birds.

THE BATTERSEA PARK WALK
Start and finish Albert Gate.
Time Allow 1¼ hours.

The fine ironwork gates and railings, touched with gilding, of the Albert Gate dated originally from 1901–2, and were inspired by the Arts and Crafts Movement, but they were cannibalized during World War II and replaced in 1986. Before entering the park, walk up Albert Bridge Road toward the river and Albert Bridge, with its delicate lattice of ironwork hung with hundreds of light bulbs – it is one of the sights of London between dusk and midnight, when it is illuminated. This Victorian suspension bridge bounces to the traffic, and on the southeast side there is a replica of a notice put there in Victorian times, requesting marching troops to break step for fear of damaging the structure. There are fine views along the river.

Return to Albert Gate and pass through it. Just inside three of Battersea Park's four gates there are typical park-keeper's lodges, fronted by neat lawns and flower beds. The garden of the one beside Albert Gate is bright with bluebells in spring, with bedding plants later in the season – and with a large notice board relating the park's history for visitors to read. Veer left past the Lodge, take the path to the right, and turn left into a walled compound. The Park offices are ahead on the left, and to the right of them is a large Herb Garden with an interesting collection of culinary and medicinal herbs, planted in roughly alphabetical order, and with a small stream running around them. Beyond it is a small garden planted with flowers and shrubs that attract birds and butterflies.

Leaving the Herb Garden, cross the North Carriage Drive to stand at the top of the West Carriage Drive. Perhaps you can identify a 'champion tree' – one of a list of the tallest or biggest trees in London published by Alan Mitchell, the author of numerous books on trees. There is one at the northern end of the car park beside the West Carriage Drive. It is a North American black walnut *(Juglans nigra)*, 110 feet (33.5 metres) high, with more leaflets than the native walnut and producing a very hard, ridged nut.

The planting of many of the trees in Battersea Park was planned by John Gibson, who became the Park's first curator in 1856. In general, he avoided rigidly straight lines, following, on the large scale, the 'gardenesque' style which was popular for parks at the time, with serpentine or wavy lines. He planted many honey locusts and planes down this west side of the park.

The Old English Garden

Now walk east along North Carriage drive for about 200 yards (180 metres), and turn right into the walled garden. This was created in 1912 on the site of a small botanic garden. It is a delightfully intimate, quiet, sunny place with dwarf box hedges, wooden pergolas smothered in roses, and seats all around. The centrepiece, a small pool that has traditionally been stocked with goldfish and lilies, was undergoing much-needed restoration as this book went to press.

Take time to stroll round this pretty garden, then leave it by the south gateway, and turn left along a winding woodland path through fenced enclosures planted with shrubs and trees. Shaded serpentine paths like this were originally a device to give some seclusion in what is public space. Toward the end of the path to the left you see an unexpected statue of a dog, an anti-vivisection memorial. Follow the path to its right and turn right at the end, passing on the left a small white house. This is a house and temple for the monks who look after the Peace Pagoda.

At the end of the path, bear left; you walk onto open ground studded with flower beds and, to left and right, water features. These were part of a Grand Vista, a sequence of shallow rectangular pools and fountains devised in 1950 or threreabouts by the cartoonist Osbert Lancaster (1908–86). To the left is a couple of eccentric colonnade erections by the artist John Piper (1903–92). They are what remain of a colourful period in the Park's history, when the area stretching from this point to East Carriage Drive was a 37-acre (15-hectare) pleasure ground, part of the Festival of Britain celebrations of 1951. The pleasure ground was planned to

BATTERSEA PARK

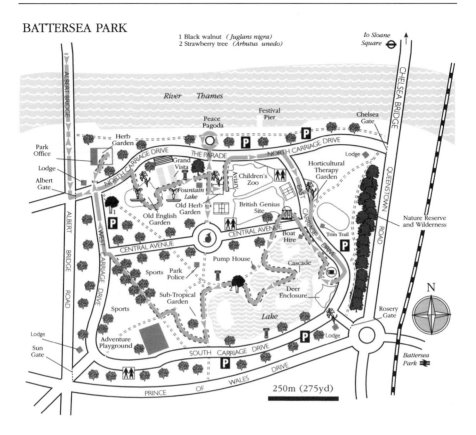

1 Black walnut (*Juglans nigra*)
2 Strawberry tree (*Arbutus unedo*)

continue for six months, but eventually it remained open for a year. At the north-east corner was a funfair with a big dipper, and although this was scaled down, it did not close until 1974. It explains the puzzling foundations you can still see in some places. The fountains in the large pool to your right often play during the weekends in summer. The Park has two engineers and when they are not busy else-where they turn them on, but they have to stay to supervise them whenever they are running.

The Peace Pagoda

Walk to the end of the broad path ahead of you, and when you reach the shrub-bery you can see ahead on a slight rise, bear left around it. This shrubbery conceals a grotto, another relic of the funfair. As you skirt it, the wooden Peace Pagoda with its four gilded Buddhas comes into view. It was a gift to London from the Japanese Buddhist Order Nipponzan Myohoji, and was erected in 1984–85, when the park was managed by the Greater London Council. It is built of Canadian Douglas fir, and its architecture is based on ancient Indian and Japanese Buddhist designs. Looking downriver from alongside it, you can see the Festival Pier, which was built for boats coming here from the South Bank, but is now closed.

The Children's Zoo

Follow the path south from the Pagoda toward the bandstand, a replica of the original Victorian structure, erected in 1988 as one of the improvements effected by Wandsworth Council. But before you reach it, turn left and climb two or three steps into a small rose garden, which leads into the old herb garden, where the rosemary plants have grown so high they look like small hedges. Turn left when you come to the aviary you can see ahead – stopping, first, to admire the plovers and other birds. It is part of the Children's Zoo – walk slowly up toward the river and you can see some of the animals enclosures between the cages of the aviary.

This zoo also originated at the 1951 Festival of Britain as a temporary feature. It remained and was expanded until, in the late 1980s, the animal houses were at last rebuilt. The inhabitants range from farm animals, such as goats, to British wild animals, including an otter, and diverse other creatures, among them wallabies, whistling ducks, pythons, and the blue-tongued skink.

Turn right again when you reach the North Carriage Drive, passing the entrance to the zoo. Just beyond to the right is a path leading to a large paved open space known as the British Genius site. It is used for funfairs, circuses, outdoor festivals, and other activities.

Horticultural Therapy Garden

Continue along North Drive and veer right along the East Carriage Drive. To the left, just past the tennis courts, is the Horticultural Therapy Garden. Pass through the gate and stroll through it – it was laid out as a demonstration garden for disabled people during the 1970s and is full of 'ideas for making gardening easier'.

You emerge from the garden facing a small leftward-leading path, which runs past the Athletics Track, but you should turn right and then left along the East Carriage Drive. To your left is an outdoor fitness circuit, with frames to swing from and balance on – a kind of outdoor gym. Beyond it, stretching away to the left, is the nature reserve, a wilderness area of thicket, boggy patches and pools, which was established to encourage British woodland plants, insects and birds. It is crossed by paths and there are boards at the entrances with maps showing the pathways.

Ahead of you to the right is a small grassy hill enclosed by a fence. Cross the East Carriage Drive and follow the path around it. This is the deer enclosure, which dates from 1888. Axis deer from India are kept in it, along with wallabies, but they are not always visible. Peacocks and guinea fowl make themselves more obvious.

By now you should have reached the lake shore. Turn right and stroll up to the waterside café (an example of 1930s architecture), from where there is a good view across to the rocky cascade signposted by a palm tree. The cascade, a feature of the Victorian park, is usually active at weekends and can often be seen at other times.

Past the café, stop to look at the news board, where news of coming events is posted, with weekly updates on the health of an injured black cygnet, maybe, or a report on the 12-inch (30-centimetre) terrapins – unwanted Christmas presents – now to be seen in the water.

Following the lakeside path westward, you pass a boat-hire yard. Take a detour northward, across Central Avenue, and walk across the grass to the War Memorial you can see to your right, surrounded by a neatly trimmed hedge. It was unveiled in 1922. The model for the soldier with the broken nose (the figure to the right, as you face the three figures, clasping the hand of the one in front) was the soldier-poet Robert Graves (1895–1985), a friend of the sculptor, Eric Kennington; the other two figures may be the war poets Wilfred Owen and Siegfried Sassoon.

Stroll across the grass to the lake shore beyond the boat hire yard, turn right, and walk past the stretch of lake which is set aside for fishing (carp, roach and perch), up to the elegant, Italianate brick Pump House. It was built in 1861 to house a massive steam engine which pumped water from a well to a cast iron tank at the top of the tower to feed the cascades and the lake. The lake was later fed directly from the Thames. The Pump House was restored in 1992 and now houses displays about the park and a small art gallery. On the grass outside is mounted the winning entry in the annual sculpture competition run by the Friends of Battersea Park.

The Lake

Retrace your steps from the Pump House, and stroll along the lake's northwest shore. The lake was a key feature of the Victorian park, just as it is today. It extends across 16 acres (7 hectares) and is only 3 feet (0.9 metres) deep. Many waterbirds, including herons, live on the lake and nest on its islands.

Too much dirty water taken directly from the Thames, algal clouding, partly the result of the lake's shallowness and lack of water movement, too many waterfowl (500 Canada geese alone), and some 1.5 tons more fish stocks than the lake should support, have put unwelcome pressure on this ornamental feature in recent years, and regular dredging was not enough to prevent rapid resilting. Recently, however, the Park won three years of funding under the European LIFE programme. This has paid for a new 300-foot (91-metre) borehole for clean water, the installation of water aerators, exchanges of fish, and the replanting of the banks with 13,000 shrubs, trees, and herbaceous plants. Under the advice of the Wildfowl Trust at Slimbridge, Gloucestershire, ecological control, including culling, has reduced the numbers of Canada geese to the recommended number of about 30. The balance is a dynamic one, however. Pinioned (captive) black swans have lived on Battersea Park Lake since the 1880s, but they recently disappeared, perhaps taken by one of the Park's 40 foxes – whose numbers are also controlled. The swans now in residence are feral. They have beaks of an intense red, and when they fly you can see their white wing flash.

Follow the serpentine lakeside path, which winds alongside the cascade, a delight of what is now clear water, with sausage-headed rushes in the pools, and stands of bamboo nearby. Follow the meanderings of the path across the stone bridge, which replaced a wooden, rustic-style bridge in 1920. The watersides nearby are newly planted. The path winds past the south side of the Pump House, past a tranquil stretch of lake, and then forks. Take the right fork. As you round the bend, watch out to the left between the path and the water's edge, for a spreading hybrid strawberry tree *(Arbutus unedo)* with dark green leaves and dusky red bark. It is another of Alan Mitchell's 'champion' trees. In the Mediterranean it produces dimpled red fruit, but they are not much like strawberries.

Around a couple of bends, to the right, is a group of three standing figures by Henry Moore (1898–1986). It is the relic of an outdoor sculpture exhibition staged in Battersea Park in 1948, the first time such an exhibition was held in a public park. Pieces were exhibited by other famous sculptors, such as Matisse and Epstein. A work by Moore's contemporary, Barbara Hepworth, also remains on the south shore of the lake.

The Sub-Tropical Gardens

Cross the path that runs along the lake's western shore onto an open lawn planted with trees. This area was the site of the Subtropical Gardens, which were a major feature of the Victorian park and aimed to challenge Kew Gardens. Curving banks were built up to give warm, sheltered conditions, and these remain, covered with trees. With its winding paths and sweeps of open lawn, this is a very attractive place. There are evergreen oaks, weeping ash, and one or two palms still to be seen, but the original plantings, including tree ferns, tender bananas *(Musa ensete)* from Abyssinia, *Begonia rex* from Assam, *Wiganda caracasana* from Mexico, black-leaved perillas from the Far East, and the castor oil plant *(Ricinus communis)* from tropical Africa, have long since disappeared.

The Sub-Tropical Gardens were only one of several extravagant displays which made Battersea Park world famous in the 19th century. This park was one of the first places where carpet bedding was tried out, in the 1850s. In this type of bedding, dwarf rosette foliage plants, such as 2-inch (5-centimetre) tall alternanthera, and succulents, such as fleshy-leaved echeverias, are used to create a patterned surface that looks like a carpet. An example can be seen in Hyde Park *(see* page 60). As the *Gardener's Chronicle* of 1864 put it, 'It hardly seems possible at first to realise that one is looking upon a group of living plants...'. Before long, parks and gardens all over the U.K. were experimenting with the idea. It was largely the brainchild of John Gibson, the Superintendent of Battersea Park at the time, who also planted many of the trees to be seen there today. To be effective with carpet bedding, gardeners must achieve perfection, so it is tricky and expensive to produce and needs constant maintenance. Nevertheless, there are proposals to research and restore an area of this bedding in Battersea Park.

The Sports Pitches

To complete the walk, leave the Sub-Tropical Gardens by the path on the west side, and take the path that leads through an avenue of flowering cherry trees (a riot of pink and white in spring) diagonally through the sports fields to West Carriage Drive. To the left are all-weather sports pitches and the largest adventure playground in London, designed for children and young people aged from 5 to 16. Beside it is a playground for under-fives and their minders. In spring, the trees either side of this path are a riot of pink and white blossom. Turn right beneath the marvellous ranked plane trees along West Carriage Drive (notice one or two recent sculptures on the lawn to the left) to return to Albert Gate, where the walk ends.

Chelsea Physic Garden

Location	About 2½ miles (4.5 kilometres) southwest of Charing Cross.
Transport	Sloane Square Underground Station (District and Circle Line) and Battersea Park and Queenstown Road stations (overground trains from Victoria and Waterloo respectively) are 20 minutes' walk away across Chelsea Bridge). Bus passing nearby are 239 (not Sundays) from Victoria; 11, 19, 22, 49, 319, 345 along the King's Road; 137, 137a along Queenstown Road. There is a car park in Battersea Park across Albert Bridge (15 minutes' walk).
Seasonal features	With your ticket you are given a detailed map showing what is of special interest where during that month.
Events	Talks and guided tours.
Admission	Open Apr–Oct: Sun, Wed 14:00–17:00 hours. Admission £3.50.
Refreshments	Tea Room open when the Garden is open.

This delightful 1.6–hectare (4–acre) secret garden was founded in 1673, when the Society of Apothecaries (the old name for pharmaceutical chemists) established a physic garden by the Thames. 'Physic' was the old term for the art of healing and the medical profession, and the aim of such gardens was to grow a library of healing plants. At that time plants were virtually the only source of medicines (even today, 80 per cent of medicines are still plant-based). In time, plants from around the world were being grown, not all medicinal, and these gardens became known as 'botanic gardens'. There are early physic gardens in Oxford and in Pisa, Italy, but only this one keeps its original name.

In the 1700s the garden was threatened by the rising cost of upkeep. It was eventually saved by the well-heeled Court doctor, Sir Hans Sloane, who in 1712 bought the manor of Chelsea. He restored the Physic Garden, then leased it back to the Society. The rent is still the same £5 a year. A key figure of the time was Philip Miller, who, while Curator from 1722 to 1770, made Chelsea the world's finest botanic garden. The 1800s saw another decline in fortune and threats from would-be building speculators, but in 1899 the garden was taken over by a parish charity, for private use by university and other students. In 1983 an independent charity was set up and the garden was reopened to visitors.

Apart from the trees, the plants will hardly be the same individuals as were growing in past centuries. However, many plants on the original lists are still grown, with many later additions, to make around 3,000 species in all. The beds are usually signposted with a plaque, telling you what category of plants they contain.

THE CHELSEA PHYSIC GARDEN WALK
Start and finish The Students' Gate.
Time Allow 1 hour.

Enter the gardens through the 300-year-old gate in the warmly aged, red-brick wall in Swan Walk. Hanging just inside is an equally old small bell for summoning apprentice apothecaries to their studies. Ahead is the kiosk where you purchase tickets. To whet the appetite, to the right close by the entrance gate is a Mediterranean pomegranate *(Punica granatum)*, with striking scarlet flowers at the tips of the shoots from June to autumn. Originally from Asia, it has been cultivated around the Mediterranean since ancient times. It often fruits in this garden, where such foreign plants (and trees) grow successfully because it offers a warm microclimate: the soil is well drained, the tall brick walls act rather like storage radiators, retaining the sun's warmth, and there is heat from traffic along the Chelsea Embankment. These factors raise the temperature up to 5 degrees higher than elsewhere and there are often frost-free areas in winter. A downside of the traffic might be exhaust pollution, but the plants seem not to suffer from this.

Useful Plants
The walk circles the Physic Garden anticlockwise, so turn along the path to the right, passing to the left a large bay tree *(Laurus nobilis)* overhanging one of this garden's many strategically placed seats, to reach the celebrated olive tree *(Olea europaea)*, the biggest in Britain at 9.0 metres (30 feet). This stalwart of the Mediterranean climate was planted in 1901 and it sometimes fruits. With the bay tree and the olive you are in that part of the garden set aside for useful plants. One of the original functions of the Garden was to teach trainee apothecaries to 'distinguish good and useful plants from those that bear resemblance to them and are hurtful'. And so, near the olive there are fruit trees and bushes, including, in late summer, succulent blackberries (visitors are not allowed to pick the fruit). There is also an apricot, usually a good fruiter although the apricots do not always ripen fully. This important fruit tree probably originated in China, was brought to Italy about 100 BC and reached England in the 13th century, at a time when the climate was warmer, with vineyards even in Yorkshire.

Turn left and left again at the end of the fruits. The path passes a bed of dye plants, with well-known species, such as American wild indigo, and madder whose roots yield a red dye. Woad can also be seen. Its leaves, when steeped, ooze a blue dye that the Celts in Britain used for tattooing; it produces dense clusters of yellow flowers in May. Dyer's greenweed produces a yellow dye. These plants are of great historic interest, for the colours they produce have now mainly been replaced by chemical dyes.

To the right are vegetables and what are termed lesser vegetables. Many are familiar, including allotment-worthy cabbages, but look also for lentil, soya bean, and less familiar native plants, such as good King Henry *(Chenopodium bonus henri-cus)*. It was one of the wild greens traditionally gathered and perhaps cultivated in Britain – its seeds have been found in the archaeological layers of Stone Age sites. It used to be sold in the old Covent Garden market, and although it has been generally discounted as a weed it is now coming back into culinary use. There is dandelion, still gathered today to make a refreshingly bitter green salad. Many of the plants in the end bed of this section will be familiar as herbs used in cooking.

At the end of this path, circle the neat herb bed. You now pass a bed of subsistence (famine) plants to the left. There is an Asian wingnut tree, which belongs to the same family as the walnut and the American hickory and carries unusual, long-hanging chains of broad-winged nuts. Then follows a bed of traditional herbalism plants, used when health was believed to be a balance of the four humours: blood, phlegm, and yellow and black biles. Black bile was said to cause melancholy and could be counteracted with an infusion of lemon balm, for example. Among the wild plants here are yarrow, or milfoil, and sanicle, found growing in chalky beech woods. 'He who keeps sanicle has no business with a doctor' states a herbal of 1578.

Mediterranean Curiosities and Aromatic Plants

Follow the path past the dye plants again and you see a Mediterranean cork oak *(Quercus suber)* to the right, hung with a necklace of corks. For commercial use, the bark of these trees is stripped every seven years or so for bottle corks to be punched out of it. Afterwards the undamaged dusky red underbark grows another layer of cork bark. Past the cork oak is the cistus bed with crinkled white or pink flowers in spring. Cistus shrubs also feature strongly in many Mediterranean landscapes. Some have highly scented leaves, and it was the smell of the cistus in the Corsican maquis scrub which lingered in Napoleon's memory. At the corner of this cistus bed, ferns are being raised.

Alongside the propagating greenhouse is a bed of plants used for perfumes (with black labels) and aromatherapy (with blue labels). Plant scents, which usually come from oils in the plant, can attract insects for pollination. However, the scents of the cistus and some other plants are in the leaves, making them distasteful to browsing animals. Roses used for attar (a volatile oil from the petals) and rose water can be seen growing here and, usually, irises of three species *(Iris florentina, germanica* and *pallida)*, whose ground-up rhizomes (orris root) can 'fix' perfumes.

Rainforest plants and poisons

Turn right at the end of the path and through the door of the glasshouse to the left. This is of pre-Victorian date and was restored in 1980. As you walk through it you become aware of the variety of climates maintained inside it, from warm temperate to what seems like a rainforest steaminess in the narrow corridor at the back.

Even today little of the vast variety of rainforest plant life has been screened for medicinal use. Yams grow here, for example; they yielded the first chemical contraceptive agents, which could never have been discovered by chance in a laboratory, and are now chemically synthesized. Another example is the poison bush from southern and western Africa, yielding an arrow poison, but also used by the Zulu

CHELSEA PHYSIC GARDEN

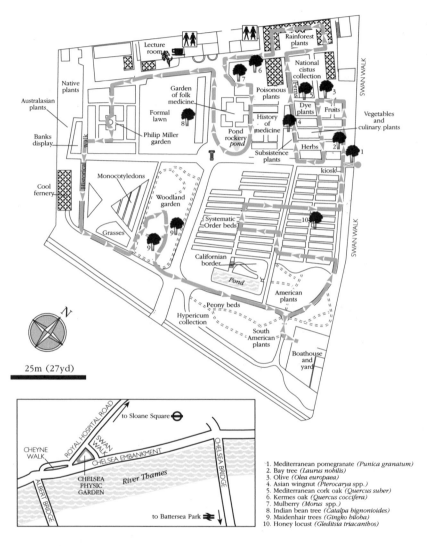

1. Mediterranean pomegranate *(Punica granatum)*
2. Bay tree *(Laurus nobilis)*
3. Olive *(Olea europaea)*
4. Asian wingnut *(Pterocarya spp.)*
5. Mediterranean cork oak *(Quercus suber)*
6. Kermes oak *(Quercus coccifera)*
7. Mulberry *(Morus* spp.*)*
8. Indian bean tree *(Catalpa bignonioides)*
9. Maidenhair trees *(Gingko biloba)*
10. Honey locust *(Gleditsia triacanthos)*

as a remedy for gut worms and an antidote for snake bite. Where the air is cooler, cinchona, the origin of anti-malarial quinine, grows, and the coffee bush.

Leaving the glasshouse, turn right and pass the shop. There is a spiny-leaved evergreen kermes oak *(Quercus coccifera)* from the Mediterranean to the left and, as you turn left down the path beyond it you see a black mulberry tree *(Morus nigra)* with sweet-and-sour dark red, raspberry-like fruit (the mulberry used to feed silk worms has white berries). Also spot the Judas tree *(Cercis siliquastrum)*, by origin from North America, southern Europe or China. In spring it can bear bunches of pink flowers looking like gouts of blood directly on its trunk and branches and on the flowering twigs, an example of what is called cauliflory.

Follow the path left through the garden beds and to your left is a bed of poisonous plants, of the kind that apprentice apothecaries had to learn to recognize. Lily of the valley is familiar, henbane less so. 'Poisonous in all parts, used in witchcraft'; reads its label; it was used by the British doctor, Hawley Harvey Crippen, who was hanged in 1910, to murder his wife. Some poisonous plants are extremely difficult to tell from their harmless relatives – those belonging to the cow parsley (carrot) family are a good example.

The History of Medicine

Further along the path on the left (east) side are the History of Medicine beds, with plants which first yielded now familiar manufactured drugs: meadowsweet, for example, which in the 19th century provided the base for aspirin; the autumn-flowering meadow saffron used in cancer research; and the lilac opium poppy, from whose seed capsules painkilling morphine is extracted. At that time, fields of this poppy were grown in Britain for its seeds, which were drunk with a tot of gin as a tincture known as laudanum.

Research continues, into the use of feverfew for treating migraine, for example. Living plants or dried leaves and stems are scanned by pharmaceutical companies for active chemicals which otherwise could only be fabricated by luck and at enormous expense - the chemical equivalent of finding a needle in haystack. The Physic Garden is a kind of library of plant chemistry and exchanges plants with organizations all over the world.

Crucial for this exchange in Victorian times (and for the introduction of exotic plants in general) was the discovery made by a Dr. Nathaniel Ward around 1829. He found that plants could survive healthily in a closed glass container. Exotic plants could be kept safely, almost in suspended animation, in this miniature greenhouse during long sea journeys. Before this, bringing back exotics was frustrating business, since most were sure to die on the voyage. Nowadays, with air travel, there is little problem. These wardian cases made it possible for Curator Robert Fortune to introduce thousands of tea plants from China to India, banana plants to Fiji, and Brazilian rubber plants to Malaya in 1876.

The bed with the white weather-record box at its west end is great fun. For many centuries it was believed that God created everything for a purpose and that plants had God-given signs or marks (signatures) which indicated what they would cure. For example, the scarlet pimpernel was used to cure blood disorders; while yellow marigolds were used to treat jaundice, an ailment whose main symptom is yellow skin. Perforate St John's wort, which is grown in this bed, has perforated leaves, obviously a cure for dagger wounds. Mandrake is also grown in a corner. This Mediterranean plant was held to shriek like a woman giving birth when its forked leg-like roots were pulled up, a sound which would kill anyone who heard it. It was used in love potions, but also as a painkiller in primitive surgery, and the story was probably put about by those who made a living collecting it. In the garden of folk or world medicine, opposite, grow medicinal plants from around the globe with similar stories.

The Rockery

Follow the path onto the main avenue, then walk round to the right, toward the statue of Sir Hans Sloane in wig and gown. It is a copy of the original by the Dutch-born sculptor, Michael Rysbrack (1694–1770), which was in place here in 1748 but is now in the British Museum for safety. Sloane's collection of curiosities founded the British Museum in 1753. Just before the statue to the right is the Pond Rockery, a rockery garden built in 1772 from lava brought from Iceland by the British botanist, Sir Joseph Banks (1743–1820). It is now a listed structure, that is, legally protected. It was an early attempt at a habitat garden, with plants growing in an environment that imitates their surroundings in the wild.

Now walk back towards the buildings, passing to the left a fine Indian bean tree which carries masses of white flowers in early summer. Turn left and walk past the lecture room. On its south-facing walls there are two plants to highlight because they are linked with Sir Joseph Banks: a lutea, a yellow variety of the Chinese Banksian rose, which flowers in spring; and the glorious ferny-leaved kowhai, New Zealand's national flower, which blooms in April. This is probably a grandchild of the original plant or seeds that Banks brought back from his voyage with Captain Cook in *The Endeavour*.

The Commemorative Beds

Follow the path to the end. Facing you are beds of native British plants, and to the left are the commemorative displays. Turn left into the largest of these, dedicated to Philip Miller (1691–1777), and justly so. As curator from 1722 he was in charge for nearly half the 18th century, making this the finest botanic garden in the world, overtaken by Kew only after his retirement in 1770. He wrote the prestigious *Gardener's Dictionary*, published in 1731, and his knowledge of plants was encyclopedic; as well as being versed in medicinal plants he was forever raising unusual plants from seed, or crossing them. His approach was down to earth – he kept melon seeds in his breeches pocket to help them germinate. He propagated the new seed which was sent to the cotton plantations of Georgia in the U.S.A., and he was the first European to grow the Chinese Tree of Heaven *(Ailanthus altissima)*.

Stroll through the Philip Miller garden and turn right at the bottom onto the main path through the commemorative beds, called the Historical Walk. Facing you is a smaller garden commemorating Sir Joseph Banks. His name is linked with Australia and the Australasian plants planted in it include the bottlebrushes (the flowers live up to that name). Banks gave his name to the Banksia genus of plants with their unusual 'cones'.

Grasses and woodland

So far, the plants on display have been dicotyledons (having two seed leaves). The other great class of plants is the monocotyledons (having one seed leaf), comprising grasses, irises, lilies and others. Following the path round to the left, you can see them growing on the left. In front are grasses with feathery bamboos; there is also a windmill palm, with leaves that look frayed. Beyond them are ranked beds of irises and other monocotyledons.

The Woodland Garden to the right is best explored by taking detours along the narrow, winding paths that cross it. There are snowdrops and hellebores to see in season. Near the cross paths are two pairs of maidenhair trees, the older pair up the path toward the statue. They have unusual fan-shaped leaves and were common in dinosaur times. Botanists thought them extinct until, in the 18th century they were found growing in the gardens of Chinese temples.

The Pond

Turn right out of the Woodland Garden and walk southeastward toward the pond. To the right, wild peonies are glorious from April to June, including the rare *Paeonia cambessedesii* from the Mediterranean Balearic Islands; Behind them are specialist's collections of hypericums. Among the waterside plants around the pool to the left grows the lovely native flowering rush, with clusters of magnificent dark-veined pink flowers in July and August. It is one of Britain's loveliest wild flowers. There are colonies of great crested and smooth newts, and toads are everywhere here on warm spring evenings when the visitors have gone.

Continue along the path to see the Boathouse Yard ahead to the right. This a relic of the days before the Victorians constructed the Embankment, when the usual way to reach Chelsea from London was by boat rowed by watermen.

The Systematic Order Beds

Return to the main path and turn right. This area of the garden is dedicated to plants from the Americas: South American plants nearest the Boatyard and North American plants beyond them. Behind the pond is a border of plants native to California. The walk turns left off the main path into the regular ranks of Systematic Order beds. These follow the geometric layout of the original garden and the many fragrant plants in these beds make pottering a delight. The plants are laid out in family groupings. One idea is to find a plant that you recognize and see what its (sometimes surprising) relations are. For example, the Ranunculaceae (buttercups and kin) include anemones, hellebores, larkspur and love-in-a-mist. There is a tree of note here in the set of beds nearest the path: a honey locust *(Gleditsia triacanthos)* with (unusually) spines on its trunk, from the Far East.

Following the paths leading north through the beds and then turning right will bring you back to the Students' Gate, where the walk ends.

Richmond Park

Location	About 7½ miles (12 kilometres) southwest of Charing Cross.
Transport	Richmond Station (Underground trains on the District Line; overground trains from Waterloo). Buses passing Richmond Gate: 371; Petersham Gate: 65, 415, 371; Kingston Gate: 371; Robin Hood Gate: 265; Roehampton Gate: 72, 265, R61; East Sheen Gate 33, 337. There are free car parks.
Admission	Open 07:00 hours–dusk in summer; 07:30 hours–dusk in winter. Admission is free.
Seasonal features	Pembroke Lodge rose garden in summer, autumn tree colour in the plantations. Isabella Plantation: camellias and azaleas in spring, heather garden in winter. Beware of deer in spring (with young) and autumn (the rut).
Events	Children's shows on weekdays, country days in summer, lunchtime light musical recitals at Pembroke Lodge.
Refreshments	Pembroke Lodge Cafeteria open Apr 1–Oct 31, Mon–Fri 10:00–17.30 hours, Sat, Sun 10:00–19:00 hours.

In 1625 Charles I moved to Richmond Palace, of which traces remain near Twickenham Bridge, to escape a plague gripping London. To satisfy his love of hunting, he purloined nearby land and eventually, in 1637, built a brick wall round it. As a concession to local opposition he kept the tracks and footpaths open, installing gates or ladders where they cut through the wall. This public access was challenged by a daughter of George II, but the threat was defeated when a local brewer won a test case. This right of public access ended the chase, but the park continued as a commercial source of venison and as a preserve for the shooting of hare and pheasant.

It was for the shooting as much as for the timber that plantations were laid; between 1819 and 1824 Sidmouth Wood and Spanker's Hill were among the areas planted with native trees, while in the 1830s, Isabella Plantation was enclosed and planted with oak, beech, and sweet chestnut. The shooting ended around 1904, when many of the plantations were opened to the public. During the world wars army camps were set up in the park; much land was ploughed during World War I, but recreational facilities for the public were restored afterwards.

The park today is a wonderfully open place, with sweeps of grass and bracken scattered with often ancient oak trees. It spreads along a terrace of the River

Thames, the ground falling away abruptly along most of the park's western edge. There are ponds and lakes in the park, and 15 or so plantations, or planted enclosures, some dating back a century and a half. One of these, Isabella Plantation, is a well-known area of gardened woodland. Tarmac roads cross the park and skirt it inside the perimeter wall, and a fair number of drivers use it as a through route. But there are many footpaths leading away from the roads, past herds of deer. By and large, except for the plantations and the grounds of a private residence or two, most of the park is freely accessible.

Deer are as much a feature of Richmond Park as they were when introduced 350 years ago. They are often seen grouped in sizeable herds. There are usually about 400 fallow deer and 250 red deer. Red deer are the largest wild animal native to Britain, measuring up to about 4 feet (1.2 metres) at the shoulder. The males (stags) have branching antlers which they shed in spring, growing a new, more elaborate set each year. The antlers are not a defence against predators, but with bellowing and other activities they are part of the mating display. Stags can often be seen locked in (rarely damaging) wrestling combat during the autumn rut, when the boss stags seek to claim and keep a harem. The animals become edgy and may attack dogs or people. The females (hinds) are smaller and lack antlers. Calves are born singly in May or June, when the mothers may be aggressive if approached.

Fallow deer were brought to Britain by the Romans for the hunt. A male is called a buck; a female, a doe; and the youngster, a fawn. They are smaller than red deer and usually have a dappled brown coat with white spots, although this can vary. Does can be aggressive when their fawns are young.

The number of deer in the park stays fairly constant, the year's births matching deaths from disease and those caused by vehicles and culling. By Royal warrant, culling supplies venison not only to the Royal household but also to the Prime Minister, the Lord Chief Justice and other prominent figures.

To some extent, the deer have helped create the Richmond parkland. They graze mainly on grass, but also on much else that grows. Grasses survive grazing because the fronds grow from the bottom, whereas a young sapling grows from the tips of the shoots and so is damaged by grazing. When deer are kept in large numbers, no saplings survive, the trees that die and fall are not replaced, and open parkland is the result. Young planted trees must be protected with others in a fenced plantation or with their own guard railings.

Most of the trees in Richmond Park are oaks. Growing in open surroundings they can have a broad shape, the branches spreading low, but many of Richmond's trees are trimmed up to a browse line by deer reaching up for the leaves. It used to be common practice in deer parks to farm unprotected trees (those outside the fenced plantations) by pollarding: the branches at the top of the trunk are cut off and the trunk then puts out a head of new branches, out of reach of the deer. As these thickened they were cut to provide smallwood, which was harvested for fencing poles, charcoal and other uses.

Most pollarding of park trees ended before the beginning the 20th century, so that the branches at the top subsequently thickened. With their head of heavy branches bunched at the top of the trunk, Richmond's pollarded trees are easy to recognize. As pollarded trees were no use for timber they were not usually felled. Some of these old pollarded oaks are, therefore, among the oldest trees to be seen in Richmond Park. Trees with dead, antler-like branches sticking up from a crown of foliage are also common in Richmond Park. Their staghead shape occurs when branches are killed by insect attack, fungal disease, or drought, and the tree subsequently puts out fresh healthy growth below them.

At 2,470 acres (1,000 hectares) Richmond Park is the largest park in London, and many different walks could be devised. This walk takes in two key features – the most interesting in the park – with a marvellous expedition across the open parkland between them.

THE RICHMOND PARK WALK
Start and finish Richmond Gate.
Time Allow 2½ hours.

Enter the Park through Richmond Gate, the stateliest of the park's dozen gates. Inside the park, cross the tarmac parking area and take the path which leads onward along the brow of the hill, parallel to the road. After about one-third of a mile (0.5 kilometres) you pass to the left, across the road, some old pollard oaks and the edge of Sidmouth Wood plantation, before reaching the gate of Pembroke Lodge. There is a deer grid across the gateway, so use the foot gate to the left and walk the drive with bushes on each side until you reach the lawns. At this point you can see Pembroke Lodge in front of you, but for the moment turn sharp right.

King Henry VIII Mound
The right turn takes you into a pretty rose garden – take another right turn to walk around it. The fall of the ground is now on your left, and straight ahead, past the end of the rose garden, is the first of this walk's key features: King Henry VIII's mound. This is a prehistoric burial mound, probably of Bronze Age date. Perched on the brow of the hill, it has magnificent views west, down the curve of the Thames and across to the west – to Marble Hill House *(see* page 166) and Windsor Castle 13 miles (21 kilometres) away. There is more green in this view than houses.

Take the path to the top of the mound. A broken ring of holly bushes encircles it, open to the west for the view. A keyhole shape cut out of the holly gives a view to the east, past Sidmouth Wood to the distant Post Office Tower and (on a fine day) St. Paul's Cathedral. At the top of the mound is a stone roundel set into the ground, cut with lines from a poem written in 1744 by James Thomson in which he describes this view.

Pembroke Lodge
Take time to enjoy the view and then retrace your steps, passing the rose garden again and keeping to the edge of the fall of ground. You pass some fine oak trees to arrive at the Lodge. This is rather a charming 18th-century building, white-painted and with wisteria around the entrance porch. In 1847 Queen Victoria gave it to Lord John Russell, then Prime Minister, as a grace and favour home. His

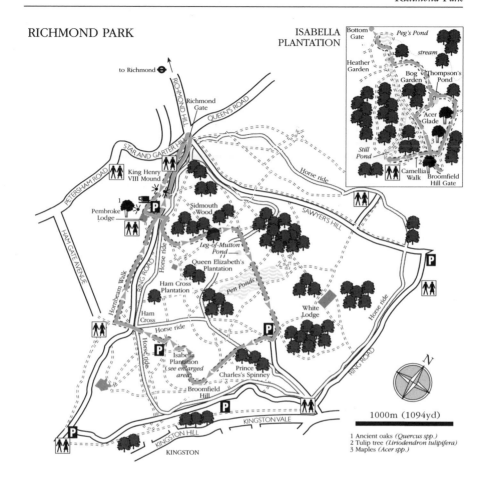

RICHMOND PARK

ISABELLA PLANTATION

to Richmond

Richmond Gate

QUEEN'S ROAD

RICHMOND HILL

STAR AND GARTER HILL

PETERSHAM ROAD

King Henry VIII Mound

Pembroke Lodge

1

Sidmouth Wood

SAWYER'S HILL

Horse ride

HAM GATE AVENUE

Hornbeam Walk

RING ROAD

Horse ride

Leg-of-Mutton Pond

Queen Elizabeth's Plantation

Ham Cross Plantation

Pen Ponds

White Lodge

Ham Cross

Horse ride

Horse ride

Isabella Plantation see enlarged area

Prince Charles's Spinney

Broomfield Hill

RING ROAD

Horse ride

KINGSTON VALE

KINGSTON HILL

KINGSTON

N

1000m (1094yd)

1 Ancient oaks *(Quercus spp.)*
2 Tulip tree *(Liriodendron tulipifera)*
3 Maples *(Acer spp.)*

Bottom Gate

Peg's Pond

stream

Heather Garden

Bog Garden

Thompson's Pond

Acer Glade

3

Still Pond

2

Camellia Walk

Broomfield Hill Gate

grandson, the philosopher Bertrand Russell (1872–1970) lived at Pembroke Lodge between 1876 and 1890. Although it is now a café, the downstairs rooms are little changed. There is an Adam fireplace in the dining room.

Cross the Lodge terraces with their superb view over the River Thames to reach the lawns on the other side, where there are some magnificent, primeval-looking oak trees, maybe 300 to 400 years old, botanical dinosaurs with twisted, contorted trunks. There is also a small gravestone of 1907 to Boy, a pet dog. There are jackdaws in these grounds, and parakeets escaped from captivity. More than 100 different bird species have been seen in Richmond Park. Leave the Lodge grounds by the gateway opposite the entrance, which leads to a car park.

The Pen Ponds

Cross the road at the car park and take the path skirting Sidmouth Wood to the left. Part of the plantation is a bird sanctuary. The rhododendrons that occupy much of the space beneath the trees were originally planted as pheasant cover. They give a showy display in May. A smaller plantation, Queen Elizabeth's Plantation, comes up on the right and when you have passed it, veer right to cross the horse ride and pass Leg of Mutton pond, a watering hole for deer. Steer toward the Pen Ponds at the bottom of the dip, probably named from deer pens. They were dug out in 1746 and are notable for their wildfowl, among them swans, grebe and gadwalls, and their fish, which include pike. Fishing permits can be obtained.

Cross the raised causeway between the two Pen Ponds and continue on the path straight ahead for about 500 yards (450 metres) until you reach a car park. On the way, on the skyline to the left, you may catch a glimpse of White Lodge through its surrounding trees. Originally an elegant, stone-clad Palladian building, it now has brick wings and other additions. It was built in 1727, the year of accession of George II, who used it as a hunting lodge, and it later became a self-contained country house for the Park's Ranger and occasional royals. Since 1955 it has been the home of the Royal Ballet School.

A narrow tarmac road at the top end of the car park is signposted 'Ham Gate' and 'Isabella'. Use this as a direction aid, for you need to steer almost due south (left) from it to cross a horse ride and then walk to the Isabella Plantation, which fills much of the horizon ahead. Follow its perimeter fence south (with Prince Charles's Spinney on the left) to arrive at the Broomfield Hill Gate.

The Isabella Plantation

Enter the Plantation – the second key feature on this walk – through this gate, erected in 1993 and adorned with a handsome nameplate in Art Deco style. Most of the tall-trunked oaks, beech and sweet chestnut were planted when the Plantation was enclosed, in 1831. Some of the common, reddish-flowered *Rhododendron ponticum* would have been planted or have seeded itself when a good bottom (thick, low cover) was encouraged for the pheasants. A second wave of planting and shaping began in the 1950s to make the Plantation more of a garden, with clearings, ponds and streams (fed by pumps from Pen Ponds). Many different rhododendrons and azaleas were planted, along with exotic trees. For example, on the spur in front of the stream just to the left of Broomfield Hill Gate is a young tulip tree *(Liriodendron tulipifera.)*

Just inside the gate to the right is a notice board giving news of things of topical and seasonal interest. In spring there are camellias and magnolias with drifts of daffodils, to be followed by bluebells. By late April and May the azaleas and rhododendrons are in flower, underpinning the fresh young tree foliage.

Euonymus (spindle), fothergillas, some deciduous azaleas, guelder roses and rowans with their bright red berries add to the autumn display of the trees in this Plantation. And in winter there are mahonias, early camellias and rhododendrons, and the bark of trees such as the snake-bark maple *(Acer rufinerve)* to admire, and winter-flowering heathers in the Heather Garden near Peg's Pond.

A stream runs straight ahead (northwest) from the Broomfield Gate, with a path on either side and frequent timber bridges between them. The stream is attractive, banked by azaleas and other flowering shrubs. In summer there is a strong show of Japanese irises, day lilies, tall *Primula floridae* and other flowers along the banks.

Some of the azaleas on the right of the central stream are among what are known as the 'Wilson 50', kurume azaleas which form the core of the National Collection. They were first collected by E.H. Wilson, a plant hunter from Kew Gardens. In his time he discovered 1,000 new ornamental plants, of which 600 species and varieties are still being grown, including 65 rhododendrons.

In early spring glimpses of colour off to the left will make you want to divert along Camellia Walk, the first path you come to on the left of the stream. It leads to Still Pond, at the end, which is shaded by shrubs and trees and rather gloomy. In autumn, a diversion along the first path on the right to Acer Glade is a must. The *Acer* species are the maple family of trees with glorious autumn colours. The path from the main stream through Acer Glade leads to Thompson's Pond, set in a wide crystal green lawn fringed by rhododendrons and other flowering shrubs. A heron is seen so frequently at this pond that it has come to be regarded as a resident. There are also resident mallards and you may see mandarin duck.

Various emergent aquatics grow along the pond's banks and in its shallows, including some native yellow flags and a handsome stand of greater reedmace *(Typha latifolia)*. These are commonly called bulrushes because the Victorian artist, Laurence Alma-Tadema (1836–1912) pictured them in his famous biblical painting of the infant Moses found among the bulrushes. Such is botany!

Thompson's Pond runs off as a stream, crossed by stepping logs, heading in the direction of Peg's Pond. Take the path alongside (this stream is also banked with shrubs) until it swings around the Bog Garden, marked by stepping logs and a stand of Gunnera. As this book went to press the Bog Garden has been overwhelmed by invasive grasses and awaited some dedicated weeding. From the Bog Garden the path rejoins the central stream. At this point the wood opens out and across the stream is a marvellous heather garden, still vivid in autumn and winter. A short distance further along is Peg's Pond, where you may see black swans. When you have reached the stream, however, you may want to spend some time wandering around this lovely plantation, or just sitting on one of the lengths of cut trunk handily positioned as seating at the foot of the trees.

When you are ready, make your way to Bottom Gate on the western side of Peg's Pond, and follow the path left to the car park for disabled drivers. From there, follow the paths west and then south (left), or walk westward across the grass to Ham Cross. Cross the road and descend toward Ham Gate, turning right to follow Hornbeam Walk back to Pembroke Lodge. The trees along this path have beech-like leaves, but fluted bark. From there follow the road north, back to Richmond Gate, where the walk ends.

The Royal Botanic Gardens, Kew

Location	About 7½ miles (12 kilometres) southwest of Charing Cross.
Transport	Kew Gardens Station (Underground District Line; overground North London Line trains). Kew Bridge Station (overground trains from Waterloo) is 5 minutes' walk via Kew Bridge, Kew Gardens Pier (boats from Westminster Pier) is 5 minutes' walk. Buses 65, 391.
Admission	Open daily from 09:30 hours–17.30 in winter, later in summer. Admission £4.50 adult, £2.50 child.
Seasonal features	Camellias and heathers in January; Crocus lawn and Rock Garden in February; cherry blossom and daffodils in March; Magnolias and spring bedding in April; bluebells and azaleas in May; Rhododendron Dell and Grass Garden in June; the giant waterlily, the Queen's Garden, and summer bedding in July; autumn colour September–November.
Events	Annual Orchid Festival in the Princess of Wales Conservatory in March.
Refreshments	The Orangery, The Bakery, and The Pavilion cafes, open daily 10:00 hours until 1 hour before the Gardens close.

In the 18th century, Kew had become a popular place for aristocratic people to live, away from the smells and diseases of London. In 1728 Queen Caroline, wife of George II, rented Kew Palace and later the Prince of Wales and his wife Augusta lived there. It was Princess Augusta who, in 1759, sowed the seeds of today's botanic gardens by laying out a 9-acre (3.6-hectare) 'exotick' garden, appointing William Aiton as head gardener, and planting an arboretum on the site. In 1767 this was named the Royal Botanic Garden. Meanwhile, Sir William Chambers (1723–96), official architect to Princess Augusta, landscaped the surrounding grounds, dotting them with temples and other follies, including, in 1761, the now-famous Pagoda. At this time, the landscape designer 'Capability' Brown (see page 10), was working in the grounds of the adjacent royal residence, Richmond Lodge. His plans of 1764 included digging out what is now the Rhododendron Dell.

When Princess Augusta died in 1771, George III merged the two estates. Their botanic importance was underlined when the botanist Sir Joseph Banks (1743–1820) became their unofficial director, beginning a collaboration with

William Aiton which lasted for 40 years. The pair sent collectors around the world in search of unusual and useful plants. Kew's bird of paradise flowers may be direct descendants of those first grown in the Gardens in 1773. At about this time the flowers called geraniums, which were, in fact, pelargoniums from Africa, were becoming popular.

Kew Gardens declined when Banks died, but in 1840 they were handed over to the government, who appointed another eminent botanist, William Hooker, director (he was eventually succeeded by his son, Joseph Hooker). This move was largely prompted by the desire to exploit to the full the new crop plants and medicinal plants to be found in the vast British Empire. Kew was to become a research centre and library for this natural wealth. Just two examples underline its importance. In 1860 the seeds of a plant known as Jesuits' Bark *(Chinchona* spp.) were collected from the slopes of the Andes Mountains in South America, and within five years 1 million trees had been distributed from special greenhouses at Kew, providing quinine to fight malaria. In the 1870s, South American rubber plants *(Ficus* spp.) grown in Kew were sent to the Far East to start the rubber industry. From 1855, Kew also supplied London's parks with new trees from its tree nursery. The last royal touch was when, in 1897, Queen Victoria donated Queen Charlotte's Cottage grounds to be added to the Gardens, stipulating that the surrounding land should be kept as a separate arboretum of native British trees, underplanted with bluebells.

Today The Royal Botanic Gardens, Kew – a charity, surviving on a basis of 70 per cent income from government grants and the remainder from admission and other charges – occupy 300 acres (121.5 hectares) planted with 30,000 different species and varieties of plants growing alongside a host of interesting buildings reflecting their history.

This is a long walk with so much to see that it could well be divided into two or three areas, each to be explored on a different day. The map on page 145 outlines the route of this walk, which takes you to features of especial interest - but there are many more to see. All are well-signposted throughout the gardens and there are maps on boards at intervals along all the paths. Exploring Kew Gardens could become a regular pleasure.

THE KEW GARDENS WALK

Start and finish: The main gate.
Time Allow 3–4 hours

Enter the Gardens through the main gate, but before proceeding to the ticket office to the left, turn to look at the handsome gateway. It was designed and erected in 1848, after the state takeover of Kew Gardens, by the architect Decimus Burton (1800–81). The double gate is for carriages and on either side of it are pedestrian entrances. The polished wrought iron is in earlier Jacobean style, with gilded highlights. The gates were once surmounted by a lion and a unicorn, but these now reside above the Lion and Unicorn gateways, respectively, in Kew Road.

From this gate stretches the Broad Walk, edged by formal beds with seasonal plantings. You will see that the trees have name-tags. Some to the left and right of this walk may be relics of Princess Augusta's arboretum. The glasshouse to the right is by John Nash. It was originally built as part of his improved scheme for Buckingham Palace, but was moved to Kew in 1836. The cylindrical pillars at each end were added from old Carlton House, which stood at the site of Duke of York's column overlooking the Mall leading to Buckingham Palace. This glasshouse is the oldest at Kew and, compared with the marvels of the Palm House and the Temperate House, it is simple, with a roof of glass tiles. It is to house a visitor centre.

Turn left into the start of Magnolia Walk and then right to reach the Orangery of 1761, a beautiful, neoclassical design by Sir William Chambers. Over to the southwest there are marvellous tree-clad vistas. It is now occupied by a shop and a tearoom, which share the interior with a marble Roman sarcophagus and 18th-century French statues of Eros and other classical figures.

Kew Palace and The Queen's Garden

At the end of the Orangery cross the southward wing of The Broad Walk and bear right across the grass toward a Tompion sundial which marks the site of the White House, a royal residence that was demolished in 1802. Tompion was a watchmaker, and the sundial has quaint instructions on how to set your watch by it. From the sundial bear northward, toward Kew Palace, the red brick house you can see ahead. (In fact, as I write, the house is invisible: the façade is undergoing restoration and is swathed in plastic sheeting, and all its gardens are closed to the public. By the time this book is in print, however, the house and its surrounding gardens should be reopened to the public).

Kew Palace is not so much a palace but an elegant merchant's house built in attractive Dutch style in red brick by one Sam Fortrey in 1631; it was once known as the Dutch house. In 1728 the Palace was leased by Queen Caroline, wife of George II, for £100 and a fat deer. It was later used by Princess Augusta, who laid out her botanic garden nearby, the kernel of today's Kew Gardens. Its rooms are furnished much as they were 200 years ago. The Queen's Garden to the west and north of the house is in 17th-century style. On the western side is a sunken nosegay garden with brick paths, a pleached laburnum walk and a fine well head from Bulstrode Park in Buckinghamshire. By late summer this garden becomes picturesquely tangled with medicinal and sweet-smelling strewing plants (pot pourri continues the tradition). Delve into the beds to read the labels enlivened with quotations from old herbals. Caraway, for example, was 'muche put among baked fruit' to help 'digest wind in them, subject thereunto'; while sunflower, its buds 'before they be flowered, boiled and eaten with butter, vinegar and pepper; are 'exceedingly pleasant meate, surpassing the Artichoke in procuring bodily lust ...'.

Walk round to the north side, facing the river, to a copy of a 17th-century geometrical parterre, laid out in 1975, extending from the house to the riverbank wall. There are termini around this garden - pillars topped by sculptured heads, a Roman garden idea popularized in the 18th century also to be seen in Chiswick House Gardens (see page 29). By the riverbank wall is a mount; climb the spiral path to the metal-framed gazebo on the top, giving prospects of the Thames beyond. This is a copy of a common 17th-century garden feature.

THE BOTANICAL GARDENS, KEW

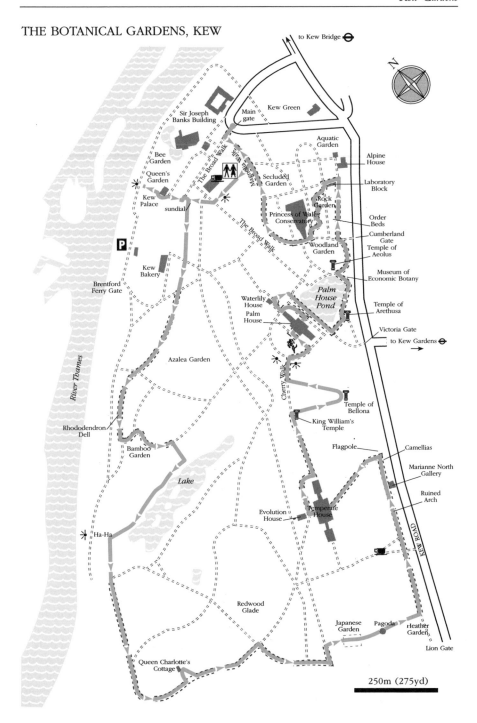

to Kew Bridge

N

Sir Joseph Banks Building

Main gate

Kew Green

Aquatic Garden

Alpine House

Bee Garden

Queen's Garden

Secluded Garden

Laboratory Block

Kew Palace

sundial

Rock Garden

Princess of Wales Conservatory

Order Beds

Cumberland Gate

Woodland Garden

Temple of Aeolus

Museum of Economic Botany

Kew Bakery

Brentford Ferry Gate

Waterlily House

Palm House

Palm House Pond

Temple of Arethusa

Victoria Gate

to Kew Gardens

Azalea Garden

Cherry Walk

The Broad Walk

Temple of Bellona

King William's Temple

River Thames

Rhododendron Dell

Bamboo Garden

Lake

Flagpole

Camellias

Marianne North Gallery

Ruined Arch

Evolution House

Temperate House

Ha-Ha

Redwood Glade

KEW ROAD

Japanese Garden

Pagoda

Heather Garden

Lion Gate

Queen Charlotte's Cottage

250m (275yd)

Follow the path leading from the mount into the Bee Garden just beyond the eastern edge of the Queen's Garden. It contains hives and is planted with lavender and sage, and is, of course, busy with bees.

The Banks Building

Leave the Bee Garden along the woodland path to your right, which leads from the Bee Garden down to a fine lawn. To your right is an armillary sundial, with metal hoops representing the equator and the paths of the zodiac. To the left there are waterside gardens and cascades, and the partly covered Sir Joseph Banks Building. This contains a botanical collection of useful plants from around the globe and an exhibition hall. Banks did much to fire enthusiasm for the exotic. He sailed with Captain James Cook (1728–79) on voyages to the Pacific – a family of Australian plants bears his name – and made several other voyages. In his time, in 1787, The Bounty under Captain William Bligh set sail to collect breadfruit in the Pacific to plant in the young West Indies colonies.

The Rhododendron Dell and the Bamboo Garden

Cross The Broad Walk, now ahead of you, then cross the grass, veering to the right of the Tompion sundial and rounding a shrubbery. Beyond it you pass The Bakery Café to the right, and take the path ahead of you. Follow it southwestward through scattered oaks, chestnuts and other trees – passing a young Azalea Garden to the left, which is well worth a diversion in spring – to the Rhododendron Dell.

The Dell, dug out in 1773, appears on 'Capability' Brown's map as a carriageway. The rhododendrons came later – they were a Victorian craze and Sir Joseph Hooker was instrumental in popularizing them; he collected 43 new species of great beauty from Nepal in the years 1847–50. They first start flowering in the Dell in January, and the rhododendrons are followed by other spectacular flowerings: a carmine magnolia in spring; and from May to late June lilacs, azaleas, late rhododendrons, and other magnolias.

From the Rhododendron Dell follow the southwestward path marked on the map on page 145 to the Bamboo Garden, which is of interest throughout the year. The leaves and stems of the bamboos are very graceful. Follow the circular path clockwise around the garden, and then turn southwest again, following the path to the left for a while, then leaving it to walk across the grass to the lake; it is just out of sight on the other side of a rise, but its position is marked by the backs of a line of lakeside benches.

The Lake

Turn right along the lakeside. Although a natural-looking lake was part of many of 'Capability' Brown's landscaping schemes, this one is not his work. It was created about a century later, in 1856–61. It has always been inhabited by unusual birds – pelicans were brought here in 1890; penguins in 1899. You may see black swans, gaudy, purple-chested mandarin duck, orange-headed pochard, and there will certainly be semi-tame black-necked Canada geese. Follow the lakeside path toward the River Thames. The trees on the northwest (right) side of the lake are native to the old world; and those on the southeast side are native to the new world – including monkey puzzle trees (Araucaria araucana) from Chile. These were first grown in Britain in the 1790s. A botanist from Kew was served some unfamiliar fruits at dinner while in Chile; he germinated the seeds on the ship home and planted them at Kew. Near the Thames there is a view across to Syon House, and, close by, a ha-ha dug in 1767.

At the top of the lake, the route turns left (south) into an area of conifers of different kinds. The paths in this area cross and recross, but are well signposted and you should follow the signs to Queen Charlotte's Cottage. The path leads deep into the conifer woodland and circles Queen Charlotte's cottage, a thatched picnic lodge built in 1772, on which restoration work began in 1996. It stands in a glade, reached by a small side path, and is surrounded by a sea of scented bluebells in late spring. The 37 acres (15 hectares) of land around it were given by Queen Victoria, and much of the area is managed as a nature reserve. Unlike other parts of Kew gardens, this is an area to explore for yourself – perhaps even to get lost in (an unusual experience so close to the centre of London). Much of it has a parkland feel, perhaps the deliberate result of 'Capability' Brown's natural landscaping.

Return to the main path and follow it through an area planted with conifers from around the world – for example, turn left at the next junction of paths and to your right, near a small pond, is a glade planted with giant redwoods *(Sequoia* spp.). The walk keeps to the perimeter path heading for the famous Pagoda and the Lion Gate. The great glass Temperate House will soon come into view to your left, along a straight path leading north. Walk a little way along this, then turn off it to reach the Japanese garden to the left.

The Japanese Gateway

An imposing gateway on a mound, a legacy of the Japan Exhibition of 1911, marks the entrance to this garden. It is made of Japanese cedar, but for protection a traditional copper roof was substituted for the cedar bark roof. The gateway is decorated with carvings of stylized, polished animals and flowers. Follow the path around the gateway on its mound past a haiku, cut in stone, but translated on a board nearby, into the garden which was completed in 1996. It is reminiscent of a Japanese tea garden, with stone-clad paths, stone lanterns, and the slight echo of water dripping into basins from bamboo pipes. A small garden opposite the gateway symbolizes activity and takes the form of water in motion in the landscape; the water is represented by raked gravel, and massive boulders symbolize mountains.

The Pagoda

Now stroll across the grass, past summer-flowering karume azaleas, to the Pagoda, which you can see clearly from the Japanese Garden. The Pagoda is one of Kew's most famous buildings. William Chambers had it built in 1761 for Princess Augusta, as a feature for visitors to discover as they promenaded around the garden. By 1763 there were 30 features in all. With ten storeys rising to 160 feet (50 metres), the Pagoda is still impressive, although it is now shorn of its chinoiserie decoration of a gilt topknot and gilt dragons at the roof angles. It was one of the first manifestations of the Chinese style in Britain, and some maintain that Chambers adopted it as a tactic in his efforts to outdo his rival, the naturalistic landscape designer, 'Capability' Brown.

Continue across the grass and you soon see the Lion Gate at the end of the path to the right. Turn left, passing to your left the Heather Garden, which is being cleared of invasive growth and restored. Further along the path you glimpse the Pavilion Restaurant set back from the path to your left. Walk on, through the Ruined Arch of stone and well-used brick. This is a mock ruin, and, like the Pagoda, it is one of the 'discoveries' erected by Sir William Chambers in 1759.

Beyond it, the path passes a charming art gallery. Its walls are crowded with 832 detailed oil paintings by a Victorian woman, Marianne North, who travelled widely to paint the plant life and scenery of several countries, among them Australia. Continue, and ahead, to the right of the path stand sturdy plantings of camellias, which flower in late winter. However, the walk takes the next path to the left, passing a mount on the right, on which stands the tallest natural flagpole in Britain at 225 feet (68 metres), cut from a 371-year-old Canadian Douglas fir. It was shipped across the Atlantic and towed up the Thames in 1958 to replace a predecessor of 1919 which had rotted.

The Temperate House

The path crosses a grove of young maples, a brilliant sight when the leaves turn colour in autumn, and you arrive at the Temperate House, This is the most elegant of the glasshouses at Kew. It was designed by Decimus Burton in 1860 but was completed years later. It is the world's largest greenhouse, containing suites of plants from subtropical and arid regions, arranged geographically. Some are endangered in their homeland (sometimes by competition from foreign plants introduced by settlers) and are being grown at Kew as a library, with an eye to their eventual reintroduction in their native habitats. One now very rare in the wild is the slow-growing dragon tree *(Dracaena draco)* from the Canary Islands. No other tree resembles it. Its bright red resin, known as dragon's blood, has been used as medicine for centuries for ailments such as loose teeth, and as a dye by Italian violin makers.

Another plant of note in the central area is the broad-trunked Chilean wine palm *(Jubaea chilensis)*, raised from seed in 1846. It is now the world's largest greenhouse plant, almost 55 feet 9 inches (17 metres) tall, and threatening the roof.

Leave the Temperate House by the west door and cross to the Evolution House, an interesting aluminium and glass construction of 1952, once the Australian House. It offers a walk through geological time, from apparently lifeless bubbling mud, and bacterial mats of 500 million years ago, past sulphur springs, to a coal-age swamp loud with frog croaks. The exhibition ends at the appearance of the first flowering plants, of which some specimens on show are live. Leave the Evolution House by the east door, turn left and walk toward a small temple you can see ahead, raised on a mound. This is King William's Temple, another of Sir William Chambers' 'discoveries'. Inside are wall plaques celebrating famous British military victories. Look back, before you enter, to admire the Temperate House, an impressive pile of architecture with the Pagoda to the left.

Continue heading north and take the next path to the right toward Victoria Gate. Chambers' handsome Temple of Bellona, built in 1760, soon comes into view to the right. It overlooks a spring crocus lawn and the Berberis Dell, berberis being a family of bushes with yellow flowers and often crimson berries. Like the mahonias that also grow in this dell, they are popular in gardens for winter interest.

Return in the direction of King William's Temple to take the northward path, now called The Cherry Walk because it has recently been planted with flowering cherries, one of the treasures discovered by the first European botanists to visit Japan. Ahead of you is The Palm House; walk along the path to the entrance halfway along its western side.

The Palm House
This glasshouse was built at the focus of Kew Gardens, and William Nesfield laid out magnificent vistas from the Rose Garden outside. The Syon Vista runs past the lake to the river (although Syon House is obscured by trees). Pagoda Vista leads the eye to Kew's famous Pagoda, surrounded by trees.

The Palm House is a magnificent Victorian creation, 360 feet (110 metres) long, 100 feet (30.5 metres) wide and 62 feet (18 metres) high, a magical construction of wrought iron and glass. Its shape is rather like an upturned ship – it was beam-built in a similar way. It was designed by the architect Decimus Burton, working with the engineer Richard Turner. The first iron rib was raised, cannily, in 1845, only months after the repeal of the glass tax levied on windows of any kind. Its original green-tinted glass was later replaced when it was realized that the vegetation did not need to be shaded. The Palm House opened in 1848, housing plants from the tropical rainforests to amaze visitors. It suffered badly from condensation, however, and in 1984 had to be closed and almost completely restored.

To a background hiss of humidifiers you can admire the coconut palm *(Cocos nucifera)*, the tall-trunked royal palm *(Roystonia regia)*, and the banana *(Musa* spp.), which has a very strange-looking end to its fruiting stem, rubber plants *(Ficus* spp.), and breadfruit *(Artocarpus* spp.). The giant bamboo is fascinating; a board alongside registers its growth - 3 feet (1 metre) in one August week, for example. The oldest plant in this greenhouse, one Encephalartos, arrived in 1775. A circular staircase leads up to a roof walkway for a canopy view of this jungle. Since heat rises, it is really torrid at the top, with water dripping from the glass roof onto viewers. In the basement is a Marine Display, with coral reef fish, a mangrove swamp tank, and a tank of living kelp and other British seaweeds.

When you have explored The Palm House, exit through the small door in the northwest wing and walk across to the Waterlily House, the small building directly ahead, also the work of Richard Turner and built in 1852. It houses lovely bluish, lilac, and white lotus blooms from Egypt and Asia. The sacred lotus growing at centre of the pool has a reddish tint. There is also a stand of papyrus from Egypt, and a loofah plant – the dishcloth gourd among the climbers on the walls.

Take the path to the left out of the Waterlily House and stroll to the Palm House Pond. Formal beds rather in the Italian style popular in the 1800s front the east side of the Palm House. Note the Queen's Beasts ranged along the Palm House, carved in stone for the coronation of Elizabeth II in 1953, among them the lions of England and of Mortimer, and the dragon of Wales.

The Palm House Pond has as its centrepiece a fountain and a statue of 1826 depicting Hercules and Achelous, a river god, which is apparently favoured as a perch by prospecting herons when the visitors have gone home. On the bank grow a couple of swamp cypresses from the southern U.S.A. Stroll clockwise around the banks and you see, standing guard alongside steps down to the water, a pair of kylins which probably date from the 18th century. They are Chinese mythological beasts looking rather like lions, of the kind seen in the Imperial Palace in Beijing. Almost opposite, across the path, is another of Chambers' temples, dedicated to Arethusa. She was the Greek nymph who turned into a spring of water. In this Temple is a record of the names of the staff of Kew Gardens who died in the two world wars.

The Specialist Gardens

The path to the right on the east end of the pond was temporarily closed as this book when to press, while the building you see to the left, the former Museum of Economic Botany, was being restored. This building once displayed curious fruits and botanical specimens brought for the first time from the ends of the Empire. Its exhibition was boosted when the East India Company made over its plant collections to Kew Gardens soon after the Indian Mutiny in 1857. Temporarily, you must now retrace your steps round the pond and follow the path to Cumberland Gate. To the left is the delicate, round Temple of Aeolus (the Winds). Atop quite a high mound and partly obscured by bushes and trees, it is another of the features built by William Chambers when working for Princess Augusta.

Turn left opposite Cumberland Gate and you have to your left the Woodland Garden. A compromise between formality and informality, it is often voted Kew's most attractive area. It is not hidden in gloomy shadow, but is full of woodland plants in sun-dappled settings. There are often drifts of colour – for example, of the spectacular, shade-tolerant white or pinkish *Trillium* spp., wood lilies from North America. The Himalayan blue poppy (Mecanopsis spp.), the Christmas rose, and other hellebores also grow here. Sprinklers are often active in this garden, keeping the ground moist, a reminder that the soil underlying Kew is poor for plants in many ways. Sprinklers may need to be turned on even after recent rain.

Turn right to walk through the Order Beds. These echo the style of the old physic gardens, planted up to teach apprentice apothecaries to recognize medicinal (and poisonous) plants and their look-alikes and relatives. There is a bed of poppies, for example, from the familiar red sometimes seen in grain fields to white, lilac, and the yellow long-horned poppy of Mediterranean beaches. One idea is to pick out a flower you recognize and see what its close relations are.

The Order beds are backed by a laboratory block, where at the start of World War II rose hips were found to be a valuable source of vitamin C. Schoolchildren collected them from the hedgerows as part of the war effort. Beyond the laboratory, to the northeast, is an Aquatic Garden, laid out in 1909, with some now-rare marsh plants and splendid collection of hardy water lilies. The imaginative pyramidal building east of it is the Alpine House, designed in 1981. As well as the Arctic-alpine collection, it houses plants such as giant lobelias from equatorial mountains.

Bear left, now, round the Grass Garden. It is botanically interesting, with examples of early grain crops planted by the first farmers thousands of years ago, and of subtropical specimens. It is more attractive than its name suggests. The leaf colours and seed heads of the edible cereals are often very decorative, and ornamental specimens range from giant growths of pampas grass to beds of delicate, low, tufted grasses.

Continue, and you pass to your left The Rock Garden. It was laid out in the 1880s, using rubble from the demolished White House which stood opposite Kew Palace, but it now has outcrops of Sussex sandstone, a cascade, streams bordered by marsh plants such as the marsh marigold and brooklime, and peaty gullies for bog plants. There are charming corners busy with bees, and in some places plants spread informally across the bare gravel. They are arranged by origin according to a plan displayed in front of the cascade.

The Princess of Wales Conservatory

Past the Rock Garden take the path to the left into the Princess of Wales Conservatory, a must on any visit to Kew Gardens. It houses plants from ten climate zones, ranging from cacti native to hot, dry deserts to plants from humid tropical rainforests, such as the giant Amazonian waterlily. This was first raised successfully at Kew in 1849. Each December it is grown anew from a pea-sized seed, and by August the leaves are nearly 6 feet (2 metres) across. In June, it is ready to produce a flower, which, white at first, then becoming pink, then deepening to red, lasts for about 48 hours. A collection of carnivorous plants grows in another climatic zone, and plants from Madagascar, such as the moth-pollinated *Angraecum,* an orchid, occupy a special area. Three-quarters of the plants on this island, which has been separated from the African continent for 70 million years, are endemic – found nowhere else. Below these zone rooms, down a slope, is an aquarium.

The Secluded Garden

From the Princess of Wales Conservatory, the path curves right, and on the right you soon come across the unexpected Secluded Garden. It makes a delightful end to the walk, and you may be glad to rest beside its unusual, spiral-plated fountain, or to wander round the collection of ferns in its small summer house, which is cool with water and has handsome wooden seating. When you are rested, exit north along Magnolia Walk to the main gate, where the walk ends.

Ham House Gardens

Location	About 9 miles (14.5 kilometres) west of Charing Cross.
Transport	Richmond Station (overground and District Line Underground). Buses 65, 371, 415 (walk past the German school at Petersham). St. Margaret's Station (overground trains from Richmond) is 1 mile (1.6 kilometres) walk away, crossing the Thames via a ferry. There is free parking at the foot of the drive.
Admission	Open Mon–Thur, Sat, Sun 10:30–18:00 hours or dusk. Admission is free.
Seasonal features	Seasonal interest through the year.
Events	Summer concerts in the gardens.
Refreshments	Garden Tearoom open Mon–Thur, Sat, Sun 10:30–18:00 hours. Orangery Restaurant open Mar–Oct from 12:30 for lunch.

Ham House is an outstanding Jacobean mansion built in the 17th century in what was then fast becoming a very fashionable purlieu, 10 miles (6.5 kilometres) from the centre of London and with convenient river transport. The house was built in 1610 for Sir Thomas Vavasour, but was remodelled in the 1630s by William Murray, later Earl of Dysart. On his death it passed to his daughter, Elizabeth Dysart, a woman 'restless in her ambition, profuse in her expense and of a most ravenous covetousness'. When married to the first Duke of Lauderdale, one of the Cabal (key members of the court of Charles II), the couple extended and luxuriously refurnished the house, and much of the magnificent interior is their work.

The house remained in the hands of the Dysart family until Sir Lyonel Tollemache (a Dysart cousin) made it over to the National Trust in 1948. By then the gardens had run to seed. Only traces remained of what the ambitious Lauderdales had created, a Prince's palace (in the view of diarist John Evelyn) with 'Parterres, Flower Gardens, Orangeries, Groves, Avenues, Courts, Statues, Perspectives, Fountains, Aviaries'. There remained only tangles of sycamore and rampant rhododendrons, not to mention unfilled bomb craters from World War II.

Gifts and donations made it possible in 1975 to begin restoring the gardens to how they were three centuries ago, as part of the Trust's contributions to European Architectural Heritage Year. A 1671 survey plan made by the Lauderdale garden designers John Slezer and Jan Wyck provided the guide for the restoration, and basically much of what remains is a simplified form of a Dutch garden (known as the New Mode at the time). Further restoration is planned for the later 1990s.

Plate 22: *The old pollarded oak trees in Richmond Park's 150-year-old plantations are among the oldest trees to be seen in the park (see page 137).*

Plate 23: *The Isabella Plantation (see page 140) is a famous enclosure of gardened woodland among the sweeps of open grass in Richmond Park.*

Plate 24: *The Japanese Gateway in Kew Gardens is a scaled-down copy of the Gateway of the Imperial Messenger, the entrance to a Buddhist Temple in Kyoto (see page 147).*

Plate 25: *Cones of box accent the geometrical Knot Garden at Ham House (see page 155), in much the same way as embroidery can be sprigged with French knots.*

Plate 26: *The walled flower gardens at Hampton Court (see page 159) provide a sheltered environment for a unique variety of flowers, and the walls encourage climbers.*

Plate 27: *William III and Queen Mary created sunken gardens in the former fish ponds which once supplied the kitchens of King Henry VIII (see page 163).*

Plate 28: Down the centre of Henry VIII's Privy Garden at Hampton Court are turf-cut patterns, and there are statues on the grass (see page 163).

Plate 29: The tall limes and elegant plane trees of the east and west shrubberies behind arcs of wall frame Marble Hill House and hide its service wing (see page 168).

THE HAM HOUSE GARDENS WALK
Start and finish The Main Gate.
Time Allow 1¼ hours.

Today, the main approach to Ham House is along an avenue of young lime and other trees, the youngest planted nearest Ham Street. Between this avenue and the River Thames to your left is the North Meadow. If you look straight ahead you can see the Star & Garter home for the disabled on the brow of Richmond Hill. A second avenue of trees leads from the main gate at the front of the house to the river bank. This was originally a main avenue because (tides willing) a barge rowed by watermen would have been a customary method of travelling from London. There are some old lime trees in this avenue, although one or two young ones now fill gaps in the procession. Turn right to face the house and walk up to the gate.

The Main Gate
Begin the walk by looking at the iron gates and stone piers of the main gateway to the house, just on the right of the avenue of trees. They were designed by Sir William Bruce, a Dysart cousin, and erected in 1671. The piers were made with stone brought from Lauderdale quarries in Scotland on the Firth of Forth. Celia Fiennes, that doughty explorer of Britain in the late 17th century, noted that iron gates such as this should be 'painted proper. Blew with gilt tops'. And the ironwork is again dark blue – not black – today. The urns date from 1671 and the carved pineapples on the pedestals along the edge of the ha-ha, or ditch, from 1799. They are fashioned from Coade stone, an artificial stone made in the 18th century to a very profitable and highly secret recipe in workshops in Fulham. Statuary was made up of pieces fired like pottery in a kiln; clay, flint and ground glass (to melt and bind the mixture) were among the constituents. The railings date from the 20th century.

Look to left and right of the gate and you see that the boundary of the estate this side of the house – the northern edge of the gravel walk – is also marked by a ha-ha. This was a ditch, a device for embracing the view, a way of bringing it into the garden without the need of a fence to keep out deer, grazing cattle, or even peasants, maybe. Wild flowers grow on the slopes of the ha-ha and wild grasses are usually also left to grow tall and seed. This is a modern ecological vogue.

The Entrance Forecourt
Walk south across the broad gravel walk that runs parallel to the front façade of the house, and into the forecourt beside the front door. Until the 1975 restorations tall shrubbery all but obscured 22 hollow heads cast in lead set in niches in the curving walls. Today the heads look very dramatic when they catch the angled sun. Originally, the walls extended further and housed 38 busts in all, and the others are now placed in niches decorating the front of the house. They portray kings Charles I and Charles II, and many Roman emperors and their wives. They look well against the damson-coloured brick.

'Two carv'd wainscot benches' referred to in a bill of 1674 are in the 'cloisters' (the covered areas) to each side of the entrance to the house. The armrests sport

HAM HOUSE GARDENS

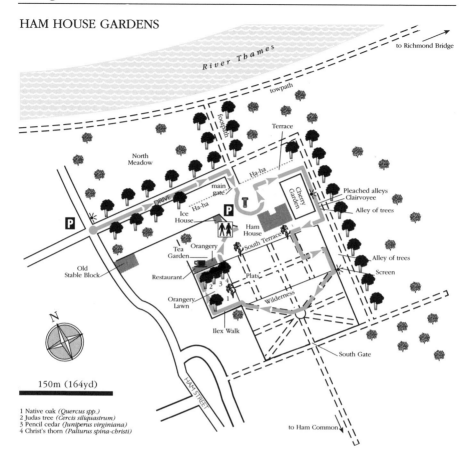

River Thames

to Richmond Bridge

towpath

Terrace

North
Meadow

footpath

Ha-ha

main
gate

DRIVE

Ha-ha

Ice
House

P

P

P

Cherry
Garden

Pleached alleys
Clairvoyee

Alley of trees

Ham
House

South Terrace

Tea
Garden

Orangery

Plats

Restaurant

Old
Stable Block

Alley of trees

Screen

2 3 4

1

Orangery
Lawn

Wilderness

Ilex Walk

South Gate

N

150m (164yd)

1 Native oak *(Quercus spp.)*
2 Judas tree *(Cercis siliquastrum)*
3 Pencil cedar *(Juniperus virginiana)*
4 Christ's thorn *(Paliurus spina-christi)*

HAM STREET

to Ham Common

charming cherubs, reclining curled. The central figure of the entrance forecourt is a Coade stone river god ('Old Father Thames', some call him) placed in this spot in 1799; he looks better the part when dampened by the modern lawn sprinkler. There is a similar figure, but in bronze, at Somerset House in London; in this forecourt he faces away, bottom toward the front door.

The topiary in this forecourt was planted by the National Trust: the clipped drums of bay, cones of yew, Portuguese laurel, and low box edging hedges reflect the late-19th century fashion.

Before moving on, stand back and look at the house. It was a favourite of Charles II, who was a frequent visitor, and it remains an authentic period piece. Although the bays on this north face look Victorian, they date from 1610.

Turn and walk back along the eastern side of the forecourt, and turn right along the wide gravel terrace that leads to the Cherry Garden. Ahead, beyond the boundary wall where the avenue of lime trees now runs, there once stretched a 'Melancholy Walk'. Running along the east side of the gardens, it was planted with trees in quincunx order – that is, in fives to a right-angle and diagonal pattern, so that the line patterns changed as you walked. It was a trick designed to aid contemplation – an old meaning of the word 'melancholy' in this context. This walk originally ended in mounds, or viewing platforms, and the one at this end also had a 'banqueting house', or garden house where light refreshments might be taken. This was a two-storied building, according to a mason's bill of 1672. If you walk right to the end of the ha-ha on this side, you see that it is armoured with lethal-looking iron spikes and saw-edges.

The Cherry Garden
Turn right into the Cherry Garden, which was restored in 1976 from the 1671 plans, although perhaps to a less elaborate design than the original. You enter a vaulted corridor of pleached hornbeam (to pleach is to interlace tree branches). Hornbeam often keeps its dead leaves in winter, so offering all-year protection. It is underplanted with box hedges. There is another, similar corridor of pleached hornbeam on the opposite side of the Cherry Garden by the house.

Between the two there is now a geometrical knot garden of diamond-shaped box-edged beds filled with clipped Dutch lavender (which is busy with buzzing skipper butterflies and bees in summer) and silvery dwarf cotton lavender, of acid hue, the rows of trimmed round heads creating (in a similar way to the Melancholy Walk) changing patterns as you walk by. And the whole display is accented with cones of box, much as embroidery can be sprigged with French knots. Note the gravel paths of this knot garden.

Fruit would have featured in a Dutch garden, and presumably cherries were espaliered against the warm brick wall in this garden, to explain the name, but old records mention only shrubs, flowers and flower pots, and vases. On the south side there is a sundial (with the old-fashioned IIII instead of IV) and there are plans to place statuary at the centre of this garden.

Walk to the end of the pleached hornbeam corridor and leave the Cherry Garden, passing to the right a trimmed alley leading to a side door to the house. You emerge on to a long terrace which runs along the south side of the house.

The South Terrace
This broad terrace ends at a railed break in the brick wall, which gives a view out toward Richmond Hill to the east. This architectural device, called a clairvoyee (literally, an 'opening to a view') predated the ha-ha, which opened the view entirely. There are more of those symbolic stone 'pineapples' along the terrace front. Pineapples at that time were a truly exotic fruit, and only a magnate with a full complement of gardeners and 'stoves' (heated glasshouses) could hope to ripen them. (There is a marvellous painting of 1670 by an unknown artist, of the royal gardener presenting one to Charles II). However, these Coade stone 'pineapples' are based on the pine cone of the Mediterranean umbrella pine, which was a Roman fertility symbol. They were called pineapples, and gave their name to the fruit.

Walk right toward the centre of the terrace and down the steps, passing more pineapples, to the beds at its foot. These have an interesting, mainly green, plant texture – grape vines clothe the drop, with sage and rosemary of the time, while other Mediterranean shrubs also flourish in the shelter of the borders: cistus with papery pink and white flowers, myrtle and scorpion senna, for example. There is an unusual chaste tree with lavender and white flowers in autumn, and magnolias along the main terrace. Where there are now terracotta vases along the outer edge of the terrace there were probably ornaments in stone or Coade stone; and maybe also oranges and other shrubs in white-painted tubs (oleander and pomegranate were mentioned in 1682).

The terrace has an open view across a grid of turf 'plats' (plots) separated by wide gravel paths. These eight plats were reshaped, in 1976, out of what had become one lawn. In the days of the Lauderdales these would have been busy with statues and other ornaments, and there are plans to replace some of these.

Follow the path to the east of the plats, where it runs in an informal alley of oak, sweet chestnut and other trees, while tightly pruned pear and other fruit trees hug the wall. There is also a fig tree. Another handsome wrought iron screen interrupts the wall at the end of the path, giving views out. From this spot, looking back to the house, you can gauge the real scale of the terrace and also notice that the two ends of the H-shaped Jacobean house have been infilled later to create more rooms. The infill has early examples of sash windows.

The Wilderness

From the screen, follow the path diagonally into the Wilderness. This is a unique example of a popular, 17th-century garden feature. It was not wild in the modern sense, but rather formal, its hedges creating garden 'rooms' entered by 'doorways'. It was not a maze; the alleys are quite wide. Writers of the day called the spaces 'cabinets', 'green arbours', and 'galleries'; they were seen as being an out-of-doors version of the more private rooms of the house, suitable for politics, chats, and even flirtations.

Before the restorations started in the 1970s there was nothing to be seen of the Wilderness but a thicket of trees and bushes. This was clear-felled and the original pattern of paths was replanted with hornbeam hedges set at intervals with taller field maples, a native tree. The four round summer houses, reproducing those seen in an early engraving, are white-walled, painted blue inside, roofed by wooden tiling topped by a gilded ball. There are wild flowers growing here and the wild grasses are left uncut in summer, except along the paths. As a result, you may see blue as well as brown butterflies: they are grassland butterflies.

This Ham Wilderness was centrally aligned to the house and to the grass plots in front of it. Walk along the path to its hub, an open space set round with a few white-painted cockleshell-backed seats, copies of the originals. There were also statues and boxes of flowering shrubs.

From this central arena you can see the fine south gateway to the left, its iron-work also painted in a copy of the 17th-century 'Smalt' blue. The elaborate coat of arms on the overthrow to the gates is of the Tollemache family, the motto (translated as 'No man can harm me with impunity') is of the Order of the Thistle. Beyond the gates, focused on the south front of the house, a great avenue of trees stretched as far as Ham Common, and traces of it can still be seen.

The Orangery Garden

Turn along the diagonal path to the right, leading westward through the Wilderness, which ends at a fine gateway leading into the southern end of the Orangery garden. The gateway, a recent copy, is gilded in places; notice the gilt flowers on top of it. Proceed along the Ilex Walk, which stretches ahead of you. Ilex trees or holm oaks (*Quercus ilex*) are evergreen oaks from the Mediterranean; they keep their dense foliage in winter. These trees first became popular in the 18th century.

Turn to admire the fine sweep of the Orangery Lawn, with a tall native oak at its centre. The lawn is edged with monochromatic rose beds – one yellow, one pink, one red, and so on. Old plans show that this garden was once wholly compartmented with plant beds and was probably a kitchen garden, and there are hopes that part of it might eventually be restored. Against the shelter of the east wall is a border with an interesting medley of herbaceous plants, including an almost black hollyhock, irises and sweet peas. These flowers are often cut for the house.

The Orangery

Turn to the right at the top of the Orangery Lawn and onto the Orangery Terrace, and walk along it. The Orangery is in rich, mellow red brick, clad in wisteria, and was probably built for the Lauderdale gardens in the 1670s. It is one of the oldest orangeries to be seen in Britain. Its west end has been converted into a café, The Garden Room. On the north side of the Orangery a door leads to a summer tea garden; and as you walk along the Terrace you will see that its east part is a restaurant. Inside there are sets of sculptured busts, 19th-century copies of antique models. Orangeries such as this were originally heated by stoves and were used to protect delicate shrubs in winter, and to force flowers to early blooming. Today in summer the Orangery terrace is set with lemon or orange bushes in tubs.

At the front of the terrace are three trees of great interest. At the west end is a Judas Tree *(Cercis siliquastrum)* from the Mediterranean, so called because Judas Iscariot is said to have hung himself on one. The central tree is a rather distressed pencil cedar *(Juniperus virginiana)* so called because it was widely grown for making wooden pencils. It is overlooked in all guide books to Ham House, yet it is especially interesting because it was introduced to Britain from North America about 1660. At the east end of the terrace is a sprawling Christ's thorn *(Paliurus spina-christi),* a very spiny Mediterranean tree, with small yellow–green flowers in July, and unusual, hatlike seeds.

The Ice House

Leave the Orangery Garden by the corner gateway. You have to your right the west courtyard to Ham House; there is a handsome lead water butt on the right. From the courtyard you can see the domed roof of the old ice house. It was built in brick, but coated in concrete during World War II, when it was used as an air raid shelter. Its entrance (which is locked – and you can't make out anything much through the small grille) is alongside the gateway leading to the front of the house and the Main Gate, where the walk ends.

Hampton Court Gardens

Location	About 10 miles (16 kilometres) southwest of Charing Cross.
Transport	Hampton Court Station (overground trains from Waterloo and Clapham Junction). Bus 11, 216, 411, 415, 431, 440, 451, 461, 513, 726. Boat from Westminster Pier.
Admission	Open daily 08:00 hours–dusk; Privy Garden 08:00–17:50 hours. Admission to the gardens is free; to the Privy Garden £2 in summer.
Seasonal Features	The Wilderness in spring; Flower Gardens in spring and summer; Privy Garden in summer; Great Vine in September.
Events	Guided tours of the gardens (£3–£5), horse-drawn carriage rides, talks by the Keeper of The Great Vine (Tue, Thur 10:00 hours). The Hampton Court Flower Show is held in July in Home Park.
Refreshments	Tiltyard Tearoom open daily 10:00–17:00 hours.

The Hampton Court estate was acquired in 1514 by Cardinal Wolsey, said to be 'the proudest prelate that ever breathed'. He built himself a magnificent palace which, in 1525, he thought politic to hand over to Henry VIII, although this did not prevent the king from stripping his offices from him. Henry set about making the place still more grand, adding the Great Hall, for example. It remained a royal palace in Elizabethan times and beyond; Oliver Cromwell stayed at Hampton Court, and after the Restoration of the monarchy Charles II put in hand changes to the park, adding the Long Water and the radiating avenues. William and Mary made it one of their main residences in 1689, when the Fountain Garden facing the park was at its most elaborate. There were also plans for Sir Christopher Wren (1632–1723) to completely rebuild the palace more comfortably, but in the event, he made only a few changes, adding the East Court and its garden face.

In the 18th century, 'Capability' Brown, famous for his gardens planned to look like natural landscapes, became Master Gardener. This may seem an odd choice to have made for grounds whose style was strictly formal. In the event, however, he changed little. Hampton Court Palace – still one of the most magnificent palaces in Britain – and its grounds were opened to the public by Queen Victoria in 1838.

This walk covers the main features of the gardens around the Palace, Beyond them is The Home Park, which merits a continuation of the garden walk. The access gates to Home Park are at the bridges across the semicircular canal, shown on the map. The Home Park's main features are the Long Water (¾ mile long and 150 feet wide/1.4 kilometres long by 45 metres wide), and avenues set out by Charles II in the 1660s. The deer 'crates' or guards round the newly planted trees resemble those used in the 17th century. Down the northern part, Henry VIII created a mile–long 'course' for the sport of deer-coursing (usually hunting by hounds alone). Later 'chaise ridings' were laid out so that gout-ridden Queen Anne could follow the hunt. There is a private residence, Stud House, in Home Park, and a golf course which was laid out in 1895.

Some features of Bushy Park, adjoining Hampton Court, are also shown on the map on the following page. One of the highlights is the Diana Fountain, the centrepiece of the Chestnut Avenue and placed there in 1713. The Chestnut Avenue was planted at a slightly earlier date – it was intended to be the grand approach to a new palace, but the plan never matured. The Waterhouse Woodland gardens are notable for their massive plantings of rhododendron and azaleas, in full flower in late May, and glades resembling the Isabella Plantation in Richmond Park *(see* page 140). The bog garden, for example, is planted with gunnera, skunk cabbage, giant plantain, iris, hostas, and rodgersias, and there is a fritillary meadow near Fisher's Pond.

THE HAMPTON COURT PALACE GARDENS

Start and finish The main entrance drive.
Distance 1.5 miles (2 kilometres). *Time* Allow 1¼ hours.

Enter the palace grounds through the main gate, but instead of walking along the drive turn left into the car park and walk across it. It occupies part of what was Henry VIII's tiltyard, an area used for jousts on horseback (the meaning of 'tilt') and for archery and other sports and pastimes. Much of Wolsey's older outer walls remain, but Henry added a wall dividing his tiltyard from the surrounding garden area, which later became the Wilderness. The cross walls were built in the time of William and Mary, when the area was divided up as kitchen gardens. In the 19th century it was also producing bedding plants (a Victorian passion) for the Great Fountain Garden. Only during the 20th century did it assume the look it has today.

The flower garden

Pass through the gate in the car park's northwest corner into a delightful walled garden with general and herbaceous beds. Take time to wander among these colourful beds, which many consider among Hampton Court's most successful gardening achievements. They date from about 1950. Leave this flower garden by the gate in its southeast corner and pass into an equally delightful rose garden to the right of it. The walk takes you the long way round to enable you to savour the delicious scents exuded by the many different species and varieties filling the beds and planted against the walls – which encourage climbers.

When you have completed the circuit of the rose garden, you find yourself walking alongside the eastern wall. The gate ahead leads to the Tiltyard Restaurant. The

HAMPTON COURT PALACE GARDENS

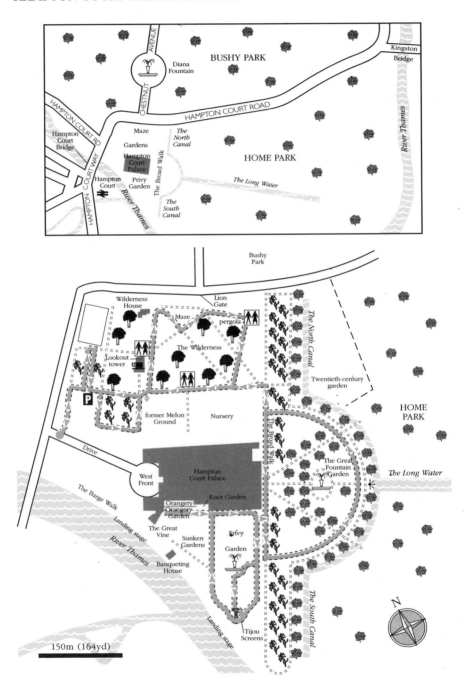

BUSHY PARK

Diana Fountain

CHESTNUT AVENUE

Kingston Bridge

HAMPTON COURT RD

HAMPTON COURT WAY

Hampton Court Bridge

HAMPTON COURT ROAD

Maze

Gardens

Hampton Court Palace

Hampton Court

Privy Garden

The North Canal

HOME PARK

The Broad Walk

The Long Water

The South Canal

River Thames

Bushy Park

Wilderness House

Lion Gate

Maze

pergola

The Wilderness

Lookout tower

P

former Melon Ground

Nursery

The North Canal

Twentieth-century garden

HOME PARK

Drive

West Front

Hampton Court Palace

Knot Garden

The Broad Walk

The Great Fountain Garden

The Long Water

The Barge Walk

Landing stage

Orangery

Orangery Garden

The Great Vine

Sunken Gardens

Privy

Garden

Banqueting House

River Thames

Landing stage

Tijou Screens

The South Canal

N

150m (164yd)

plot to the left beyond it has been grassed and planted with ornamental trees. Along the wall to your right there once stood a line of heraldic beasts, now gone.

Go through the gate and turn left along the path on the other side. You pass an old lookout tower on the left which can be seen rising above the café on the other side of the wall. This was one of five built in 1537 to overlook Henry's tiltyard.

The Wilderness

The grassy area to your right is the Wilderness. In Tudor times this area was a kind of orchard planted with fruit trees and other trees, such as oaks and hollies, but in 1699 under William and Mary it was replanned as a Wilderness. The term did not then mean a wild place, but a geometric pattern of paths and hedges creating room-like areas outdoors. A similar wilderness has been restored at Ham House (*see* page 156). This garden feature fell out of fashion in the 18th century and Hampton Court's Wilderness was neglected, becoming rather overgrown. In the course of this century the area has been cleared of scrub and planted with many exotic trees. In spring the grass becomes a carpet of nodding daffodils and bluebells.

Follow the path past the tower, and to the left, just before you reach the perimeter wall, is Wilderness House, a solid brick building of the late 17th century, with a long, narrow walled garden joining it to Wilderness Cottage, once a coach house. This is where 'Capability' Brown lived when, in 1764, he became Master Gardener at Hampton Court. Wilderness House was a mark of the esteem in which he was held, and his annual salary of £1,107 plus £100 for growing pineapples was high by the standards of the time.

The Maze

Turn right now to see, ahead of you, Hampton Court's celebrated Maze. Like the Wilderness of which it forms part, the Maze dates from the late 17th century, when it would have been planted with hornbeam hedges (they keep their leaves in winter); today it is mainly yew. It was probably designed by Henry Wise who later, in 1702, became royal gardener to Queen Anne. It is a puzzle maze: there is a knack to finding your way around it and you can find yourself lost in dead ends. This Maze is one of the most famous in Britain and has been visited by many well-known people; for example, in 1828 the novelist Sir Walter Scott and the poet William Wordsworth met there with their families. It still draws crowds.

Just past the top of the Maze, to the left, you come to the Lion Gate. The stone piers date from 1713–14, and the iron gates from a later visit by George I. Wren's plans for the new palace included a new main entrance facing north, hence the grand approach avenue in what is now Bushy Park, and these gates suggest that the idea was still alive at this later date.

From the Lion Gate, the path takes you through a shady planted pergola and then veers right across The Wilderness. The name-tags invite you to look more closely at the trees. Behind the shrubbery at the end of the path is the maintenance depot and about 1 acre (0.4 hectares) of glasshouses, producing over 100,000 bedding plants a year, all destined for the gardens. Many of the plants, propagated by cuttings rather than seed, have historic links with the Palace grounds: the ivy-leaf geranium 'Madame Crousse' has been raised at Hampton Court for most of the 20th century; and the heliotrope 'President Garfield' is another example.

Broad Walk

Now turn left, walk to the southeastern corner of the Wilderness, and pass through the gate into the Broad Walk. This magnificent half mile stretches past the Real (Royal) Tennis Court and the front of the Palace to the River Thames. Until 1689 a protective moat ran along it in the shadow of the Palace walls, and the park grass lapped right up to it. Today it is a gravel path bordered most of the way with a classic herbaceous flower border, 10 feet (3 metres) wide – a long garden, in effect. This is a Victorian addition dating to 1890, although it was grassed over in World War I and replanted afterwards. In the summer, horse-drawn carriages offer visitors a tour of this walk and of the Great Fountain Garden as was the fashion three centuries ago.

Stroll along toward the end of the palace. Immediately to your right is a kiosk where you buy a ticket to enter the Privy Garden. Once through the gate, climb the steps to the left which lead to the top of a bank, where you have a good viewpoint into an ornamental garden.

The Privy Garden

In the days of Henry VIII, the Palace's intimate gardens lay in this area, between Palace and river. There was a mount with a lookout, a pond yard for supplying fish, but also the king's privy (private) garden for the exclusive use of the royal family and their close court. The Privy Garden was entirely unlike any modern garden, chequered with squares of turf, brick dust and sand, and even black iron scrapings supplied by local blacksmiths, while carved unicorns and other heraldic beasts bristled over poles and railings painted green and white. There were 20 sundials, but few flowers – lavender, rosemary, thyme maybe, and roses, and clove-scented 'gillyflowers' (usually carnations or wallflower).

This symbolic garden was later simplified into grass plots set with statues, one of which, Arethusa, was brought to this garden from Somerset House by Oliver Cromwell. She is now the centrepiece of the great Diana Fountain in Bushy Park. Under William and Mary, the grass plots were converted into *gazon coupé*, that is, patterned turf, and later intricate dwarf box borders were added, with yews and variegated hollies clipped into obelisks and globes, and bulbs and flowers planted. Apparently, Henry Wise played a hand, for his bills of 1702 survive: '32 large round headed Holleys at 50s each, 76 yews for ye sloopes at 5s each, 161 Standard honeysuckles in Basketts at 2s 0d'.

This garden grew out under Capability Brown to a virtual shrubbery. But recent archaeological investigation has revealed the original design, and the garden you are now looking at is its recreation. In 1994–5, the scrub and heavy growth was cleared. There were protests against the felling of 38 trees, by then nearly 300 years old, but the result is a marvellous evocation of a past age.

Stroll halfway along the walkway and descend the steps to your right. Take the path to the left, then turn right to walk through the beds into the centre: 30,000 small box were used to sculpture the flowing parterre beds; and curling borders of earth have been set with clumps of auriculas, daffodils, tulips, small, obelisk-trimmed topiary, and mop-headed hollies standing sentry. Flowers popular in the past have been replanted, including descendants of 17th-century hyacinths and the single red-flushed yellow tulips *Tulipa* 'Grand Duc' – no longer commercially available – from a bulb gene bank in the Netherlands. There are patterns cut in the turf and statues on the grass. It is a superb reconstruction.

The Tijou Screens

Now walk south to the river end of the garden where the Tijou screens, one of the many marvels of Hampton Court gardens, have been reerected. They are screens of wrought and beaten iron made as gates for the Great Fountain Garden by the French-born metalworker Jean Tijou *(fl.*1689–1712), who produced ironwork for Christopher Wren for St. Paul's Cathedral. The English art critic Sir Sacheverell Sitwell (1897–1988) described them as 'the absolute embodiment of the age, as personal as the cut of the courtiers' clothes'. It is said that nothing more beautiful was ever made in iron. There are 12 linked gates, each with a different design of birds, flowers and heraldic shields. As I write, some are being gilded as they may have been originally.

The Privy Garden was originally surrounded by stepped terraces, but Brown in one of his few positive innovations gravelled the one near the Palace and replaced most of the other steps with the grass slopes there now, 'because we ought not to go up and down stairs in the open air'. Take the path along the western terrace on the west side. There is a first mention by John Evelyn in 1662 of a 'Hornbeam Walk' along the privy garden's west side. This is long gone, but the terrace was replanted with pleached hornbeam in 1970 and is known as Queen Mary's Bower (in the original garden, Queen Mary II, wife of William III, sat on this terrace knitting, so it is said). In summer, orange trees in tubs are set on the gravel.

The Sunken Gardens and the Great Vine

At the gateway in the west wall of the Privy Garden inspect the charming ornamental brick niche to the right – this is a 1690 Christopher Wren original (its partner and those at the entry gate are copies, as the bricks reveal). Through the gate, there is to the right a small knot garden, laid in 1924 in Tudor style, brighter in colour, however, than it would have been. Past it, a rose garden extends alongside the Orangery. In Tudor days, this whole area was known as the Pond Yard, for to the left were three largish fish ponds supplying the kitchens. Parts of the old surrounding walls remain, but under William and Mary, the tanks were drained and in their place sunken, sheltered gardens were created for exotic plants from warmer climes (the south-facing situation helped protect them). The plants were raised in early greenhouses, called 'glass cases', and planted out in summer. These sunken gardens have been recreated – the smaller (to the west) in 1950 in 17th-century style, in what was called the auricula quarter (auricula being a spring bedding plant).

At the end of the path is the entrance to the famous Great Vine, planted in 1768 by 'Capability' Brown, whose main job was probably to grow fruit for the palace.

It was once surrounded by one of the original glass cases, but it is now housed in a greenhouse made in 1969. It is a Black Hamburg dessert variety, its branches, 100 feet (30.5 metres) long producing more than 500 bunches a year, which are sold when ripe. The vine was originally fertilized from Palace sewers – or maybe its roots even reached the river – but it is now nourished by fertilizing the ground alongside it.

The Banqueting House

From the walkway you may turn left into the Orangery to see the cartoons by the Italian Renaissance painter Andrea Mantegna, which are on permanent exhibition there. As I write the Banqueting House, along the path between the Sunken Gardens, is closed for restoration, but the public will soon be able to visit it again. It is a rather charming 17th-century castellated building in red brick, built on the site of a mount, a feature of Tudor gardens. You can enter it to admire the two main rooms, the first with painted scroll panelling, the second magnificent, painted by the Neapolitan painter Antonio Verrio (1639–1707), his Minerva dominating the ceiling, with woodwork carved by Grinling Gibbons (1648–1721), its windows looking out over the river and its walls hung with nostalgically faded pier glasses (mirrors). In the days of William and Mary a banquet might be a large meal, but it could also be a small snack between meals, perhaps of wine and sweetmeats, taken while chatting to cronies. This Banqueting House makes a magnificent garden house.

The Great Fountain Garden

Now return to The Broad Walk and turn right along it. This roadway was eventually continued to veer left along the river bank on an embankment. There was a bowling green there in William III's day, with four pavilions originally, one of which survives.

Now cross The Broad Walk and walk around the perimeter of the Great Fountain Garden. Note its symmetrical layout: three paths flanked by avenues of trees dissect a semicircle, and a fountain plays at its centre. A semicircular avenue of lime trees was first planted in this area by Charles II, but not until the 1690s did William and Mary replan it as the Great Fountain Garden. A Huguenot designer, Daniel Marot (1663–1752), created a very elaborate Dutch-style parterre, with scrolled patterns of close-trimmed dwarf box hedges set in gravel, and *gazon coupé*, or turf cut into patterns highlighted by coloured sand. His parterre was an intricate design of yews and hollies clipped into obelisks, the whole surrounded by railings. Walk up the central avenue to the fountain. His garden had a more elaborate pattern of paths with a total of 13 fountains at the points where they crossed.

Apparently, however, this great parterre had a short life. It is said that Queen Anne, who succeeded to the throne in 1701, disliked the smell of box and had much of it dug up. The fountains, except for the central one, were removed, but the semicircular canal was dug. Later, however, Queen Caroline, wife of George II, apparently replaced the box. Apart from these changes, the basic pattern of the garden remained, even when Capability Brown was Master Gardener. Noted for replacing anything resembling formal gardens with the natural look, he was 'solicited by the King to improve the grounds' but 'he declined the hopeless task, out of respect to himself and his profession'. He did, however, let the yews grow untrimmed. Clipped until the 1760s, then left to grow freely, some of them, with their massive trunks, look like giant toadstools. Each tree can now take one gardener a couple of days to prune.

In Victorian days, following the current fashion, this Fountain Garden and its wings to each side were dotted with gaudy colour-clashing bedding, including carpet bedding. This was grassed over in World War I, and today's beds are models of their kind, with the emphasis on foliage and structure rather than colour alone.

The Park Vista

Walk to the canal and admire the vista three quarters of a mile (1,200 metres) down Long Water. When Charles II took the throne he was enthused with French ideas of style, with the avenue (signifying authority) and the long canal. In 1661, he had both constructed at Hampton Court. The Long Water had trees marching down each bank and two angled side avenues forming goosefoot, aligned to the centre of Wren's new Palace front. The diarist John Evelyn noted at the time that 'the Park, formerly a flat, naked piece of Ground, is now planted with sweete rows of lime-trees, and the Canale for Water neere perfected'. You might glimpse some of the 300-odd fallow and red deer which are direct descendants of those of Wolsey's day.

The great storm of 1987 decimated the trees in the avenues of the park, which were already rather gappy. There has been recent restoration: the glorious Cross Avenue, laid out around 1700 and nearly ⅔ mile (1 kilometre) long, was clear-felled and replanted between 1991 and 1995 with 1,247 lime trees in the original positions. There was some opposition to this work, but it is now seen to have been a resounding success.

Cross the Broad Walk and reenter the Wilderness through the gate on the north side of the palace, and head back through the rose garden and the car park to the main gate, where the walk ends.

Marble Hill Park

Location	About 8½ miles (13.7 kilometres) from Charing Cross.
Transport	St. Margaret's and Twickenham stations (overground trains from Waterloo and Clapham Junction) are 10 minutes' and 20 minutes' walk away respectively. Buses 65, 371, 414. There is a ferry across the Thames to Ham House *(see* page 152). There is a car park off Beaufort Road on the east side of the park.
Admission	Open daily dawn–dusk. Admission is free.
Seasonal features	Horse chestnuts in flower in late spring; ancient black walnut and other fine trees in leaf in summer.
Events	Concerts on the south lawn in summer.
Refreshments	Coach House Café open daily 10:00–17:30 hours Easter-Sept; open weekends Oct-Easter.

Its surrounding park forms a marvellous setting for Marble Hill House, a perfect small Palladian villa which dominates its park. Its setting is not as it was originally. The shrubberies which embrace it to each side have grown up where once its out-buildings stood, while the gently sloping lawns reveal only slight traces of the original terracing (despite its name, the house is not on a hill). Nevertheless, the park makes a very satisfying visit, with some historic trees, an ice house and (especially) a grotto, a landscape conceit which was very fashionable when the house was built.

And when the house was built there could have been no better placing for it. Twickenham was then a riverside village in charming countryside, yet within easy enough reach of London to guarantee entertaining neighbours – the poet, Alexander Pope (1688–1744), and the novelist and politician, Horace Walpole (1717–1797) among them – for the fashionable residents.

The house was built in 1724–9 for Henrietta Howard *(c.* 1698–1767), the mistress of George II, who paid for it with money given her by the king. She was also Mistress of Robes to Queen Caroline, and later became Countess of Suffolk. Colen Campbell was one architect, but Henry Herbert, later Lord Pembroke (an amateur architect) was among the many friends who flocked to help with the work. The restrained façades were to be copied many times. Jonathan Swift, author of *Gulliver's Travels,* advised Henrietta Howard on her wine cellar; while Alexander Pope helped with advice about the gardens and grounds, which were laid out by the queen's landscape designer Charles Bridgeman *(see* page 9). Lord Bathurst sent lime trees from Cirencester Park and Lord Islay (later Duke of Argyll) planted a black walnut *(Juglans nigra)* – which is now huge. 'Every thing as yet promises more

MARBLE HILL PARK

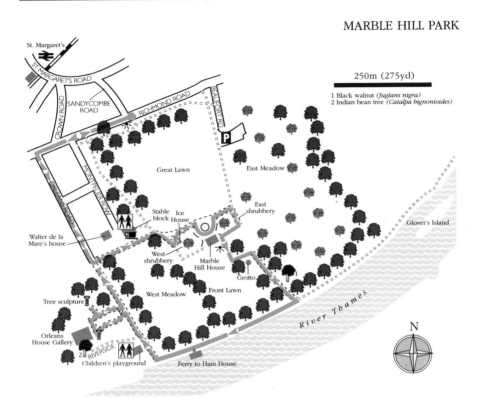

250m (275yd)

1 Black walnut *(Juglans nigra)*
2 Indian bean tree *(Catalpa bignonioides)*

happiness for the latter part of my life than I have yet had a prospect of', wrote Henrietta Howard in 1731 to John Gay, the author of *The Beggars' Opera*, who lived in Richmond. 'I shall now often visit Marble Hill'. Having had a disastrous first marriage, she lived happily at Marble Hill for 36 years with her second husband, George Berkeley, until his death in 1753.

The house was later occupied by another royal mistress, Mrs Fitzherbert (1756–1837), secret wife of the Prince of Wales who later became George IV. It became empty for some years around the turn of the 20th century, until, in 1902, London County Council took it over for use as tea rooms. It was restored and opened in 1966 as a museum of paintings and furniture, some of which had survived from its first years. In 1986 English Heritage took charge of it.

THE MARBLE HILL PARK WALK
Start and finish The Orleans Road gate. ***Time*** Allow three-quarters of an hour.

Enter the park via the gate in Orleans Road, and walk straight ahead until you come to converted stabling, now the Coach House Café, to the left. From about the 1720s, the 'Gothick' style came into vogue, and among its adherents were some of Henrietta Howard's neighbours, including Horace Walpole, who had built

Strawberry Hill House in 'Gothick' style. Under their influence Henrietta Howard was persuaded to convert a barn into a Gothick 'priory' somewhere in this area, but it was pulled down by 1770. Horse chestnut trees were popular when the estate was planted, and some good specimens survive in this part of the park. There is also a magnificent plane tree.

Continue ahead, past the stabling and a fenced minipark for toddlers and parents, and you come to a corner of one of the densely tangled shrubberies which form natural wings to each side of the house. Turn right down the short path at the corner of this to see the 18th-century ice house, in which river or lake ice packed tightly in straw could last up to two years. It originally had a domed brick roof, but it is now capped with smooth mortar, and ivy has covered it completely. All ice houses were domed, presumably because the dome shape was found most efficient in controlling the circulation of air; while drainage considerations meant that they were always sited some distance from the main house. This ice house is kept locked, unfortunately, so visitors are unable to admire the skilled brickwork inside.

Ice was a summer luxury in the 18th century, its value shown by some lines of a friend of Henrietta Howard, Jonathan Swift: *No more the Dean, that grave Divine,/Shall keep the Key of my No-wine;/My Ice-House rob, as heretofore,/And Steal my Artichokes no more...*

The North Front

Continue along the main path to the north face of the house. The Great Lawn, to the left, is now often occupied by sports pitches. The house is elegantly winged by arcs of wall. In front of these walls are lollipop-trimmed bay shrubs in white-painted containers; ornaments such as these were popular in the 18th century. From the east shrubbery opposite, which hides the site of the service wing of the house, to Richmond Road stretches a superb double avenue of horse chestnut trees. This was the original main driveway to the house. The path skirting the eastern shrubbery has been planted with lime trees and two right turns along it bring you out in front of the elegant Palladian south face of the house.

The river, to the south, is obscured by trees for most of the year, but in winter, when the trees are leaf-bare, you can see how well chosen was the situation, with the river and the misty distance beyond, the Thames providing a ready-made water feature. The lawn bears traces of broad turf terraces, now framed by trees on each side; these terraces were possibly Bridgeman's contribution to the garden scheme. Eighteenth-century prints of the house from the river show what Pope called an impression of 'amiable simplicity' produced by the grass terraces and curved lines of trees. The atmosphere at that time may have been much the same as today, although some argue that the bankside trees should be cut down to leave the river view open, as it was originally.

Lady Suffolk's Grotto

Follow the edge of the east shrubbery round to the left, and you come to a grotto on the right, down in a small hollow ringed by fencing. Grottoes were a popular fad of the 18th century, somewhere to walk to when promenading the grounds, or to sit while chatting with friends. The idea for such a feature came originally from Italy, and there was a well-known example in Alexander Pope's villa, nearby. To the right of the path you see steps descending to the grotto. Go down them and look inside, where you see a puzzling, well-like pit and a round stone table. The walls would probably have been decorated with sea shells and maybe pieces of coloured glass. From outside the grotto there is a view to Richmond Hill, but in summer it is obscured by foliage.

The Black Walnut
From the grotto, continue right along the path towards the river. To the left is a giant black walnut *(Juglans nigra)*, one of the largest in the country, protected nowadays by a fence. Its girth at shoulder height is 17 feet 6 inches (over 5 metres), and its massive side boughs do not need support. It was planted for Henrietta Howard by Lord Islay (later Duke of Argyll). A native of North America, its leaves have more leaflets than our native walnut, they are sharply toothed, and the ridged nut is very hard. This tree miraculously survived the great storm of 1987 which felled some tall Lombardy poplars nearby.

The River Walk
Follow the path down to the river, go through the gate that leads to the river walk, and turn right (westward) along it. From this walk you catch glimpses through the trees of what is now a famous aspect of the house.

Follow the walk past Orleans Road and the childrens' playground to the left, to the signposted entrance to Orleans House Gallery. The name is explained by a French connection: the Duc d'Orléans, Louis Philippe lived in Orleans House between 1793 and 1814. After 1830 he became King of the French. All that really remains of his house is the 1720 octagon by James Gibbs, a handsome pavilion in ochre-coloured brick with red-brick pilasters and dressings of Portland stone. There is an art gallery in the wing to one side.

In front of the gallery is a magnificent Indian bean tree *(Catalpa bignonioides)*, with largish light green leaves, intricate white blossom in July, and hanging pods looking like beans in winter. And on the shade alongside the Octagon is a cast (slightly dented) of Diana the huntress in her short tunic; 1944 is the earliest record of her.

The Tree Sculpture
But there is a more surprising work still to be seen. Walk back, as if to return to the river, and where the path curves to the right by a lamp post, a winding earth path leaves to the left, into the open woodland. It brings you to a recent tree sculpture, not all that large, on top of a post in a small clearing. It is the root end of a tree trunk, with eight root spokes radiating from a central face, each ending in a club of rootlets. It is partly gilded with melted sheets of green glass attached to some roots. Return to the main path and continue along it to the gate leading into Orleans Road, where the walk ends.

Further Information

Opening times

LONDON HISTORIC PARKS AND GARDENS TRUST
Duck Island Cottage, St. James's Park, London SW1A 2BJ. Tel: 0171 839 3969.
Membership: Standard £12, concessionary £6.
An independent charity concerned with conserving and restoring London's historic parks and gardens, and providing education about them. The Trust organizes guided walks and visits, exhibitions, study days and seminars.

OSTERLEY PARK
Jersey Road, Isleworth TW7 4RB. Tel: 0181 560 3918.
Events information line 01494 522 234.
Osterley Park House open 26 Mar–2 Nov: Wed–Sun 13:00–17:00 hours (last admission 16:30 hours). Bank Holiday Mon: 11:00–17:00 hours. Admission £3.80 adults, £1.90 children (National Trust members free). Facilities for the disabled.
The house and park are in the care of the National Trust.

SYON PARK
Park Road, Brentford, Middlesex TW8 8JF. Tel: 0181 560 0881.
Syon House open Apr–Sep: Wed–Sun 11:00–17:00 hours; Oct–Dec: Sun 11:00–16:00 hours. Admission £5.50 adult, £4 child.
Syon House and park are in the care of the National Trust.

CHISWICK HOUSE GARDENS
Burlington Lane, London W4. Tel: 0181 995 0508.
Chiswick House Tel: 0181 995 0508. Open Apr–3 Sep: daily 10:00–18:00 hours (or dusk); Nov–Mar: Wed–Sun 10:00–16:00 hours. Admission £2.50 adult, £1.30 child, under-5s free.
Chiswick House is in the care of English Heritage. The park and gardens are managed by Hounslow Borough Council.

FULHAM PALACE GARDENS
Bishop's Avenue, London SW6. Tel: 0171 736 7181/7989/3233.
Museum and shop open Wed–Sun 14:00–17:00 hours.
Admission 50p adult, children free.
The Palace and its grounds are under the care of English Heritage. A detailed tree map is available from the Museum shop.
Bishop's Park is managed by The London Borough of Hammersmith & Fulham. For information tel: 0181 748 3020.

HOLLAND PARK
Abbotsbury Road, W14. Tel: 0171 602 9483.
Ecology Centre Tel: 0171 603 2129.
Theatre box office Tel: 0171 602 7856.
Holland Park is managed by The London Borough of Kensington and Chelsea.

THE KENSINGTON ROOF GARDENS
99 Kensington High Street, London W8 5ED. Tel: 0171 937 9774.
The Roof Gardens are owned and managed by The Virgin Group.

KENSINGTON GARDENS
The Magazine Storeyard, Magazine Gate, Kensington Gardens, London W2 2UH. Tel: 0171 298 2117.
Kensington Gardens are managed by the Royal Parks Agency.
The Events Booklet is available from The Old Police House, Hyde Park, or call the Publications Department: 0171 298 2113 ext. 2019.
Kensington Palace, the State Apartments and Royal Ceremonial Dress Collection open daily 10:00–18:00 hours (last admission 17:00 hours). Admission £6.50 adult, £4.50 child.
The Serpentine Gallery tel: 0171 402 6075 for details of shows.

HYDE PARK
The Ranger's Lodge, Hyde Park, London W2 2UH. Tel: 0171 298 2100.
Hyde Park is managed by The Royal Parks Agency.
The Events Booklet is available from The Old Police House, or call the Publications Department: 0171 298 2113 ext. 2019.
The Lanbury Lido is open from 09:00 hours in summer, and an early morning swimmers' club is based there all year round.

THE REGENT'S PARK
The Storeyard, Inner Circle, The Regent's Park, London NW1. Tel: 0171 486 7905.
The Regent's Park is managed by The Royal Parks Agency.
The Events Booklet is available from The Old Police House, Hyde Park, London W2 2UH, or call the Publications Department: 0171 298 2113 ext. 2019.
London Zoo open daily from 10:00 hours. Tel: 0171 722 3333.

KENWOOD ESTATE
Hampstead Lane, London SW3 7JR. General information and events line: 0181 348 1286; 0181 340 5303; Estate Office: 0181 340 5303.
The Kenwood Estate is managed by English Heritage. The Estate Office Manager and Rangers, based at the Estate Office, Mansion Cottage, near the Brew House Restaurant, provide information about planting and new developments on the estate and answer visitors' queries.
Open–Air Concerts: book through Ticketmaster, tel: 0171 413 1443.
Kenwood House open 1 Apr–Oct: daily 10:00–18:00 hours. Tel: 0181 348 1286.

BLOOMSBURY SQUARES
The squares are managed by The London Borough of Camden. For information, contact the Parks and Open Spaces Department. Tel: 0171 278 4444.
British Museum Great Russell Street, London WC1. Tel: 0171 636 1555. Open Mon-Sat 10:00–17:00 hours; Sun 14:30–18:00 hours. **Jewish Museum** 129 Albert Street, London NW1. Tel: 0171 284 1997. Open Sun-Thur 10:00–16:00 hours.0

GREENWICH PARK
Park Office, Blackheath Gate, Charlton Way, London SE10 8QY. Tel: 0181 858 2608.
The park is managed by The Royal Parks Agency.
The Old Royal Observatory open 1 Apr–30 Sept: Mon–Sat 10:00–18:00 hours, Sun 12:00–18:00 hours; 1 Oct–31 Mar: Mon–Sat 10:00–17:00, Sat, Sun 14:00–17:00 hours.

The Ranger's House open 22 Mar–31 Oct: daily 10:00–18:00 hours; 1 Nov–31 Mar: Wed–Sun 10:00–16:00 hours. Tel: 0181 853 0035. Admission £2.50 adult, £1.30 child.

CRYSTAL PALACE PARK
Thicket Road, London SE20 8UT. Tel: 0181 778 9496/9612.
The park is managed by the London Borough of Bromley.

VICTORIA EMBANKMENT GARDENS
The gardens are managed by Westminster City Council. For information contact the Parks and Open Spaces Department. Tel: 0171 641 2616.

VICTORIA TOWER GARDENS
The Gardens are managed by Westminster City Council. For information contact the Parks and Open Spaces Department. Tel: 0171 641 2616.
The Museum of Garden History Lambeth Palace Road, London SE1 7LB.
Tel: 0171 401 8865. The museum is run by the Tradescant Trust. Admission is free.
Lambeth Palace Garden is open to the public three times a year: in April (the date is published in the National Gardens Scheme diary); and in June and September. For information call Lambeth Palace: 0171 928 8282.

THE GREEN PARK
The Ranger's Lodge, Hyde Park, London W2 2UH. Tel: 0171 298 2000.
The Events Booklet is available from The Old Police House, Hyde Park, or call the Publications Department: 0171 298 2113 ext. 2019.
The park is managed by The Royal Parks Agency.
Spencer House, entrance: 27 St. James's Place, London SW1A 1NR. Tel: 0171 499 8620 (recorded information); 0171 409 0526 (office).
Public tours Feb–end Jul, and Sep–end Dec: Sun 10:30–16:45 hours. Ticket £6, under-16s £5.

ST. JAMES'S PARK
The Park Office, Horse Guards Parade, London SW9 2BJ. Tel: 0171 930 1793.
The Events Booklet is available from The Old Police House, Hyde Park, London W2 2UH or call the Publications Department: 0171 298 2113 ext. 2019.
The park is managed by The Royal Parks Agency.

BATTERSEA PARK
Wandsworth, SW11. Tel: 0181 871 7530.
The park is managed by The London Borough of Wandsworth.
Children's Zoo open 1 Apr–30 Sept: daily 10:00–17:00 hours; 1 Oct–31 Mar: Sat, Sun 10:00–15:00 hours. Admission £1.10 adult, 60p child.

CHELSEA PHYSIC GARDEN
66 Royal Hospital Road, Chelsea, London SW3 4HS. Tel: 0171 352 5646.
The garden is run by an independent charity.

RICHMOND PARK
Superintendent's Office, Holly Lodge, Bog Lodge Yard, Richmond Park, Surrey TW10 5HS. Tel: 0181 948 3209.
The park is managed by The Royal Parks Agency.

THE ROYAL BOTANIC GARDENS, KEW
Richmond, Surrey TW9 3AB. Tel: 0181 332 5922.
The Royal Botanic Gardens are run by an independent charity.
Annual season ticket £18 adult, £35 family; Friends' annual membership £33 adult, £44 family, £33 senior family.

HAM HOUSE GARDENS
Ham, Richmond, Surrey TW10 7RS.
Tel: 0181 940 1950.
Ham House open Easter–end Oct: Mon–Wed, 13:00–17:00 hours; Sat, Sun 12:00–17:00 hours (last admission 16:30 hours).

HAMPTON COURT PALACE GARDENS
Surrey KT8 9AU. Tel: 0181 781 9500.
Hampton Court Palace open mid-Mar–mid-Oct: Mon 10:15–18:00 hours, Tue–Sun 09:30–18:00 hours; mid-Oct–mid-Mar: Mon 10:15–16:30 hours, Tue–Sun 09:30–16:30 hours. Last admission 45 min before closing. Admission £8.50 adult, £5.60 child, under-5s free.

MARBLE HILL PARK
Richmond Road, Twickenham. Tel: 0181 892 5115.
Marble Hill House and gardens are managed by English Heritage.
Marble Hill House open 22 Mar–31 Oct: daily 10:00–18:00 hours; 1 Nov–31 Mar: Wed–Sun 10:00–16:00 hours. Admission £2.50 adult, £1.30 child.

IDENTIFICATION GUIDES

Press, Bob *Photographic Field Guide to the Trees of Britain and Europe* (New Holland Publishers 1993).
Sutton, David *Field Guide to the Trees of Britain & Europe* (Kingfisher, 1990).

Index